An Introduction to the
New Testament Apocrypha

AN INTRODUCTION TO THE
NEW TESTAMENT APOCRYPHA

F. Lapham

T & T CLARK INTERNATIONAL
A Continuum imprint
LONDON • NEW YORK

Copyright © 2003 T&T Clark International
A Continuum imprint

Published by T&T Clark International
The Tower Building, 11 York Road, London SE1 7NX
15 East 26th Street, Suite 1703, New York, NY 10010

www.continuumbooks.com

Reprinted 2004

British Library Cataloguing-in-Publication Data
A catalogue record for this book is available from the British Library

Typeset by CA Typesetting, Sheffield
Printed on acid-free paper in Great Britain by MPG Books Ltd, Bodmin, Cornwall

ISBN 0-8264-6978-7 (hardback)
     0-8264-6979-5 (paperback)

CONTENTS

PREFACE

The exciting discovery at Nag Hammadi, some 60 years ago, of quantities of Christian books and tractates hidden during the fourth century, many dating back in origin to two centuries before that, somehow took the Church at large by surprise. It is true that textual scholars had long been familiar with a variety of documents loosely associated with the New Testament, some of Gnostic orientation; but these works, by and large, had neither been given wide popular dissemination, nor accorded the same serious critical attention that the canonical books had always enjoyed. Since the discoveries at Nag Hammadi, there has been a veritable explosion of apocryphal scholarship, particularly on the several Gnostic Gospels and Dialogues which seem to challenge traditional Christian ideas and belief; but such critical appraisal has yet to make its mark upon the local congregation. It is hoped that this book may make a small contribution towards introducing these important Christian works of the early centuries to clergy and teachers within the Church, and to students of theology, ecclesiastical history and New Testament interpretation.

Uncertainties of authorship, provenance, date and genre make it almost impossible to arrange the many and diverse books of the Christian Apocrypha into distinct categories. Most of the writings, however, do present at least a tenuous relation to some particular geographical region; and for the sake of convenience, and in order to facilitate study of the documents in manageable groups, this arrangement has been adopted. It is not intended that the book should represent an exhaustive survey of all the writings of the New Testament Apocrypha; but it may be that the present selection, which includes most of the important works of the second and third centuries, will encourage further reading of the texts, and help to bring fresh insights to the study of early Christianity.

English translations of the texts discussed in this book may be found in one or other of the general introductory works listed in the Further Reading section.

FURTHER READING

English translations of all the Apocryphal texts referred to in this book may be found in one or more of the following general works:

Elliott, J.K., *Apocryphal New Testament* (Oxford: Clarendon Press, 1993).
James, M.R., *Apocryphal New Testament* (Oxford: Clarendon Press, 1924).
Robinson, J.M. (ed.), *The Nag Hammadi Library in English* (San Fransisco: Harper & Row, 3rd edn, 1988).
Schneemelcher, W. (ed.), *New Testament Apocrypha* (trans. R. McL. Wilson; 2 vols.; Cambridge: James Clarke, 1991).

The following is a select list of general reading on the early history of the Church, and the Christian apocryphal literature:

Bovon, F., A.G. Brock and C.R. Mathews (eds.), *The Apocryphal Acts of the Apostles* (Cambridge, MA: Harvard University Press, 1999).
Bremmer, J.N. (ed.), *The Apocryphal Acts of Peter: Magic, Miracles and Gnosticism* (Leuven: Peeters, 1997).
Bremmer, J.N. (ed.), *The Apocryphal Acts of John* (Kampen: Kok Pharos, 1995).
Burrus, V., *Chastity as Autonomy: Women in the Stories of the Apocryphal Acts* (Lewiston, NY: Edwin Mellen Press, 1987).
Carrington, P., *The Early Christian Church* (2 vols.; Cambridge: Cambridge University Press, 1957).
Chadwick, H., *The Early Church* (Harmondsworth: Penguin Books, rev. edn, 1993).
Frend, W.H.C., *The Early Church* (London: SCM Press, 1991).
Grant, R.M., *Gnosticism and Early Christianity* (New York: Columbia University Press, 1959).
Klauck, H.-J., *Introduction to the Apocryphal Gospels* (Edinburgh: T. & T. Clark, 2003).
Klijn, A.F.J., *The Acts of Thomas* (Leiden: E.J. Brill, 1962).
Koester, H., 'Apocryphal and Canonical Gospels', *Harvard Theological Review* 73 (1980), pp. 105-130.
Lapham, F., *Peter: The Myth, the Man and the Writings* (Sheffield: Sheffield Academic Press, 2003).
Logan, A.H.B., and A.J.M. Wedderburn, *The New Testament and Gnosis* (Edinburgh: T. & T. Clark, 1983).
Lohse, E., *The New Testament Environment* (London: SCM Press, 1998).
Pagels, E., *The Gnostic Gospels* (London: Weidenfeld & Nicholson, 1980).

Patterson, S.J., *The Gospel of Thomas and Jesus* (Sonoma, CA: Polebridge Press, 1993).

Peel, M.L., 'Gnostic Eschatology and the New Testament', *Novum Testamentum* 12 (1970), pp. 141-65.

Perkins, P., *The Gnostic Dialogue: The Early Church and the Crisis of Gnosticism* (New York: Paulist Press, 1980).

Roberts, C.H., *Manuscript, Society and Belief in Early Christian Egypt* (London: Oxford University Press, 1979).

Robinson, J.M., and H. Koester, *Trajectories through Early Christianity* (Philadelphia: Fortress Press, 1971).

Uro, R., *Thomas at the Crossroads: Essays on the Gospel of Thomas* (Edinburgh: T. & T. Clark, 1998).

Vaage, L.E., and V.L. Wimbush (eds.), *Asceticism and the New Testament* (London: Routledge, 1999).

Wilson, R. McL., *Gnosis and the New Testament* (Oxford: Basil Blackwell, 1968).

INTRODUCTION

1. *The Discoveries*

One of the most far-reaching consequences of the Second World War, it is sometimes asserted, is that it changed for ever human perceptions of God and his relationship to the world, bringing a new honesty and realism into religious thought and inquiry. What may not yet be so generally recognized is that events of another kind, taking place in the desert sands of Egypt during the closing years of that conflict, were to have equally significant repercussions for our understanding of Christianity. In 1945 an Arab named Muhammad Ali, with his brother and friends, digging by some ancient burial caves at Jabal al-Tarif, close to Nag Hammadi in Upper Egypt, came across a large sealed earthenware jar buried underneath a slab of stone. With some trepidation they ventured to open it. What the young Arabs had gone out to collect was the rich, soft earth, close by the caves, which they used to fertilize their crops; what they found, however, when they smashed the jar, were 13 priceless books—codices—bound in sheepskin or antelope hide, each containing several different texts written on papyrus leaves in a language which none of them could understand.

Muhammad was understandably disappointed that his discovery was not materially valuable, worth nothing more, perhaps, than a little extra fuel for his hearth; yet these texts—more than 50 in all—were mercifully (and quite literally) saved from the fire, and later identified to be fourth-century Christian documents written in Coptic, the ancient language of Egypt. When biblical scholars began to examine the texts more closely, they soon realized that most of them, if not all, were Coptic translations of considerably earlier Greek originals, dating from the beginning of the second century onwards. Some of the texts paralleled material found in the New Testament books themselves, though often with an unfamiliar slant. Others were characteristically Gnostic (a term which, because it is commonly and loosely used in many different ways, we will shortly need to define), presenting to the reader a very different view of Christ and his teaching than has traditionally been handed down. Here, preserved for centuries in the sands of Egypt, was a whole new picture of what the Christian faith meant to groups of Christians living not only in Egypt, but in Palestine and Syria, in Asia Minor and Mesopotamia, and perhaps further east than that. The important questions that needed to be answered, of course, were how representative and widespread were these strange forms of belief, and in what ways, if at all, did Gnostic Christianity relate to more normative forms of the faith.

The discoveries at Nag Hammadi were by no means the first Christian Apocryphal works to be discovered in Egypt;[1] but the burst of research into these extraordinary documents unquestionably proved to be the catalyst for a renewal of serious interest in many other important works unearthed at various sites during the twentieth century, and which hitherto had received only perfunctory, if not dismissive, attention. Perhaps the most important of these sites was at Oxyrhynchus, south of Cairo, chosen for investigation because there seemed to be some evidence here of early Christian monastic life. In 1897, after one or two unsuccessful trial excavations, the archaeologists B.P. Grenfell and A.S. Hunt began to dig in a rubbish mound close to the ancient ruins of an early Roman temple in the town. During the months that followed, literally thousands of scraps of Greek papyri which, for some reason, had been hidden or discarded so many centuries before, began to come to light; and one of the first to be unearthed was noticed to contain part of the story, found also in the New Testament, of the mote and the beam (Mt. 7.5). This was one of a number of passages in this particular papyrus fragment which appeared to consist of 'sayings' of Jesus—though many of the 'sayings' (or Logia) were unfamiliar and strange. Other fragments of a similar nature were later discovered, and scholars began to wonder whether they comprised part of a hitherto unknown 'Sayings Gospel'. Not until the discoveries at Nag Hammadi in 1945 was the work positively identified, for one of the Coptic manuscripts found there was a complete text of what was entitled the *Gospel of Thomas*, including all the passages unearthed at Oxyrhynchus a century and a half earlier.

---

1.   Excavations in a cemetery at Akhmim in Upper Egypt in 1887, for instance, uncovered the grave of a Christian monk. In the grave were found some parchment fragments of texts later identified as the *Apocalypse of Peter* and the *Gospel of Peter*. For a study of these documents, refer to Chapter 4.

2. *Apocrypha and Pseudepigrapha*

Before proceeding further with our survey of the 'hidden Scriptures', it will be important to define some of the terms already used which have come to be associated with these fascinating but relatively unknown texts —for no field of study has suffered more from the vague and inconsistent use of its terminology. First, the word 'apocrypha' itself. It is derived from a Greek word meaning 'hidden' or 'secret', and is used at one level to describe those scriptural texts which, though regarded by some to be spiritually valuable, nevertheless failed to meet the criteria set by the early Christian scholars who settled the 'canon' of the New Testament. The word 'canon', in its Christian usage, has a complex history. Its primary meaning (again from the Greek) is a 'rule' or 'norm'; and so it came to represent the standard measure by which scriptural texts were adjudged to be either authentic and profitable, or false and dangerous. The formulation of the canon of the New Testament, like that of the Jewish Scriptures for the Old Testament, was a gradual process; but by the fourth century there had emerged an agreed list or catalogue of writings which Christians could safely regard as authoritative. Thus, for example, the two Epistles of Peter, and the three of John, were included (though, in some instances, rather late), while those of Ignatius of Antioch, and the so-called *Shepherd* of Hermas, were not. And since, by its very nature, the canon was a closed catalogue, no writing discovered after that date, even if it purported to have been composed by one of the Apostles, could find a place within the New Testament.

We may feel that such a selection was both arbitrary and unfair, as well as limiting to the Church's growth, and this may indeed be a valid criticism. We must understand, however, that some such measure of orthodoxy was deemed at the time to be expedient because of the rapid proliferation of sects whose teachings and way of life were regarded by the mainstream Church to be heretical and dangerous. One of the chief aims of this present study will be to allow readers to decide for themselves whether the proscription of these non-canonical books has been beneficial or detrimental to the Church over these many centuries, and, if the latter, how they might now find an appropriate place within Christian study and worship.

It is important to recognize that the primary reason why a particular book was not included in the New Testament canon was its presumed pseudonymity; and it was because such works were thus disputed and set aside—and therefore effectively banned—that they earned the designation

'Apocryphal' or hidden. There was, however, another important reason for this categorization. Many of these books purported to contain esoteric or 'secret' teachings of Jesus which only the elect could understand; and it was thought necessary by the author, or by those who later came to treasure the works, to shield them from the eyes of undiscerning and unscrupulous critics. It is not difficult to understand why, in times of persecution, such precious books were quite literally hidden away in suitable places in order to preserve them for posterity. A cautionary note in the *Letter of Peter to James* (*Epistula Petri*)[2]—a covering letter accompanying the books of Peter's teachings which he herewith sends to the leader of the church in Jerusalem—will illustrate the anxiety of the various Christian groups to preserve what they considered to be the true teaching of Christ:

> I earnestly beseech you (my brother) not to pass on to anyone of the Gentiles the books of my preachings which I (here) forward to you, nor to any one of our own tribe before probation. But if some one of them has been examined and found to be worthy, then you may hand them over to him... (*Epistula Petri* 1.2).[3]

The other term frequently used in Apocryphal study is the word 'pseudepigrapha'. Literally, it means 'false writings', books, that is, which, either by their title or superscription, claimed an authorship which was not genuine. It should be realized, of course, that the literary convention of the age would not have frowned upon the prevalent custom of pseudonymity, so long as there was no intention to deceive. Most of the pseudepigraphical writers of the early centuries would have wanted only to add gravity to their works by associating their teachings with the great apostolic names of the past. If they were guilty of stretching that apostolic teaching (whatever that may have been) to suit their own purposes, that is as far as they might be indicted. On the other hand, their pseudonymity did create real problems for those self-styled guardians of orthodoxy of later generations

2.   The *Epistula Petri* is a short covering letter purporting to accompany and explain the books of Peter's Preachings which he sends to James of Jerusalem. This introductory letter, attached to the so-called Pseudo-Clementine literature, together with James's reply (*Contestatio*), will be discussed in Chapter 2.

3.   The translation used here is that of the *New Testament Apocrypha* (*NTA*) edited by Wilhelm Schneemelcher (rev. edn of Edgar Hennecke; trans. R. McL. Wilson; Cambridge: James Clarke, 1991). Unless otherwise stated, all translations will be from the *NTA*. In this quotation, and generally throughout the book, square brackets denote either a lacuna in the text, or a reconstruction of an indistinct word or passage. Round parentheses indicate explanatory supplements by the translator.

(Irenaeus, Hippolytus and others) who needed to decide which of the extant documents were genuine, and which were not. Inevitably there were some whose authenticity was generally disputed; and some (like the Epistles of Peter, James and Jude) came to be accepted as worthy reading for the Church only at a comparatively late stage in the formulation of the canon.

It will be recognized that not all pseudepigrapha may be categorized as Apocryphal. Several of the books which passed early canonical scrutiny are now acknowledged by most New Testament scholars to be pseudepigraphical, notably one (if not both) of the Petrine Epistles, all the Johannine Epistles, and one or two of those letters, such as Ephesians, which have traditionally been ascribed to Paul. In the same way, not all of the books designated as Apocryphal are pseudepigraphical, for not a few make no claim of authorship at all. In the main, this present study deals with the early pseudepigrapha—by far the most important of the Apocryphal works; but the more significant of the anonymous writings of the period, usually associated with the apostolic group as a whole, will also be examined.

Before leaving the definitions of terminology, it is important to note the distinction which is usually made between Apocryphal writings and those other works which are classified as 'patristic' (of the Church Fathers). Clearly there is a fine dividing line between them. Ignatius, for instance, an early Bishop of Antioch, is thought to have written his short Epistles to the several churches of Asia Minor at the beginning of the second century. Certainly they have been revered by the Church ever since, for they form inspirational and instructive reading for Christians in all kinds of situations. Like other highly prized literature, however—the writings of Clement of Rome and Clement of Alexandria, for instance—they do not conform to the most fundamental of the canonical criteria, apostolicity, and were thus not in serious contention for inclusion in the New Testament.

3. *Earlier-known Writings*

As exciting as the more recent discoveries in Egypt have proved to be, we need to be aware that they represent by no means the totality of the non-canonical Christian writings that have come down to us from antiquity. As we read the works of the early Church historians and theologians—Eusebius's *Ecclesiastical History*, for example, or Origen's *Homilies* and *Commentaries*—we encounter the occasional mention of works which were evidently very familiar at the time of writing, but which have subsequently been lost in the course of the centuries which followed. The fourth-century writer Epiphanius cites an *Itinerary of Peter*,[4] for instance, and Clement of Alexandria a book which he knew as the *Preaching of Peter*,[5] the tracing and identifying of both of which works has exercised the minds of textual scholars ever since. Again, although early attestations of works purporting to describe the 'Acts' of named apostles—Andrew, John, Peter, Thomas and Paul—appear in Origen, Eusebius and other second- and third-century writers, it was only later that manuscripts containing these texts came to light; and it may well have been the use of this collection of Acts by the heretical Manichaean sect,[6] in preference to the canonical Acts of the Apostles, that contributed to their eventual decline. Inevitably, as the more orthodox and widely accepted Scriptures became more accessible and generally affordable (for manuscript copies were extremely expensive), those texts that had only limited circulation, with teachings that were increasingly suspect, would be mentioned largely in order to refute or condemn them. There is no doubt that the adverse criticism of respected and learned Fathers of the Church such as Clement of Alexandria and Tertullian contributed greatly to the gradual wane in popularity of these once highly prized works. Happily, some of these 'lost' documents have survived, and have been identified and preserved—though in some cases only by a single copy; and modern re-evaluation has shown how important these texts are for our understanding of the development of early Christian thought.

One particularly interesting example of a work once thought to be irretrievably lost is the second-century *Apocalypse of Peter*, cited by Clement of Alexandria,[7] Methodius of Olympus,[8] and Theophilus of Antioch,[9] and clearly a work of some importance at that time. A fragment of a work which seemed to correspond to quotations in those early citations was discovered at Akhmim in Egypt in 1887; but it was not until the recognition in 1910 of a closely related Ethiopic text that the citations of Clement and the others were positively identified. In one of the codices discovered in 1945 at Nag

---

4.   Epiphanius, *Refutation of All Heresies* (*Panarion*) 30.15.1: 'They (the Ebionites) also use other books, namely the so-called *Itinerary of Peter* written by Clement, adulterating some of what is in it and leaving some that is true.'

5.   Clement, *Stromata* 1.29 and 6.5.

6.   The third-century Iranian Mystic Mani sought to synthesize eastern and western religious thought into a world religion which was essentially dualistic and Gnostic in outlook—a commixture of Buddhism, Zoroastrianism and Christianity.

7.   *Eclogae Propheticae* 41.

8.   *Symposium* 2.6.

9.   *Ad Autolycum* 2.19.

Hammadi, a completely unrelated and very different Coptic text came to light with the same title of the *Apocalypse of Peter* (see Chapter 4), and we shall need to keep in mind the totally different style and purpose of these two documents. For the present, however, all we need to note is the great variety of books of different genre—some of them in the style of Gospels or Dialogues, some composed in the style of 'Acts', some Apocalypses, as well as 'Sayings' texts. The dating, authorship and provenance of these works, as might be expected, are complex questions; but it will be recognized that scholarly research into all of these matters is vitally important for our investigations into the development of Christianity in relation to other current beliefs and philosophies in the early centuries.

4. *The Manuscripts*

It may be useful at this stage to say something about the physical characteristics of the manuscripts upon which the documents we shall be considering were written. The earliest form of writing material, so far as the Hellenistic period is concerned, was manufactured from the inner bark of the papyrus plant which grew in abundance along the banks of the Nile. Narrow strips of this material were plaited, pressed and joined together to form lengths up to about 30 centimetres. Where these were insufficient for longer documents, papyrus lengths were joined end to end, and rolled to make up a single scroll. Scribes would write in ink, usually in a single column, and often on only one side, with a pen made from a length of reed. It was, of course, quite possible to write on the reverse side, and many of the scrolls and fragments found at Oxyrhynchus are written on both the verso and the recto sides. It was not uncommon for scrolls to be reused, the original text being erased, and the new occupant of the scroll replacing it, sometimes at right angles to the former script. Such so-called 'palimpsests' (from a Greek word meaning 'reversed' or 'back again') present obvious additional difficulties to the textual scholar.

Fortuitously, the dry climatic conditions of Egypt have preserved many papyrus documents and fragments; and doubtless many more have yet to be uncovered. The very impermanence of the papyrus itself, however, encouraged the gradual change, from the third century onwards, to the use of parchment or vellum. Parchment, the dried and stretched skin of sheep or goats, owes its name to the city and region of Pergamum in Asia Minor, noted in early times for its book making, as well as for its library, which is said to have rivalled that of Alexandria. The more expensive and finer vellum, from calf or antelope skin, was used for the superior quality manuscripts. One of the most highly treasured of these, for example, is the fourth-century Codex *Vaticanus graecus* which once contained substantially the entire Bible between its covers, though a few books of the New Testament are now missing. Despite their relatively greater cost, vellum and parchment gained favour because these materials could be folded and stitched in sections, and sections joined in book or codex form, allowing long documents to be contained in one volume. The Codex *Vaticanus graecus*, in its present state, for instance, has 759 leaves, and the text is written in 3 columns. The 13 codices from Nag Hammadi, as was mentioned earlier, each contained a number of different works (usually described as tractates) bound together in one codex, either because the editor or compiler thought he had identified some common theme, or simply for reasons of practical convenience.

The earliest form of Greek script has the name 'uncial'—rounded capital letters with neither space between the words nor accents to assist pronunciation. Sometimes the scribe would draw a short horizontal line in the side margin to denote a new paragraph (our English word 'paragraph' derives from the Greek 'to write alongside'). By the ninth century the script in general use had moved away from the uncial to the minuscule, small cursive letters, with separated words, and breathing marks and accents to facilitate reading. It is important to note that while our earliest manuscripts are clearly the uncials, the later minuscules, produced as late as the eleventh and twelfth centuries, might quite conceivably represent an earlier tradition than some of the uncials of the third and fourth centuries.

Much of the laborious task of transcribing and translating the early Church documents was performed in monasteries or by professional scribes. Modern palaeography is sometimes able to detect, from the characteristic style and form of the writing itself, the particular scriptorium that produced the manuscript. Again, scholars are able to speculate, with some degree of accuracy, on the original length and content of a document which is not now complete, by the science of Stichometry (see Chapter 3, n. 5); and the age of a manuscript can often be ascertained from the mode of its binding and seaming, as well as by such well-established procedures as carbon dating. This, of course, tells us little or nothing about the origin and date of the primary source which in many cases will go back as far as the late first or early second century. Some of the more interesting and exciting discoveries of recent years have therefore been the papyrus uncial fragments, such as those discovered in recent years at Oxyrhynchus. Some of these are no easier to interpret than they are to decipher; yet careful and painstaking study of these fascinating fragments brings us very close to the original documents themselves. Piece by piece, then, as new finds add to our knowledge, the picture of the early Church, its Scriptures and beliefs, its life and its worship, becomes ever clearer.

5. *The Classification of the Documents*

The literary style and content of early documents, both within the New Testament and outside it, varies so widely that it has been considered useful to categorize them broadly according to type. The oldest method of grouping the material has been to follow the pattern of the New Testament itself, with its clear sections of Gospels, Acts, Epistles and Apocalypse. Within the New Testament, however, it has long been recognized that the Synoptic Gospels are very different in character from St John's Gospel; and many of the books designated as Epistles might be more aptly described as theological treatises than letters. It will be no great surprise, then, to discover that the Apocryphal writings are even more difficult to type, for many even of those pseudepigraphical documents which have long borne the title, for example, of 'Gospel' or 'Acts', bear little resemblance either to their canonical counterparts or to each other. However, we must briefly take note of the various literary types.

a. *The Gospels*
Firstly, there are just a few early Gospel-type books, known only through a brief citation or quotation, here and there, by one or other of the Church Fathers, and which have come to be known, traditionally, as the 'Jewish-Christian Gospels'.[10] Though only short excerpts of these works are now in existence, it would appear that they were written in the same form and style as the Gospels which came to be included in the New Testament. Some of them may have contributed to the formulation of the New Testament Gospels. Alternatively, they may have been adaptations of those for use within the Jewish-Christian communities—that is, those groups of traditional and conservative Christians who followed the teaching of the primitive church in Jerusalem, and maintained their observance of the Jewish Law. These important fragmentary excerpts are from works which Jerome, Epiphanius and Clement of Alexandria knew as the Gospels of the Hebrews, the Nazaraeans, and the Ebionites. While there is still some uncertainty and confusion about the names and origins of these various works,

10. J.K. Elliott (*The Apocryphal New Testament* [Oxford: Clarendon Press, 1993]) calls these the 'Lost Gospels'.

they are at least identifiable as 'Gospels'. By way of contrast, the Nag Hammadi *Gospel of Thomas*, being simply a collection of Sayings of Jesus without any recognizable historical setting, hardly shares the same genre (or *Gattung*, to use the German equivalent) as the New Testament Gospels; and the *Gospel of Peter*, while manifestly in the same form as the canonical four, and undoubtedly dependent upon them, comprises in its present form nothing more than a truncated account of the Crucifixion and Resurrection narrative, and there is no certainty that it ever contained much more. The *Gospel of Philip*, despite its clear title, is even more difficult to classify. More often than not it is described as a *florilegium*—an anthology of Gospel sayings and comments loosely strung together, with few narrative links.

No greater degree of uniformity is exhibited by a group of documents which have obvious literary similarities to the Apocryphal Gospels, but are given the generic title of 'Dialogues of the Saviour'. Typical of these is the Nag Hammadi document called the *Apocryphon of James*, consisting chiefly of a discourse between Jesus and the disciples which occurred some considerable time after the Resurrection, followed by an account of a revelatory experience as the disciples recalled his teaching in the days of his flesh. Another work in this Dialogue form, though purporting to be a letter from the Apostles to the churches, and given a vague Gospel-type historical setting, is the so-called *Epistle of the Apostles* (*Epistula Apostolorum*), originating, perhaps, from the second century. The author describes, embellishes and comments upon incidents in the Gospel story, as the following post-Resurrection passage will illustrate:

> That you may know that it is I, lay your hand, Peter, and your finger, in the nailprint of my hands; and you, Thomas, in my side; and also you, Andrew, see whether my foot steps on the ground and leaves a footprint. For it is written in the prophet, 'A ghost, a demon, leaves no print on the ground.' (*Epistula Apostolorum* 11; cf. Jn 20.27)

b. *The Acts Literature*

At first acquaintance, the Apocryphal *Acta* present a bewildering array of books purporting to tell the story of one or other of the Twelve as they set out to preach the Gospel, with word and miracle, in their allotted regions. This, certainly, is a concept which is easily grasped; and there are great insights to be gained simply by taking these books at face value. It quickly becomes evident as we read, however, that there are interconnecting textual and thematic links between several of the Acts, and we shall need to take these into account when, in later chapters, we begin to examine how and why these books were written. Was the intention of these several books merely to entertain, like the Greek novels of an earlier age? Or was their purpose to instruct in the faith? Did the stories and traditions they contain have some historical foundation? These are important questions we must leave for later consideration.

The *Acts of Peter* is a fairly straightforward document, in the style of the canonical Acts; but we shall discover, even here, that some passages in the text were probably not part of the original work, being added at a later date by an editor. We shall consider shortly why such editing, or redaction, took place, and how far it is possible to uncover the original work. In this present chapter, all we need to do is to recognize that very many of the documents we shall examine have suffered some redaction during the course of their transmission—words and even whole passages changed, or added to the original text, whether accidentally or deliberately—and that the complex task of modern textual scholarship is to try to retrace the original text of the author. One thematic parallel, between the *Acts of Paul* and the *Acts of Peter* (the well-known *Quo Vadis* story) will serve to show why many believe that there has been some borrowing by one author from the other's work—unless, of course, both authors have used a separate common source:

> Paul fell asleep, fatigued by the fastings and the night-watches with the brethren. And the Lord came to him, walking upon the sea, and he nudged Paul and said: 'Stand up and see!' And he, awakening, said, 'Thou art my Lord Jesus Christ… But why so gloomy and downcast, Lord?…' And the Lord said, 'Paul, I am about to be crucified afresh.' And Paul said: 'God forbid, Lord, that I should see this!' But the Lord said to Paul: 'Paul, get thee up, go to Rome and admonish the brethren that they may abide in the calling…' (*Acts of Paul*, Pap. Ham., p. 7).

> As Peter went out of the gate he saw the Lord entering Rome; and when he saw him he said, 'Lord, whither goest thou here?' And the Lord said to him, 'I am coming to Rome to be crucified.' And Peter said to him, 'Lord, art thou being crucified again?' He said to him, 'Yes, Peter, I am being crucified again.' And Peter came to himself; and he saw the Lord ascending into heaven; then he returned to Rome rejoicing and giving praise to the Lord, because he said, 'I am being crucified'; since this was to happen to Peter. So he returned to the brethren (*Acts of Peter* 35).

c. *The Epistolary Writings*
It is now generally agreed that many of the Epistles that gained inclusion in the canon of the New Testament are pseudonymous, attaining their privileged status because they were then considered to be genuine. Most of

the Apocryphal 'Epistles' (like some within the New Testament) are not really letters at all. One such document, despite its title, is the *Epistula Apostolorum*. The *Epistle of Peter to Philip* is another, commencing in the style of a letter, but immediately turning into a Gnostic catechetical treatise. There are, however, a small number of brief, but very important, documents in letter form which have come to be associated with a collection of writings traditionally attributed to Clement of Rome. Clement, according to several early and apparently authentic lists, was the third or fourth Bishop of Rome, and was celebrated and revered throughout the entire western Church. After his death, the legendary stories of his acquaintance with the Apostle Peter, and their missionary journeys together in Palestine and Syria, were widely circulated, and much of Peter's teaching and preaching was reputedly enshrined within the so-called Pseudo-Clementine books. The introductory writings associated with these books are in the form of letters —from Peter to James (the *Epistula Petri*) and from Clement to James (the *Epistula Clementis*); and because these letters refer to the secret teachings of Peter, thought to be contained in the Pseudo-Clementines (the *Homilies* and *Recognitions* of Clement), they are clearly important documents which we will want to examine closely.

d. *The Apocalyptic Writings*
The last major literary type consists of that group of documents referred to as Apocalypses, having much in common with the last book of the New Testament, the Revelation of St John the Divine. The word 'apocalypse' (not to be confused with 'apocrypha') means an 'uncovering' or 'revealing'; and apocalyptic works are essentially concerned to describe visions of things that are yet to come—involving, of course, the blessing and salvation of the fortunate elect, on the one hand, and the eternal punishment of those whose faithlessness and moral turpitude in this life has guaranteed their suffering in the life to come. These revelatory visions, experienced sometimes in dreams, sometimes in ecstatic states, usually include exhortations and warnings of the dangers of impiety. The study of these apocalyptic writings falls into the wider category of 'eschatology' (from the Greek word meaning 'the last things').

The eschatological passages of the New Testament Gospels (Mt. 24 and 25; Mk 13; etc.), as well as the Johannine Apocalypse, will doubtless have had some impact on the development of the Christian apocalyptic writings of the early centuries. A much more significant influence, however, must have been the equivalent writings within Judaism whose popular appeal was immense—works such as the book of *Enoch* and the Jewish *Sibylline*

Oracles. Clear parallels between some of these pre-Christian writings and the Christian Apocalypses show that passages may well have been adapted for Christian use. Other wholly Christian works (as, for instance, and despite its title, the *Ascension of Isaiah*) have been modelled on Jewish forms of apocalyptic literature. Whether Jewish or Christian, the message of the apocalypticists is stark and uncompromising:

> And he showed me in his right hand the souls of all men and on the palm of
> his right hand the image of that which shall be fulfilled at the last day; and
> how the righteous and the sinners shall be separated and how those will do
> who are upright of heart, and how the evil-doers will be rooted out for all
> eternity. We saw how the sinners wept in great distress and sorrow, until all
> who saw it with their eyes wept... (*Apoc. Pet.* 3).

This passage from the traditional *Apocalypse of Peter* might provide a clue to the rationale of this type of writing. Jews and Christians held in common the belief that the creation was finite, and would in the course of time be brought to a cataclysmic end. For Christians, of course, that end would be concomitant with the Second Coming (the parousia) of Christ, a happening which was at first considered to be imminent. As time elapsed, the apparent delay in the parousia, together with both the pressures of state persecution of Christians, and the lure of worldly gratification, encouraged increasing apostasy. It was essential to remind Christians of the grave dangers they faced, so far as their eternal salvation was concerned, if they lapsed their faith and followed the ways of the world. All genuine apocalyptic writing is therefore dualistic—emphasizing, as did Jesus himself, the essential choice facing the Christian, between the things of this world and the things of God.

Several smaller Apocalypses of uncertain date, pseudonymously attributed to Paul, Thomas, Peter and others, have come down to us, some discovered at Nag Hammadi, others having been known for many centuries. Not all of these can be said strictly to be of the apocalyptic genre;[11] but all will need our perusal if we are to gain a thorough acquaintance with the New Testament Apocrypha. Again, however, we must recognize the inadequacy of the traditional mode of literary classification; and we must now ask whether a grouping according to theological orientation might afford a

---

11. The word 'apocalypse' properly means a 'revealing'—an uncovering of what has been hidden; as such it does not necessarily refer to eschatological expectations. Gnostic Apocalypses are concerned with the revealing of divine truth to those who are able to understand.

better way to help us to relate the wide variety of scriptural writings to the several different Christian communities of our period.

6. *Theological Types*

a. *The Gnostic Writings*

We have used the term 'Gnostic' several times already, and it is now imperative that we try to define this elusive and ambiguous term. It derives from a Greek verb meaning 'to know' (our English word 'knowledge' is from the same root). We might begin by noting that all Gnostics reckoned themselves to be possessed of special esoteric knowledge which was denied to others. It will be evident, then, that the term 'Gnostic' encompasses a whole range of differing views and beliefs. Many Christians who would certainly have considered themselves to be of the mainstream Church valued their special status as the 'elect', claiming superior insights into God's purposes for the world through Christ. We have only to look at the Pauline Epistle to the Ephesians to see how the claim to privileged insight was by no means confined to the so-called Gnostics:

> He has made known to us in all wisdom and insight the mystery of his will, according to his purpose which he set forth in Christ as a plan for the fulness of time, to unite all things in him, things in heaven and things on earth (Eph. 1.9, 10).

It will be recalled, too, that Jesus himself is reputed to have given secret teaching to his disciples, if we may rely on the accuracy of St Mark's account of his ministry. They were chosen and special; and part of their special status consisted in the fact that insights into God's purpose were vouchsafed to them, and not to others:

> To you has been given the secret of the kingdom of God, but for those outside everything is in parables; so that they may indeed see but not perceive, and may indeed hear but not understand, lest they should turn again and be forgiven (Mk 4.11, 12).

It was only a short step from such 'Gnosticizing' Christianity to the gradual development, from the second century onwards, of a variety of sophisticated Gnostic systems largely based on the belief that some human beings were *by nature* capable of salvation, while others were not. Clearly, this represented a crucial departure from the generally understood tenets of Christianity, as these are reflected in the canonical writings; and the split between what we have come to call 'orthodoxy', and those groups castigated as 'heretical' sects, became ever wider. Many of the writings we shall be examining, especially those from Nag Hammadi, exhibit these Gnostic characteristics.

Two facts about Gnosticism in general need to be recognized before we can have an adequate understanding of its place within, and its relationship to, Christianity. First, Gnosticism did not spring up as a fully developed system to rival Christianity. Like every other systematic development, it *grew*, emphasizing one particular aspect of primitive Christianity—spiritual awareness and knowledge. We might indeed compare its growth to that of Christianity itself, from the primitive 'Jesus Movement' of Palestine, to the powerful and hierarchical edifice of the worldwide Church. Secondly, like Christianity, it was syncretistic—that is, it was susceptible to outside influences, assimilating ideas from Judaism, eastern philosophies and the mystery religions of Asia, as well as from the mythology of Greece and Rome. Our knowledge of the various Gnostic systems is largely derived from the anti-heretical writings of the orthodox Fathers of the Church (Irenaeus and Hippolytus, for example) who describe their sectarian beliefs in some detail; and the Gnostic documents produced by these sects to some extent confirm the accuracy of these polemical accounts.

Having recognized that Gnosticism is not a single philosophical or religious system, but representative of a wide range of syncretic belief, we must now try to identify some of the more important Gnostic principles that we shall encounter within the scriptural literature of the various groups. Gnostic belief is essentially dualistic. It presupposes a fundamental dichotomy between spirit and matter; and the ultimate goal of the Gnostic is to transcend the material aspects of his or her nature, and to return to his or her original and true state of oneness with God. The secret teachings of Christ enable that transforming process to take place.

The Gnostic dualism extends, of course, to creation itself; for since matter is essentially evil (so the Gnostics believed), the cosmos could not have been brought into being by the great spiritual power who is God, but must owe its creation to an inferior (and perhaps even malevolent) power. We do not at this stage need to enlarge upon the complicated systems of elemental powers and divinities devised by the Gnostics to explain how some mortals are destined for union with God, and some for ultimate extinction. It will be sufficient here merely to recognize that works such as the *Gospel of Philip* and the *Pistis Sophia*, which reflect the esoteric ideas of the second-century Gnostic Valentinus, while very different in character from less sophisticated and earlier works such as the *Gospel of Thomas*, nevertheless have this matter–spirit dualism in common.

The other important characteristic of 'Christian' Gnosticism, clearly associated with its dualism, is the belief that the true Christ could not actually have been a fleshly human being, since all matter is essentially evil. He must therefore have only *seemed* to be a human being. This belief, widely held among Gnostics, though not limited to them, came to be known as 'Docetism' (from the Greek verb 'to seem'). All truly Gnostic writings tend, therefore, to represent the physical form of Jesus as an unreal image of his essential and true spiritual self, and his suffering, Crucifixion and Resurrection as mere semblance. It cannot be stressed too strongly, however, that although these several theological emphases are typically and characteristically Gnostic, they present themselves in the various writings in very different forms and intensities, and are not confined to particular geographic regions.

b. *The Jewish-Christian Writings*
In direct contrast to Gnostic thought are the writings of the more conservative Christians who were tenaciously determined to integrate their understanding of the teachings of Christ with the observance of the Jewish Law. Jesus was himself content, as a Jew, to observe the customs and laws of his people, proclaiming that he had not come to overthrow the Law, but to fulfil it (Mt. 5.17); and many Christians of Jewish origin—not only in Palestine, but spread abroad in every part of the known world—were insistent that salvation was still dependent upon a strict observance of the Law. This, of course, meant not only adherence to the Commandments, in all their intricate detail, but also the recognition of the initiatory and symbolic rite of circumcision. We shall see in the next chapter how this insistence on the Law divided the Church for a century and more; and the harm incurred to its peace and unity reverberates down to the present day.

Had Jewish forms of the faith been limited to Judaea, it might be considerably easier than it is to settle the provenance of those works that contain legalistic elements. For historic reasons which we must leave aside for the present, however, communities of former Jews (generally referred to as 'Jewish-Christians')[12] living outside Palestine were sometimes as jealous as their Judaean counterparts for their legalistic heritage; and many of

12. The term 'Jewish-Christianity' covers a variety of meanings. In the broad sense, all Christians could look back to their Jewish religious ancestry. The term is used here, however, to denote those converts from Judaism who regarded Christianity as a progression from their former faith, rather than an entirely new religion, and who continued to observe Judaic Law and custom.

the Jewish-Christian writings probably originated not in Judaea, but in Syria and Asia Minor, or perhaps even in Egypt, where in earlier times Jews had settled in considerable numbers.

A further complication is that some of these writings show signs of editorial redaction—alterations or additions made to the text at a later date with the intention of slanting the teaching of the work towards a particular theological view. The Clementine *Homilies* and *Recognitions*, two quite different versions of the Clementine stories about Peter and Clement,[13] afford an especially good example of this kind of editing, certain passages concerning eating and washing regulations having been added, in all probability, by a later Judaizing hand. In those Jewish-Christian documents where little redaction is suspected, but where the text is extant only in either Coptic or Ethiopic, it is often impossible to be certain about the date or the provenance of the work. Such documents include the *Epistula Apostolorum*, composed perhaps in Egypt, and the traditional *Apocalypse of Peter*, whose two extant versions (Greek and Ethiopic) have given rise to much scholarly debate.

c. *The 'Orthodox' Writings*

We need to tread warily with our use of the term 'orthodox' (literally it means 'the right or true opinion'), for in some parts of the second-century Church, particularly east of Antioch, Jewish forms of Christianity were not only widespread, but considered to be normative. Nevertheless, lying between the literature of the Gnostics, on the one hand, and of the Judaizing Christians, on the other, there is a large collection of works that contain none of the excesses of the two extremes. Many of these books, other criteria having been satisfied, found a place within the New Testament canon. Equally 'orthodox' writings, such as the *Acts of Peter and the Twelve Apostles*, may have been relatively unknown in early times, and have only recently come to light; while others which were deemed to veer, however slightly, from the orthodox scriptural norm, and capable of a Gnostic interpretation, were categorized as 'dubious'.

7. *Stylistic Differences*

Attempts to classify the Apocryphal books must also take into account the various stylistic devices employed by their authors which might well pro-

---

13. Clement of Rome, who, according to tradition, was one of the early bishops of Rome. Refer to the Pseudo-Clementine literature, discussed in Chapter 3.

vide some clue as to the origin and purpose of the works. The Acts literature, for example, purports to recount actual historical events as they occurred; yet there is no doubt that they are composed in the style of the ancient Greek novel, with no less an intention to entertain than to inform. Furthermore, those who compiled the works were not averse to the interspersion of allegory and symbolism among the legends and folk-stories that form the main structure of their work. In the *Acts of Thomas*, the compiler has incorporated a wholly analogical story—the so-called 'Hymn of the Pearl'—based, perhaps, on the Gospel story of the Prodigal Son, to illustrate the fallen soul's return to his former blessed state of union with his heavenly Father. The author of the *Acts of Peter and the Twelve Apostles*, on the other hand, makes extensive use of symbolism to convey Christ's teaching on the dangers of worldly acquisition. In the story, the city called Habitation represents the world; and the city called Nine Gates, towards which the Apostles are journeying, is the heavenly and eternal city. The task of the exegete is to determine which parts of a document, if any, might be taken as historical, and which are purely representational.

Again, in the apocalyptic literature, scenes of heaven and hell, often depicted in lurid detail, are full of poetic imagery borrowed from the Scriptures, and intended to disturb, persuade and encourage those in danger of apostasy. The individual style of visionary writing yields some information about its origin to the practised reader—whether, for instance, the vision is couched in the present or future tense, suggesting either a Jewish or a Hellenistic provenance (respectively); but such criteria are not always reliable.

Faced, then, with the obvious inadequacy of any single classificatory mode, we might begin to suspect that the Apocryphal writings could tell us very little about the Christian communities that lay behind them. If we are able to fit and combine all pieces of evidence together, however—the literary *Gattung*, the theological orientation, the stylistic elements—and incorporate information we may derive from the texts themselves, and the early attestations in other works, we might be in a position reasonably to speculate about the kinds of communities that produced and used them. In Apocryphal research there are, of course, few certainties; but the comprehensive and holistic approach I propose to follow should furnish us with as true a picture of the early centuries of the Church as at present it is possible to have. Few, if any, of the extant early Apocryphal works began life in Greece or Rome. It will therefore be my plan to examine how each of the more eastern centres and regions of Church activity developed: beginning with Judaea, then moving north to Samaria, then to Antioch and Syria, then to Mesopotamia, and finally moving west into Asia Minor—the traditional respective missionary areas of James, Philip, Peter, Thomas, John and Paul. I shall add a chapter, too, on the beginnings of Christianity in Egypt, so far as this is known—an intriguing subject in view of the discovery there of so many of the early documents we shall be studying. It should here be made clear that this division of the documents into regional groups is as much a device of convenience as it is a statement about the precise origins of the various books—though in most cases the documents will be found to have associations with their allotted region. It would be difficult, for example, to avoid associating the writings of the Philip tradition with Samaria, or those of the Thomas tradition with Mesopotamia. The primary advantage of our modus operandi, however, is that the documents are assembled in manageable groups, thus avoiding unnecessary confusion for the reader. Before we can begin to look at the books themselves, however, we need briefly to trace the early history of the Church from its inception in Jerusalem, to the middle of the second century; and to that task we must now turn.

Chapter 1

THE EARLY HISTORY

1. *The Sources*

Rarely do the fortunes of early Christianity figure in secular documents of the period; and even when they do, it is largely in relation to matters of civil law and order. We are therefore obliged to rely on the Christian historians, polemicists and apologists of the early centuries for whatever information may be gleaned about the progress and development of the faith. In this, of course, lies one of our chief difficulties, for we can never be quite sure of the strict objectivity of their accounts and comments. Irenaeus, Bishop of Lyons, and Hippolytus, Bishop of Rome, devoted much of their writing to the exposure and castigation of heretical doctrines which they considered to be inimical to the Church's well-being. For insights on the development of Gnosticism we turn to the works of Clement of Alexandria, Tertullian and Origen, from whom also we derive invaluable quotations from early Christian documents which have not otherwise survived. The writings of the Palestinian scholar Hegesippus, for instance, are known to us only through brief extracts in the works of Eusebius, Irenaeus, Epiphanius and Philip of Side; but even these few quotations from the *Memoirs* (*Hypomnemata*) of Hegesippus shed important light on the life and history of the primitive Jerusalem Church.

We should not fail also to mention the apologetic writings of the Christian philosopher Justin Martyr who wrote, probably in Rome, during the first half of the second century. In the Church's ongoing controversy with both Jews and Judaizers, Justin's *Dialogue with Trypho the Jew* and his two *Apologies*, together with other work known to us only through Irenaeus and Hippolytus, help us considerably not only to understand the issues involved in that crucial controversy, and the different nuances of theological opinion, but also to trace the development of Christian doctrine and liturgical practice.

It is not our purpose here to attempt a comprehensive historical survey of the early Church. Few subjects have been more adequately covered. Because we want to locate each of the Apocryphal books within some specific geographical area, however, insofar as this is possible, it will be helpful to say something about the initial movement and spread of the faith in earliest times, beginning from Jerusalem, and spreading out in all directions. Complementing what is recorded in the canonical Acts about the evangelistic activities of the individual Apostles, several of the Apocryphal writings themselves make mention of the distribution of missionary responsibility:

> Then the Apostles separated to 'the four words' that they might preach. And they went in the power of Jesus in peace (*Epistle of Peter to Philip*, p. 140).[1]

> While Jesus was saying this, Thomas, Andrew, James and Simon the Canaanite were in the west, with their faces turned towards the east, but Philip and Bartholomew were in the south with their faces turned towards the north...and Jesus cried out, turning towards the four corners of the world with his disciples... (*Pistis Sophia*, ch. 136).

Eusebius of Caesarea, undoubtedly the most important of our historical sources, records what is probably the oldest tradition concerning the movement of the Apostles. His information derives from the writings of Papias, Bishop of Hierapolis in Asia Minor in the early decades of the second century. Papias is described by Irenaeus as 'the hearer of John (the Apostle) and the companion of Polycarp'; and in the preface to his five books of *Oracles of the Lord*, Papias claims to have inquired carefully into the lives and words of the Apostles Andrew, Peter, Philip, Thomas, James, John and Matthew. The traditional areas of responsibility which Eusebius records provide us, therefore, with as good a starting point as we might find:

> The holy Apostles and disciples of our Saviour were scattered throughout the whole world. Thomas, as tradition relates, obtained by lot Parthia, Andrew Scythia, John Asia (and he stayed there and died in Ephesus), but Peter seems to have preached to the Jews of the Dispersion in Pontus and Galatia and Bithynia, Cappadocia, and Asia, and at the end he came to Rome and was crucified head downwards, for so he demanded to suffer (*Ecclesiastical History—HE* 3.1.1).

---

1. All page nos. for the *Epistle of Peter to Philip* refer to Codex VIII of the Nag Hammadi Library.

2. *The Judaean Church*

It will be noticed in the above passage that Eusebius has no mention of James, the Lord's brother (or step-brother)—presumably because James neither left Jerusalem, apparently, nor was one of the Twelve. That he assumed the leadership of the Christians in Jerusalem following the departure of Peter for wider mission seems beyond question. In the Epistle to the Galatians, Paul speaks of James as one of the three 'pillars' of the Church, Peter (Cephas)[2] and John being the others (Gal. 2.9). In this same Epistle, Paul seems to refer to James as one of the Apostles, an indication that Paul's use of the word 'apostle' was, understandably enough, wider than most. The Acts of the Apostles does not corroborate Paul's view of James's standing in Jerusalem prior to Peter's departure 'to another place' (Acts 12.17). Thereafter, however, James comes to the fore, taking the lead in all subsequent meetings of the Apostles. It would certainly seem reasonable to suppose that, since the Twelve were generally to be found about their missionary tasks, returning to Jerusalem only for conference and review, a coordinating and administrative role performed by James would provide order and stability to their labours. Doubtless it is in this context that we must interpret Peter's apparent recognition of James's supervisory position in the opening words of his Apocryphal letter to James:

> Peter to James, the lord and bishop of the holy church: Peace be with you always from the Father of all through Jesus Christ. Knowing well that you, my brother, eagerly take pains about what is for the mutual benefit of us all... (*Epistula Petri* 1.1, 2).

While we must allow that the writer of this introductory epistle might well have had reasons of his own for exalting James's status and authority within the Church, there is sufficient textual evidence to show that for three decades until his death, somewhere between 62 and 67, he was in fact the leading Christian in Jerusalem. It is in this supervisory capacity that James is seen to act when Paul, his missions now ended, reports to James and the Apostles in Jerusalem (Acts 21.15). Paul brings with him a problem. His preaching had alienated the Jews, for it seems that he was encouraging Jewish converts living among the Gentiles to forsake the Law. The advice Paul is given from 'James and all the elders' is that he

2.   Cephas is the Aramaic form of the Greek 'Petros' ('a rock'). Both forms are used by Paul in the account of his confrontation with Peter in Antioch.

and his companions, while in Jerusalem, should themselves be seen to observe the Law by submitting to a rite of purification. We shall examine James's attitude to the Law more closely in the next chapter, but we should here note the circumspect and conservative character of the Jerusalem church. We must also note the significant judgment, recorded and sent out to all Gentile Christians by James, that they too must observe Jewish food regulations, and avoid fornication according to the Law. Such legalistic strictures, albeit of a moderate nature, were far from the spirit of Pauline preaching, and marked an important stage in the burgeoning struggle between Gentile and Judaizing Christianity.

That James was given the title 'the Just' (Hegissipus says, 'from the Lord's time') is witnessed by several early writers, the earliest of which being the authors of the *Gospel of the Hebrews* and the *Gospel of Thomas*. This latter work is especially germane to our study, for it testifies also to the tradition regarding the pre-eminence of James:

> The disciples said to Jesus: We know that you will depart from us; who is it who will be great over us? Jesus said to them: Wherever you will come, you will go to James the Just, for whose sake heaven and earth came into being (*Gos. Thom.* log. 12).

What is not clear is why the title was given. Hegesippus, writing about 180 in his *Hypomnemata*, extols James's holy manner of life, claiming that he spent such long periods in prayer and intercession for his flock that 'his knees grew hard like a camel'. The more likely derivation of the title 'Just' is suggested in the *Gospel of the Hebrews* which emphasizes James's asceticism. In this early Jewish-Christian work, James is said to have witnessed an appearance of the risen Lord (cf. 1 Cor. 15.7), having vowed that he would fast until such a vision had been vouchsafed to him. It must surely be in the sense of 'one who observes the Law' that James is called 'Just'; and this, certainly, is the chief meaning of the Greek word *dikaios* ('righteous') which we translate 'just'. Even Hegesippus remarks that James neither drank strong wine nor ate meat, and refrained from shaving his head—practices very characteristic of the ascetic piety of the sect known as the Nazirites. Clearly, for all his apparent moderation, in some respects at least he adhered strictly to Jewish Law and custom.

For the best part of three decades, then, the mother-church in Jerusalem, under James's leadership, clung to its Jewish heritage. It may be that this was more prudential than pragmatic, for it would not otherwise be easy to understand how James avoided the charge of blasphemy for so long, despite the apparent high esteem in which he was held even by some of his opponents. When his inevitable seizure by the Jewish authorities came, it was as the leader of the heretical sect of Christians that he was flung headlong down the steps (or perhaps from the pinnacle) of the Temple, and murdered. There are in fact two chief accounts of his martyrdom—those of Josephus and Hegesippus—which differ considerably in their details. A third version of the attack on James on the steps of the Temple is woven into the Pseudo-Clementine *Recognitions*, but in this account it is the persecutor and 'enemy' Saul of Tarsus who is represented as James's adversary. In this story, perhaps based on the account of Hegesippus, James recovers, and continues his supervision of the Church, warning his colleagues to flee from Jerusalem, north to Jericho—an interesting insight, however problematical, in view of later tradition.

Both Hegesippus and the author of the *Second Apocalypse of James* make the disturbances surrounding the martyrdom of James the immediate cause of Vespasian's sack of the city in 67; and the tradition recorded by Eusebius that Christians left Jerusalem to its well-deserved fate prior to that catastrophic event, escaping north to the city of Pella, seems to be well founded. There is, of course, no certainty that Christian migrants to Pella remained there. Eusebius informs us that the Apostles appointed a worthy successor to James, placing the see of Jerusalem in the hands of one Simeon, the son of Clopas; and it might well be the case that, once the war was over, many of those who had fled would feel it safe to return. There is little doubt that Christians would be in as much danger from state persecution as the Jews themselves; and it may be that many suffered the same fate, either during the siege itself, which is described in such vivid detail by the Jewish historian Josephus,[3] or in subsequent years.

Unfortunately we have no record, apart from the Pella tradition itself, of the movement of Christians within Judaea, or, for that matter, south towards Egypt. It may be, as some scholars have suggested, that primitive Jerusalem-type Christianity ceased to exist after 70, and that Hellenistic Jewish forms of the faith that developed later in Syria and Asia originated outside Judaea. We shall shortly discuss how Hellenistic forms of Christianity developed in different ways from Judaean Christianity; but to make the assumption, simply from lack of evidence to the contrary, that primitive Jewish Christianity died out completely, would seem to be unwarranted. Eusebius does in fact relate that the Church maintained its presence and work among the Hebrews of Jerusalem from the

3.   *War* 5. Cf. Eusebius, *HE* 3.5.6-25.

time of the Apostles to the destruction of the city by the Emperor Hadrian in 135, and provides us with details of the episcopal succession.

3. *The Church in Samaria*

Pella was, in fact, one of the original ten cities that, about the time of the birth of Christ, formed an alliance for mutual trade and defence. The region, south and east of Galilee, and largely on the eastern side of the Jordan, had come to be known as the Decapolis. Here, according to Mark's Gospel, Jesus had toured with his disciples, restoring the demoniac at Gadara, and preaching and healing throughout the region (Mk 7.31). Matthew relates how great crowds from Decapolis and beyond the Jordan followed Jesus (Mt. 4.25), and we might reasonably speculate that if the Jerusalem Christians did indeed flee to Pella in the late sixties, they might well have found support there from like-minded Christian friends.

To the west of the Decapolis, and on the western side of the Jordan, lay Samaria, with its chief coastal city of Caesarea. The Acts of the Apostles suggests that this was the missionary area of Philip the Deacon. In the persecution that followed the martyrdom of Stephen, all except the Apostles themselves 'were scattered throughout the region of Judaea and Samaria' (Acts 8.1); and Philip's highly successful evangelistic activity in Samaria was brought to the attention of the elders in Jerusalem. Such, at all events, is the evidence of the New Testament, which also gives us the story of the chief Apostles sharing in Philip's achievement (Acts 8.4-17). It may be that these accounts of the conversion of the Samaritans, and of their subsequent receipt of the Spirit, reflect two distinct traditions which Luke here attempts to harmonize; for, according to different traditions, both Peter and Philip are credited with establishing the faith in Caesarea. Certainly the authority of the mother-church seems to be an issue of importance; and the note of tension which some exegetes have identified in this passage is reflected, perhaps, in the opening words of the Apocryphal *Epistle of Peter to Philip*:

> Peter, the apostle of Jesus Christ, to Philip, our beloved brother and fellow-apostle, with the brethren who are with you, greetings! I wish you to know, our brother, that we have received commandment from our Lord, the saviour of the whole world, that we should come together, in order to teach and preach concerning the salvation which was promised to us by our Lord Jesus Christ. But you held yourself apart from us and had no liking for our coming together... (*Epistle of Peter to Philip*, p. 132).

It will be noticed that Peter here addresses not Philip the Deacon, who settled in Caesarea, but Philip the Apostle from Bethsaida, who, according to early tradition, went to live and work in Phrygia in Asia Minor. There is a confusion here, replicated in other works concerning 'Philip', and we shall address this in due course. So far as this particular work is concerned, we may suggest that its author shared in the general confusion between the two Philips, but that his intention was to refer to Philip the Deacon, appointed with six others, to assist the Twelve (Acts 6.1-6), and whose unilateral mission in Samaria met with such success.

The other figure of considerable significance in the early history of the Samaritan Church was the enigmatic Simon Magus who features prominently not only in the canonical Acts, but also in the Apocryphal *Acts of Peter*, and in the Pseudo-Clementine *Recognitions* and *Homilies*. It would seem incontrovertible that some such person did exercise considerable esoteric influence in this region—and possibly later in Rome, for his magical exploits are attested by Eusebius, and in the work of Justin Martyr. Irenaeus refers to him as the progenitor of all sorts of heresies, and it cannot be denied that many of the beliefs of the Gnostic sects emerging in Syria and Egypt during the second century had much in common with the Simonian cult. Once again, the somewhat confused account in the Acts of the Apostles seems to reflect two distinct traditions. Philip's preaching resulted in the conversion and baptism of Simon; but Peter's opposition to Simon, despite the latter's show of penitence after trying to purchase the Spirit, was implacable, and we are left wondering whether Simon was ever rehabilitated into the Church's fellowship (Acts 8.9-24).

It would be impossible to ignore, and difficult to exaggerate, the widespread ramifications of Simon's teaching, and his clash with the Church. His immediate following was confined, according to Justin, largely to the Samaritan race, whether in Samaria itself, or in Rome, where, so it was said, he was honoured by the erection of a statue.[4] His wider influence, however, was immense; and his extravagant claims to divinity for himself and his consort Helen, together with the attraction of his peculiar blend of mythology, astrology and occult philosophy, found fertile ground not only in Samaria, but throughout Syria and Egypt. Irenaeus makes the claim that Jewish and Syrian Gnostic systems devised by Menander, Saturninus, Carpocrates and Basilides all played their part in the concepts of Valentinus and Elchasai, the more sophisticated development of whose teaching found expression in some of the documents from Nag Hammadi.

---

4. Justin Martyr, *First Apology* 1.26.3.

In Chapter 3 we shall consider in some detail the two non-canonical documents which portray Simon Magus as Peter's great antagonist, the *Acts of Peter* and the Pseudo-Clementine *Recognitions*. Both narratives describe the contest between Peter and Simon, designed to allow the people to choose which of them was the worthier. It will soon become obvious as we read, however, that Simon seems to symbolize the 'enemy' Paul, hated by the legalistic Jewish-Christians, and that the contest between the two Simons was intended to represent the bitter and ongoing struggle between Gentile and Jewish forms of the faith—between the legalism of Jewish Christianity, on the one hand, and the liberalizing, all-inclusive Christianity of Paul, on the other. The New Testament itself bears witness to the tension, if not animosity, that seems to have existed between the Apostles Peter and Paul in the early years concerning the vexed question of who might be eligible for full membership of the Church. In his Epistle to the Galatians, Paul himself recounts how on one occasion he accused Peter of hypocrisy and inconsistency on the issue of the equality of Jewish and Gentile Christians (Gal. 2.11). Peter, in fact, answers this charge in the Epistula Petri, referring to Paul as 'the man who is my enemy'. While modern scholarship tends to feel that earlier biblical historians have exaggerated the long-term effects of this bitter personal quarrel (which certainly seems to have been speedily and amicably resolved), we shall discover that the underlying conflict between Gentile and Judaizing Christians would recur in a variety of ways for the best part of another century.[5]

We cannot leave the Samaritan Church without a mention of the two important sects that came to be known as the Nazaraeans and the Ebionites. It is almost impossible to unravel the many different, and sometimes conflicting, strands of information that have come down to us from the early Church Fathers concerning these sects (whether they might be described as Jewish, or Jewish-Christian); but we cannot begin to understand primitive Palestinian Christianity without having some acquaintance with them. We first meet the term 'Nazaraeans', as a description of a particular sect among the Jews, in the Acts of the Apostles, where Tertullus accuses Paul of being a ringleader of the sect (Acts 24.5). There is no evidence that the earliest Christians referred to themselves as Nazaraeans. Indeed, the contrary indication is that the term 'Christians' soon became the norm (Acts 11.26). By the middle of the second century, however,

---

5.   Second-century evidence of this may be found, for instance, in Ignatius (*Magnesians* 10, and *Philadelphians* 6); Justin Martyr (*Dialogue with Trypho* 10 and 17); and in the *Epistle of Barnabas* 11. See also Chapter 3 below.

Justin Martyr was able to identify among the Jews and Samaritans a variety of different beliefs about Christ which later writers (Epiphanius and Jerome) came to associate with the Nazaraeans and Ebionites.

We shall look in vain for some definitive consensus about the Christologies of these groups, but it might not be too far from the truth to say that in the years following the migration of Christians to Pella, there were in this region significant numbers of Jews who adhered to the law, but who also recognized Jesus to be the awaited Messiah. Some at least of these acknowledged his divinity, some even his pre-existence. By the fourth century, groups of such Christian believers, though still holding to their former Jewish obligations, had come to be known in some areas as Nazaraeans. It would be a mistake to be dogmatic about their Christology, for even Epiphanius, who had some knowledge of the sect through his friend Jerome, was himself uncertain. We must remember, too, that different groups of Nazaraean Christians would be unlikely to develop in exactly the same way. Those living in Coele Syria or Beroea, for instance, where the sect was said to be strong, might have a somewhat different view of Christ from the Nazaraeans of Pella and the Decapolis, where, according to Epiphanius, the 'heresy had its beginnings'.[6] How far Nazaraean belief could be said to be representative of 'Jewish Christianity' is difficult to say. There is no doubt, however, that some converts from Judaism who were reluctant to forsake the Law, but who believed Christ to be in some sense the 'Son of God', were known, at least in Samaria and as far north as Coele Syria, as Nazaraeans.

The other Jewish sect on the fringe of Christianity have been given the name of Ebionites. The word *ebion* (from a Hebrew word meaning 'poor') is frequently used in the Old Testament for the devout and pious ones. It would be in this sense that it is used in the first of the Gospel Beatitudes—'Blessed are the poor in spirit...' (Mt. 5.3). Irenaeus was the first to employ the term 'Ebionites' to describe this distinct sect, stating that their teaching was similar to that of Cerinthus and Carpocrates who denied both the divinity and the virgin birth of Jesus. The Ebionites, however, did regard Christ as in some sense the fulfilment of prophecy; and if they might not have been generally recognized as Christians by others, there is no doubt that they professed an allegiance to Christ as the anointed one of God. Epiphanius was considerably more certain about Ebionite belief than about the Nazaraeans, as the following passage from his *Panarion* reveals:

6.   *Panarion* 29.7, 8.

> Besides the daily bath they [the Ebionites] have a baptism of initiation and
> each year they celebrate certain mysteries in imitation of the Church of the
> Christians. In these mysteries they use unleavened bread and, for the other
> part, pure water. They say that God has established two beings, Christ and
> the Devil. To the former has been committed the power of the world to
> come, and to the other the power of this world. They say that Jesus was
> begotten of human seed, and chosen, and thus called by election Son of
> God, Christ having come upon him from on high in the form of a dove.
> They say he was not begotten by God the Father, but that he was created,
> like the archangels, but greater than they (*Panarion* 30.16).

Several key points in this important passage tend to corroborate the
evidence of Justin and other early writers about this sect. The Christology
of the Ebionites was unequivocally Adoptionist—that is, they believed
Jesus to be wholly human, a man whom God endowed with his divine Spirit
at his baptism, making him in some sense his 'Son'. The manner of their
observance of the Christian 'mysteries' (the Eucharist) showed a definite
proclivity towards asceticism (the use of water instead of wine), as did their
custom of ritual and habitual washing. Other passages from Epiphanius
and Hippolytus indicate that they used only the Gospel of Matthew (or their
version of it), and they rejected completely the Epistles of Paul. They insisted on the rite of circumcision as a prerequisite of Christian initiation;
and they seem to have surpassed the Nazaraeans in their devotion to the
Jewish Law, though they rejected the concept of Temple sacrifice. We may
also detect a hint of Gnostic dualism in their ideas concerning the ongoing
struggle within creation between the power of this world, and the power of
the world to come.

Of the origins of the Ebionite sect there is some uncertainty. Most ecclesiastical historians believe that it was not merely a continuation of primitive
Jerusalem-type Christianity, but that it developed as a counter-reaction to
burgeoning Gentile Christianity, at a time when rabbinic Judaism was
beginning to reconsolidate following the destruction of the Temple in 70.
The theory that Ebionism developed as an offshoot of Nazaraean Christianity during the second century would require some modification, however,
in the light of scholarly investigations into the more recently deciphered
texts of the Dead Sea Scrolls. Several of the documents found in Cave 4,
for example, refer to the members of the Qumran Community as the
Ebionim ('Poor Ones'), a description which seems to have been applied to
Judaic sects, around the time of Christ, whose manner of life was based on
piety, frugality and holiness. The initial discoveries at Qumran gave rise to
the popular expectation that these papyrus texts would provide exciting

new evidence of earliest messianic Christianity in the Jordanian desert, for many passages in the documents seemed to have clear parallels in the Gospels. Furthermore, it was recognized that some of the characteristics of the Jewish sect of the Essenes, as described by Hippolytus, were reflected in these fragmentary documents. Could Jesus himself have been an Essene—and John before him? Were the Ebionites a branch of Essenism? Did some of James's church move into the desert to await the final struggle between good and evil, and the coming of the new age?

That there are positive links between early Christianity and Jewish desert piety is beyond question; but which movement borrowed concepts from the other, or whether both were dependent upon a common fund of thought, is at this stage of research impossible to be sure. What may be said is that the Ebionites, whatever their origin, in some way represent the link between Nazaraean Christianity and Jewish piety, being influenced, perhaps, by both, to form a distinctive 'Christian Judaism' (rather than a form of 'Jewish Christianity'). As in the case of the Nazaraeans, the lifestyle and teaching of Ebionite communities would develop in different ways, leaning one way or another towards either Christianity or Judaism. The general picture remains true, however, that at a time of turmoil in Jewish life following the fall of Jerusalem, when conservative Jews were trying to re-establish their cultural and social identity within the empire, many Jews would feel the need, while acknowledging Christ as the true Prophet, to stand firm against the liberalizing Gospel of Paul and Gentile Christianity.

With the gradual spread of Christianity to the east and north of Samaria, a number of charismatic teachers and prophets began to appear whose teachings, while owing much to the Gospel, had more in common with the ancient religions of Parthia and India. One such figure, who came to be known as Elchasai (meaning 'hidden power'), taught at the close of the first century an intriguing mixture of Judaism, Christianity and astrology. His insistence on observance of the Law, of circumcision and the Sabbath, suggests a Jewish background; and, like John the Baptist, he emphasized a new baptism of repentance—a second ritual washing for the forgiveness of sins, with the penitent calling upon seven witnesses—heaven, water, holy spirits, angels of prayer, oil, salt and the earth—as guarantors of his lasting conversion. Yet Elchasai repudiated both the Jewish Prophets and the Temple sacrificial system; and the pre-existent Christ was represented as the 'the Greatest and Highest God'. The angels (both good and bad) and the stars figured prominently in his system, an indication of the influence of Persian thought. The contents of the *Book of Elchasai*, citations of which are found in the *Refutations* of Hippolytus,[7] were said to have been revealed to its author by the Son of God, whose height, Elchasai averred, was 96 miles, and whose female companion (the Holy Spirit) was of similar proportions. We will encounter such strange imagery in several of the Apocryphal books before us.

The nascent Gnosticism of Elchasai's system would develop in a number of different ways. A century and a half after Elchasai, the Mesopotamian founder of a world religion which was to prove a serious rival to Christianity—Manichaeism—was to spend his formative years within an Elchasaite community whose teachings he subsequently repudiated. Mani must certainly have been familiar with, and influenced by, the teachings of Zoroaster, as well as those of Jesus and Buddha; but while he acknowledged these as prophets, he considered them to be his forerunners; for it had been revealed to him by his 'angel-twin' that he was no longer a human being, but in reality the awaited Paraclete, the Apostle of Light, and his followers lost sparks of divinity, trapped here on earth, and awaiting release through knowledge. Such information about Mani, and his Gnostic system, comes to us from books recently rediscovered, including an account of his early life and extensive missionary journeys in the *Cologne Mani-Codex*. We have, of course, moved ahead of our period somewhat, with this brief mention of Manichaeism. Our reason for doing so is that the documents reveal Mani's acquaintance and extensive use of important Christian Apocryphal writings, notably the *Gospel of Philip* and the *Acts of Thomas*—and, it may be, with the *Gospel of Peter*.

We shall leave for later consideration several other key philosophical and religious systems comprising ideologies associated with Marcion, Menander, Saturninus, Basilides, Valentinus and Bardesanes—all influential in their differing ways in the rise of Gnostic, Ascetic and Encratite groups throughout Palestine, Syria and beyond. What is important here is to recognize that mainstream Christianity was compelled to struggle desperately against a host of conflicting and competing theories concerning human origin, purpose and destiny, a fact which makes more understandable the apparently frenetic and obsessive concern of the early Christian polemicists to disparage and discredit the 'heresies' all around them.

---

7. Hippolytus, *Refutation of All Heresies* 9.8.3.

4. *The Syrian Church*

The spread of Christianity to Antioch in Syria, some 300 miles from Jerusalem, was the direct result, so the Acts of the Apostles informs us, of the persecution of Christians following the death of Stephen (Acts 11.19-26). Luke's evidence is certainly credible, for the city, under both Seleucid and Roman rule, was noted for its cosmopolitan liberality. Here Christians would be free to pursue their own way, relatively safe at least from state intervention. The groundwork for later internal dissent, however, was laid at Antioch with the arrival of Christians from Cyprus and Cyrene whose preaching attracted the first Gentiles into the Church. Luke is anxious to show that such a significant step met with the full approval of the Jerusalem elders by recording the visit of Barnabas to Antioch, and his subsequent ministry with Saul of Tarsus among the Gentile Christians in that city. It was at Antioch, however, that the Church had to deal with the beginnings of conflict between Jewish and Gentile Christians on the vexed question of circumcision; and here also, according to Paul himself, as we noted earlier, that Peter showed his apparent ambivalence in the matter of Gentile status within the Church (Gal. 2.11-21).

Clearly, the spread of the faith into the Hellenistic world, and among Gentiles as well as Jews, was unstoppable, despite considerable Judaizing opposition; and Antioch proved to be a convenient and suitable base for the Pauline missionary activity. There is no firm evidence that Peter ever visited Antioch, though both Origen and Eusebius seem to know a tradition that he was in fact its first bishop, and Ignatius his successor.[8] Only the Pseudo-Clementine *Homilies* and *Recognitions*, whose historicity is more than dubious, actually record his presence there; and neither the Acts of the Apostles nor the *Acts of Peter* suggest that he ventured any further north than Caesarea. This latter work does in fact assert, doubtless for political reasons, that Peter journeyed eventually to Rome, a claim which is nowhere else attested except in popular tradition. The canonical Acts merely states that after his miraculous release from prison, Peter went to 'another place', an expression which might have meant either a safe haven away from Jerusalem, or, indeed, to a final haven in heaven.

Leaving aside any Petrine involvement in Philip's evangelistic work in Samaria (Acts 8), it would certainly appear that Peter was initially drawn to (or believed himself to be charged with) the conversion of the Gentiles,

---

8.   Cf. Eusebius, *HE* 3.36.2; cf. Origen, *Homily on Luke* 6.

concentrating on the Hellenistic coastal cities of Judaea and Phoenicia, and moving always towards Caesarea. The Lukan account of Peter's association with Caesarea focuses on his phenomenal success among the Gentiles, to the amazement of Jewish believers (Acts 10.45); and it was this first Gentile mission at Caesarea that Peter pointedly refers to in his speech at the Conference of Apostles and Elders at Jerusalem, claiming to have been the chosen instrument of God in the task of bringing the Gentiles to faith (Acts 15.7). If all this seems to contradict Paul's unequivocal statement about an earlier agreed division of work, with he, himself, being charged with going to the Gentiles (Gal. 2.9), and Peter to the Jews, it may be that Paul's understanding of the outcome of Conference differed from that of the Apostles; for, when Paul and Barnabas (with Judas and Silas) were entrusted with a letter to the Gentiles of Antioch, it was, in fact, the start of the first *authorized* Gentile mission into Asia and beyond. It is evident, however, that Peter recognized no bounds to his work. At Caesarea, where the Acts of the Apostles informs us he 'remained for some days' (Acts 10.48), residing, it may be, with Philip and his family, many Gentiles received the Holy Spirit; and it was here, according to the Pseudo-Clementines, as he prepared to leave for Tyre, that he laid hands on Zacchaeus as his successor, giving him the 'chair of Christ', and the power to 'loose what is to be loosed and to bind what is to be bound'. The pattern of Peter's ministry at most of the cities along his route was the same—preaching, healing, baptizing and, finally, appointing one of his own entourage to stay behind as bishop.

The tradition that Peter came to Antioch as its first bishop, following the conversion of the first Gentiles, has at least one strand of circumstantial support. The First Epistle of Peter is addressed to 'the exiles of the Dispersion in Pontus, Galatia, Cappadocia, Asia and Bithynia, chosen and destined by God...' (1 Pet. 1.1). Who, precisely, these Christians of the 'Dispersion' were is not immediately obvious. Some have identified them (or the majority of them) as Gentiles, and others a mixture of Gentiles and Jews. There would seem to be no compelling reason, however, to abandon the more traditional view, propounded by the early exegetes of the patristic age, that 'Peter' was writing largely to Christians of Jewish background and race (cf. 1 Pet. 2.12); and if we take into account the traditional division of missionary responsibility which made Peter the 'Apostle of the Circumcision', we might see 1 Peter as the counterpart for Jewish-Christians of the 'Pauline' letters to the Gentiles of that same area—Colossians and Ephesians. If this were so, it would go some way to explaining the close similarities between these three Epistles. We might, then, reasonably

speculate that Peter made Caesarea or Antioch his base for missionary
journeys into Asia. While no such activity is anywhere recorded in extant
literature, the testimony of Paul concerning the division of missionary
responsibility (Gal. 2.7, 8) would seem to suggest that both Peter and Paul
were working, separately, in that area. If this were, indeed, the case, we
could well imagine that a Petrine source would want to endorse, for Jewish-
Christians, the 'Pauline' message to the Gentiles (Eph. 2.11) concerning
the privilege of their calling, and the high quality of life which, in Christ,
they must now exemplify.

What is certain is that so much of the early Petrine Apocryphal literature
seems to originate in the vicinity of Antioch. The *Gospel of Peter* first
came to the notice of the ecclesiastical authorities in the small town of
Rhossos (so Eusebius tells us), some 30 miles north of Antioch. Here,
towards the close of the second century, a group of Christians was using
this Gospel, attributed to Peter, unaware that its docetic overtones, and its
textual deviations from the accepted norm, would shortly curtail its authorized use. The *Acts of Peter* and the original Greek version of the traditional *Apocalypse of Peter*, as we shall later try to show, both have strong
links with the region known as Coele Syria. It is this area, of course, which
is generally associated with the so-called 'Matthaean Church'—the Jewish-
Christian community for which Matthew's Gospel was probably compiled;
and because this Gospel is cited far more extensively than any other Gospel
in the Apocryphal writings, we need to be aware of the current thought
about its origin and compilation.

It has long been recognized that the Gospel as we now have it owes
much to the earlier Markan Gospel, large portions of which were used
with little change by the authors of both Matthew and Luke. However,
some passages that are common to Matthew and Luke do not appear at all
in Mark; and for many years the majority of textual scholars have postulated that a common unknown source once existed which they have called
'Q' (from the German *Quelle*, meaning 'source'). A significant number of
scholars reject this 'Two Source Theory' (Mark and Q) for the compilation
of Matthew and Luke, preferring to believe that the author of Luke possessed a copy of Matthew, and filled out from Matthew what was lacking
in Mark. The recent discovery of the *Gospel of Thomas*, however, which is
not a Gospel in the conventional sense, but rather a collection of Dominical
'Sayings', has tended to confirm the view that such 'collections' or *florile-
gia* might well have been in circulation, Q being one of them. The debate
continues. In a subsequent chapter we shall examine whether the *Gospel of*

the Nazaraeans, which seems to have been written in Aramaic, was the precursor of the Matthaean Gospel, and whether it reflected, as Matthew's Gospel itself appears to do, a distinctive Petrine tradition.

5. *The Church in Mesopotamia*

A fourth-century hagiographical work, discovered in Asia Minor, and displaying some evidence of textual revision in the course of its transmission, would seem to be a most unlikely place to begin to look for evidence of early Christianity in Eastern Syria and Mesopotamia; yet a document entitled the *Life of Abercius* contains a transcription of a Greek epitaph of one who describes himself as 'a disciple of a holy shepherd', and who evidently travelled widely in this area shortly before his death in Phrygia in the early years of the third century. Abercius, who might well have been a priest or bishop at Hierapolis, is said in the *Life* to have composed his own epitaph, in which he describes something of his journeys both to Rome, and to places of special interest in Syria and Parthia, before returning home to Asia Minor. Archaeological corroboration of the existence of the epitaph came in 1883 with the discovery within the walls of the public baths at Hierapolis of a number of fragmentary inscriptions, among which was found clear evidence of Abercius's epitaph. So impressed was this Asian Christian with the reception he had been accorded among Christian brethren at Nisibis and elsewhere along his route, that he was anxious to have his journey recorded for posterity.

That there were Christians in some numbers at Nisibis by the end of the second century, and in other cities of northern Mesopotamia, notably Edessa, is beyond question. The *Diatessaron* of Tatian, compiled in his Syrian homeland, was certainly in general use in the region shortly after the middle of the century; and Bardaisan, whose strange amalgam of Christian teaching and astrology was proving immensely popular in Edessa only a generation later, testifies in his *Laws of the Countries* to the presence of Christians in Parthia, Media and Persia. There is, it is true, little direct textual evidence from the period to show in what ways the form of the faith east of Antioch differed from its western counterpart. The important question of how Christianity first came to this region is a matter of continuing research; but here we might just observe that, though in the course of time the city of Edessa became the undisputed headquarters of the eastern Syrian Church, to imagine that Christianity spread into Syria and beyond exclusively from neighbouring Antioch would be unwarranted. Undoubtedly the Church at Antioch played as important a role in extending the faith east along the great 'Silk Road' as it did west into Asia Minor, Greece and Rome. The ancient tradition of expansion from Jerusalem, however, cannot be ignored; and we will want to explore the strong possibility that not only was Christianity introduced into Edessa and the cities of northern Mesopotamia along more southerly routes as well as from Antioch, but that this may in some measure account for the variety of forms of the faith which seem to have developed in this region.

There are several oblique references in the text of Abercius's epitaph to sustenance, as much ethereal as material, which the traveller was delighted to receive along the journey, and in one line he seems to indicate that he had Paul (presumably the Apostle) as his spiritual companion. Despite the lacuna at this point in the text, and the obvious uncertainty about its interpretation, it has been thought that Abercius might have been following (in reverse) the path of Paul's journeys. If this were indeed the case, we would need to recall that Paul's only recorded excursion into eastern territory (Gal. 1.17)—into what he called 'Arabia'—was not from Antioch, but from Damascus. Since according to his own submission Paul spent three years in this region, his influence here (if we can rely upon the accuracy of Luke's account) must have been extensive and prolonged. It has generally been assumed that Abercius would enter Mesopotamia through Edessa, taking the road south to Nisibis, and returning, perhaps, by the same route. A more likely journey from Rome, however, would bring him by sea to Tyre or Caesarea on the Syrian coast, whence he could take the Damascus road through Caesarea Philippi, visiting the cities beyond the Euphrates before returning to his native Phrygia through Edessa. It could well have been by this same route that the first Christians came to Mesopotamia, and perhaps even to India.

It might seem a trifle perverse to begin this short survey of early Syrian Christianity with the precarious evidence of a crumbling memorial discovered in Asia Minor, when there is to hand the well-documented story of Edessa's literary link with Jesus himself. Eusebius relates, in his *Ecclesiastical History*, how King Abgar, the 'celebrated monarch of the nations beyond the Euphrates', wrote to Jesus to beg him to come and heal his infirmity.[9] Jesus' reply, by letter, was to the effect that after completing his work in Palestine he would return to his Father, and therefore could not come; but he promised to send one of his disciples to heal Abgar, and bring the message of life to his people. After the Ascension (Eusebius

---

9.   Eusebius, *HE* 1.13.6-22.

records), one of the Twelve—Judas, called Thomas—sent Thaddaeus,[10] who not only cured the king of his illness, but preached so convincingly that the whole city became Christian. Were the Abgar legend, as Eusebius presents it, historically reliable, we should indeed have little need for Abercius; for the outcome of the reported correspondence between the Edessan king and Jesus, elaborated and confirmed in the fifth-century *Teaching of Addai*, testifies persuasively to the widespread adoption of Christianity in the city. There is at present, however, no definitive consensus on the historicity of the story, or on the question whether the tradition derives from its ostensible date during the second period of the reign of Abgar V Ukkama, or, as some have suggested, from the much later reign of Abgar VIII the Great. Because of the obvious links between the reported correspondence and the 'Judas-Thomas' tradition in the Syrian Church, much in evidence in the Thomasine literature, we shall defer discussion on this important question until Chapter 5. Without wishing to anticipate that discussion, however, we might just observe here that while we may want to agree with the majority of scholars that the legend, in its present form, bears all the hallmarks of later invention, designed to give apostolic origins to the Edessan Church, we ought not to exclude the possibility that a simpler form of the tradition could be very much earlier, and one which, like many legends, is not entirely without historical foundation.

If we are not able, then, to admit the Abgar story, in its present form, as primary evidence of the introduction of Christianity into Syria, we may find ourselves on rather safer ground with other early traditions concerned with eastern expansion. Luke's description of the Pentecostal outpouring of the Spirit (Acts 2) mentions 'Parthians and Medes, Elamites and residents of Mesopotamia' among the Jews of the Dispersion visiting Jerusalem for the Festival. We must accept, of course, that Luke's comprehensive list might well be no more than an imaginative device to emphasize the rapidity of the spread of Christianity to the entire world; but we must also recognize that, whenever the passage was written, it would surely have been based on the then known extent of Christian penetration into these several parts of the empire. That there were Christians beyond the Euphrates, and perhaps even as far south as the Persian Gulf, must have been

---

10. Also one of the Twelve according to the lists of Apostles in Matthew (10.3) and Mark (3.18). Eusebius's use of the name 'Thaddaeus' in this tradition may reflect a confusion with the name 'Addai' (traditionally one of the 'Seventy' whom Jesus appointed; cf. Lk. 10.1) who, according to one account, was the first evangelist of Edessa. See Chapter 2, section 6, and Chapter 5.

known by the close of the first century. Little documentary evidence exists to show how the faith developed here, however, and we shall look to the Apocryphal writings, notably the *Gospel of Thomas*, the *Acts of Thomas*, and the *Book of Thomas the Contender*, to shed some light on this fascinating problem.

6. *The Asian Church*

If the Edessan Church belongs to Thomas (or Judas Thomas, as he is called in many of the writings),[11] the churches west of Antioch would seem, according to the evidence of the New Testament, to be Pauline. We will recall, however, that the ancient tradition, attributed to Papias, Bishop of Hierapolis, was that Asia was the territory of the Apostle John, who lived long, and died in Ephesus. Eusebius's interpretation of Papias's testimony clearly assumes that there were two 'Johns'—the Apostle, who wrote the Gospel and the Epistles, and John the Elder who was responsible for the Revelation. That these respective works are very different in style and character has been evident from the beginning; but that there are unmistakable theological links, particularly between the Gospel and the First Epistle, is also generally recognized. It is happily not our task to try to determine to what extent the Johannine canonical writings share a common authorship, though we might venture that, notwithstanding early tradition, this seems unlikely. What is quite fundamental to our understanding of the Asian Church, however, is that the writings reveal the influence not only of Pauline thought, but also—and perhaps chiefly—of the so-called Hermetic literature of the period; and because of the signal importance of these writings for the development of Gnosticism, we need to be clear about what is encompassed by the term *Hermetica*.

The *Corpus Hermeticum* is a collection of those extant writings composed, for the most part, under the representative name of the Egyptian sage Hermes Trismegistus who, after his death, was deified as the God Thoth. Appearing originally in Greek, from the end of the first century to about the fourth, these writings have been described as a cross-fertilization of Greek and oriental thought, a popular mixture of Stoic ethics and Platonist ideology. Many of the writings are in Dialogue form; and the teaching

11.   'Thomas' is not a name. It means, from the Hebrew, 'twin' (as does the Greek form 'Didymus'). Several disciples of Jesus bore the name of Judas. No doubt 'Thomas' was one of them; but whose twin he was is problematical. Was it, perhaps, Thaddaeus?

is put into the mouth of Hermes, the messenger of the Gods. Human salvation is to be achieved by knowledge—that is, the knowledge of God; and to know God is to partake of his nature. The power of God permeates the world in the form of rays of light. Concepts of the immanence of God in the world, of the meeting of human mind (Nous) and reason (Logos) with the being of God, of enlightenment, rebirth and immortality, all abound in this literature; and it will be quite evident that the underlying philosophy of the *Hermetica* is clearly reflected in the Fourth Gospel, not least, as Augustine of Hippo observed in his *Confessions*, in the Johannine Prologue. If the Evangelist was not directly influenced by the Hermetists, at least we must allow that he drew from a common ethos and outlook which pervaded the entire Hellenistic world of his time.

It will have been noticed that there are remarkable similarities between the thought-forms of the Hermetic writings and those of emergent Gnosticism, parallels which will become increasingly obvious as we examine in particular the manuscripts from Nag Hammadi. If the Fourth Evangelist may be shown to draw from the pre-Gnostic ideas that permeate the *Hermetica*, however, he must also be reckoned to be quite as indebted to the Jewish (and Alexandrian) philosopher Philo, whose idea of the divine Logos as the creative power emanating from God is fundamental to his thought—as indeed are many of the symbolic concepts used to describe the nature of the deity. In view of the incontrovertible links between the Johannine writings and these important Egyptian sources, we may feel that there is some justification for the minority view that John's Gospel was composed in Alexandria, rather than in Ephesus or Antioch. It does seem to have been known by Ignatius, however—though he quotes only sparsely from any of the Gospels; and Polycarp appears to have been familiar with the Johannine Epistles, if not the Gospel and Revelation, confirming Papias's tradition about his own association with John the Elder. While it is not within our scope to determine the origin of the Johannine writings, it is important that we recognize that, notwithstanding clear Alexandrian influence, all the Johannine literature seems to focus on the Church in Asia. There is presently no evidence weighty enough to encourage us to discard the ancient tradition recorded by Eusebius that the Church in this region, after the death of Paul, looked for its leadership to the (ageing) Apostle John.

How then did this strange Alexandrian mix of Platonist thought characteristic of the *Hermetica*, and the Hellenistic Judaism of Philo, find so ready a home in Asia? Perhaps to some extent the answer lies in the fact that the ideas and language of Alexandria were in some measure current already in the well-established mystery cults of Cybele in Phrygia, and Artemis in Ephesus. More fundamentally, so many of the concepts of Hermes and of Philo were already familiar from the Old Testament itself – the idea, for instance, that God is the fountain of light and life, and that to know him is the goal of human endeavour. Again, geographical links across the Mediterranean between Egypt and Asia Minor would ensure a steady flow of ideas, and a constant interrelationship of cultures. We recall, for instance, that the Alexandrian Jew Apollos brought to Ephesus, and subsequently to Achaia, an eloquent, charismatic and perhaps even allegorical interpretation of the Scriptures (Acts 18.24, 25) which would allow Christianity to compete on equal terms with the popular mysteries and attractive ideologies of Asia.

The Apocryphal *Acts of John*, though possibly of Syrian rather than Asian origin, nevertheless recounts the missionary activity of the Apostle in the provinces of Asia Minor, as he journeyed to many of the cities whose churches had been the recipients of admonishing letters in the Johannine Apocalypse. Its author highlights the Church's struggle with rival cults and religions in an idealized account of John ascendancy over Artemis (Diana) in Ephesus, culminating in the destruction of her temple:

> While John was saying this, of a sudden the altar of Artemis split into many pieces, and all the offerings laid up in the temple suddenly fell to the floor and its glory was shattered, and so were more than seven images; and half the temple fell down, so that the priest was killed at one stroke as the pillar came down (*Acts of John* 42).

Of particular significance for our purpose in this work is the portrayal of Christ in distinctly other-worldly terms, reminiscent of other books of the Johannine 'School',[12] and with remarkable affinities both to Philo and the *Hermetica*. We might instance a passage in the section entitled 'Revelation of the Mystery of the Cross' (*Acts of John* 97–102) in which the author, with Gnostic and Docetic overtones, writes of the cross in terms of the Logos of God:

12. During the course of the second century, notable Christian teachers in Rome and elsewhere (Justin Martyr, for example) began to gather around them hearers and disciples for instruction, after the manners of the Greek and Roman philosophers. Schools of some particular theological orientation inevitably became associated with one or other of the Apostles. The Johannine 'School', strong in Ephesus, may have been responsible for producing some, at least, of the Johannine literature of the New Testament.

> And I saw the Lord himself above the Cross, having no shape but only a
> kind of voice; yet not that voice which we knew, but one which was sweet
> and gentle and truly (the voice) of God, which said to me, 'John, there must
> be one man to hear these thing; for I need one who is ready to hear. This
> Cross of Light is sometimes called Logos by me for your sakes, sometimes
> mind, sometimes Christ...' (*Acts of John* 98).

Before moving on from the Asian Church, mention must be made of one
who was schooled in Alexandria, but whose later influence in Asia might
well have been considerable at the start of the second century. Like the
Ebionites, Cerinthus taught that Jesus was a mere man—though one endowed with great wisdom and spiritual gifts. At his baptism Jesus received
the Holy Spirit from a higher deity than that of the Jews; and before his
death, the heavenly 'Christus' separated from Jesus, and returned to the
heavens. This combination of Judaizing Christianity with Alexandrian
Gnosticism, popular in every age, would be of profound influence for
christological thought for centuries to come. Its immediate impact in Asia
is very clear as we read the Epistles of Ignatius to the several churches of
Asia. Ignatius seems to have been troubled both by Judaizers and by Docetics. It is not easy to decide from the texts of the Epistles whether these
'heretical' groups or individuals were identical or different. If Cerinthus
did indeed teach in Ephesus, as tradition suggests, it would not be unrea-
sonable to imagine that he was the root cause of many of Ignatius's problems. An amusing and telling legend, recorded by Irenaeus, recalls how
the Apostle John, about to go into a bath-house, and hearing that Cerinthus
was inside, refused to enter the building lest the roof should fall in.

7. *The Egyptian Church*

So little is reliably known or recorded about early Christianity in Egypt
prior to the time of Clement that many have doubted whether the faith
began to take hold at all until the middle of the second century. If Origen
was nurtured in Christianity from his infancy, however, as Eusebius seems
to suggest,[13] at a time in Alexandria when 'countless numbers were being
wreathed with the crowns of martyrdom', this would certainly attest that
the faith was already firmly established in this city. It might also indicate
that Eusebius's line of episcopal succession in Alexandria could well have
some basis of fact. Philo writes of a sect, whether of the Jews or of the

13. Eusebius, *HE* 6.2.2. See also *HE* 4.1.1.

Church, called the Therapeutae (meaning 'Healers') who lived an ascetic and monastic life in the desert south of the city. His description of the worship and customs of this sect might argue for at least a Christian influence, if nothing more; and it may well be the case that links had been forged between migrant Christians from Jerusalem, moving into southern Arabia, and like-minded ascetic souls from among the vast enclave of Hellenistic Jews in Alexandria. It is at least feasible, then, that by the early second century there were Christian communities, albeit of a Gnostic persuasion, in various locations in Upper Egypt, a conjecture which the stores of Christian manuscripts unearthed at Nag Hammadi, Oxyrhynchus and Akhmim tend to endorse.

Such reasoned speculation receives additional support from the fact that Clement of Alexandria obviously knew a work entitled the *Gospel of the Egyptians*, which he claims to have been used by Encratite Christians, presumably in this region. Only a few short quotations from this work now survive, and it is difficult to draw firm conclusion. Some have suggested that the *Gospel of the Hebrews* was used by Greek-speaking Jewish Christians in Alexandria, and the *Gospel of the Egyptians* by the Gentile Christians. In a later chapter we shall discuss what might be learned from these and other documents of the second century about the progress of Christianity in this southerly region.

Chapter 2

THE JUDAEAN CHURCH

The Epistle of Peter to James and the Contestatio of James
The Preaching of Peter
The Ascents of James
The Apocryphon of James
The Two Apocalypses of James
The Protevangelium of James

In this chapter we shall examine some of the important early writings which appear to relate directly to the tradition and teaching of the primitive Church both in Jerusalem under the leadership of James, and in the more remote desert regions to the south and east of the city. We might have expected to examine in this chapter those Gospels (or, rather, fragmentary quotations of Gospels) written largely in the Hebrew language for the use of Jewish Christians. However, we shall defer the study of the *Gospel of the Hebrews*, the *Gospel of the Nazaraeans* and the *Gospel of the Ebionites*, to later chapters, for these works have only secondary associations with the Christians of Judaea. Instead, we shall concentrate on those few documents, whether of early origin or late, which will help to illustrate and illuminate the way of life of the Judaean Church.

The so-called Pseudo-Clementine literature has been mentioned on several occasions in the foregoing pages, and we must now briefly introduce this highly complex set of related writings. Two codices were discovered, in the mid-nineteenth century, containing several documents bound together, and all of them in some way associated with Peter, James (the Lord's brother) and Clement of Rome. The major work was entitled the *Homilies*, and purports to relate the mission and teaching of Peter throughout Samaria and Syria, accompanied by Clement, who later became Bishop of Rome. Two accompanying letters, one from Peter to James, and one claiming to be James's reply, seem to have literary associations with the *Homilies*, but were undoubtedly constructed at a later date. A third letter—from Clement to Peter—is of a somewhat different character, and is of even later composition. Another work, entitled the *Recognitions*, sub-sequently came to light, with remarkable parallels to the *Homilies*, but this time written in Latin rather than Greek; and a great deal of scholarly research has been expended on attempting to discover the relationship between these two works. We might have examined all the Clementine literature together in one chapter. However, since some of the documents clearly relate to the James tradition of Judaea, and others (the *Homilies* and *Recognitions*) to the Petrine tradition of Samaria or Syria, the several works, though clearly related through Clement, are here being studied in their different regional groups. We begin this present chapter with two interrelated Epistles of the James tradition whose brevity belies their importance for the history of early Christianity—the *Epistula Petri* and the *Contestatio of James*.

1. *The Epistle of Peter to James (Epistula Petri)*

Peter and James (the Lord's brother) are often portrayed in the Apocryphal writings as both recipients and revealers of secret teaching vouchsafed especially to them (as distinct from the Twelve) by the risen Lord. Not always are they represented as being in accord; for while there is no evidence that either was unduly legalistic, it does certainly seem that Peter, of the two, inclined rather more than did James towards the universalism of Paul. It was clearly important for the Judaean Church to claim Peter's support, as the large number of early Petrine documents attests. This short letter, from Peter to James in Jerusalem, purports to introduce the books of the Apostle's teachings or preachings (the so-called *Kerygmata Petrou*; see below) which he herewith sends to James, emphasizing the need for extreme caution and discretion in the matter of who might be allowed to see them:

> I urgently beseech you not to pass on to any one of the Gentiles the books of my preachings which I here forward to you, nor to any one of our tribe before probation. But if some one of them has been examined and found to be worthy, then you may hand them over to him in the same way as Moses handed over his office of a teacher to the seventy (*Epistula Petri* 1.2).

The letter has come down to us, as has been mentioned, as one of the three introductory documents prefixed to the Pseudo-Clementine *Homilies*, the early sections of which are thought to contain the very teachings referred to in the letter. There is no precise indication of the content of Peter's teaching in his letter, except that it is fundamentally opposed to

the liberalizing doctrines of Paul. The Law is paramount, and not by any
to be set aside:

> For some from among the Gentiles have rejected my lawful preaching and
> have preferred a lawless and absurd doctrine of the man who is my enemy.
> And indeed some have attempted, whilst I am still alive, to distort my
> words by interpretations of many sorts, as if I taught the dissolution of the
> law and, although I was of this opinion, did not express it openly. But that
> may God forbid! (*Epistula Petri* 2.3, 4).

Clearly, as was intimated in the previous chapter, we have here an allusion
to the acrimonious confrontation between Peter and Paul to which the latter
refers in his Epistle to the Galatians (Gal. 2.11). It may be the case that the
nineteenth-century Tübingen School of Theology laid rather too much stress
on the historical and theological consequences of the antipathy between
the two Apostles; but this Epistle, and the pseudo-historical *Homilies* to
which it was attached, testifies to a very real and continuing Jewish–Gentile
problem throughout the whole of the second century, and one which has
its repercussions to the present day. Taken at face value, Peter's letter was
self-evidently despatched before the death of James in the mid-sixties, and
while the 'Seventy' (Lk. 10.1) were still alive. It is far more likely, however, that the letter is not genuine, and that these archaizing features in the
text were intended to authenticate the point of view of its legalistic Jewish-
Christian author.

2. *The Contestatio of James*

In similar vein, the second of the introductory writings—usually referred
to as the *Contestatio*, a testimony of James's receipt of the Epistle—confirms the need for secrecy and discretion with regard to Peter's Books of
Teaching, adding weight to the theme that Peter and James were united on
the question of the requirement of the Law for all Christians. Here again,
however, the text belies the authenticity of the work, assuming a far more
established ecclesiastical regime than is conceivable for the first century.
Those to whom James will entrust the Books must stand by a river or fountain of running water and make this vow:

> As witnesses I invoke heaven, earth and water, in which everything is com-
> prehended, and also in addition the all-pervading air, without which I am
> unable to breathe, that I shall always be obedient to him who hands over to
> me the books of the preachings and shall not pass on to any one in any way
> the books which he may give to me, that I shall neither copy them nor give

a copy of them nor allow them to come into the hands of a copyist...
(*Contestatio* 2.1).

It would certainly seem to be the case that these two short documents
were composed at the time of the compilation of the Pseudo-Clementine
corpus; and we need now to determine what sources the compiler had at his
disposal. Epiphanius mentions an *Itinerary of Peter* which he disparages
as an Ebionite construction deliberately distorting the truth, and representing a largely biased view of Peter's teaching. He also knew a work entitled
the *Ascents of James*—evidently the account of the martyrdom of James
the Just on the Temple steps in Jerusalem. Neither of these two documents,
nor the *Kerygmata Petrou*, is discretely extant; but it is generally agreed
that all three are embedded in the Pseudo-Clementine literature; and much
scholarship has been expended on attempts to identify and isolate these
several sources of the work. It is not yet clear whether there was in existence a basic document (a *Grundschrift*) to which the compiler added the
introductory writings, nor whether it was he, or some subsequent editor,
who was responsible for the undisputed Ebionite redaction throughout the
work.

3. *The Preaching of Peter (Kerygmata Petrou)*

Interspersed with the romantic and episodic 'journey' material in the
Homilies and *Recognitions* are elements of systematic teaching which are
attributed to Peter, whose special commission it was to transmit the teaching of Christ, the True Prophet. The early chapters (*Recognitions* 1–3)
raise fundamental issues concerning Providence, the Nature of God, of
Good and Evil, of the Law, the Scriptures and of Baptism. It should be
noted, however, that a good deal of this same teaching appears in much
the same way in excerpts quoted at the end of the second century by Clement of Alexandria. In a work entitled *Stromata*, Clement makes a number
of citations from what he called the *Kerygma Petrou*, or the *Preaching of
Peter*. It is important here to observe the difference, purely to avoid confusion, between the *Kerygmata Petrou* (of the Pseudo-Clementines) and
the *Kerygma Petrou* (of Clement of Alexandria's *Stromata*). Was the
document that Clement of Alexandria apparently knew the same as the
Petrine teaching in the *Homilies* and *Recognitions*? The majority of modern scholars reject this idea on the grounds that there appear to be no
close textual parallels between the *Kerygma* and the *Kerygmata*. There
are, however, very many *thematic* parallels; and we cannot assume that

the compiler of the Pseudo-Clementine *Recognitions* would slavishly reproduce the exact text of his source material.

We may not discount the possibility, then, that a *Book of Peter's Preaching* (or Teaching) was in wide circulation in Egypt and Palestine during the second century, and was quoted in its pure form by Clement and others, and which was substantially incorporated—and perhaps embellished by a later Judaizing editor—into the material that made up the Pseudo-Clementine writings. Space will not allow me to show more than one comparison between the *Kerygma* quoted by Clement and the *Kerygmata* of the Pseudo-Clementines; but the following short passages on the theme of Christianity being the third way, neither Jewish nor Greek, but altogether a new thing, will serve to demonstrate the very real possibility that these works were substantially one and the same:

> For we find in the Scriptures, as the Lord says: 'Behold, I make with you a new covenant, not as I made with your fathers in Mount Horeb.' He made a new covenant with us; for what belonged to the Greeks and Jews is old. But we, who worship him in a new way, in the third form, are Christians. For clearly, as I think, he showed that the one and only God was known by the Greeks in a Gentile way, by the Jews Judaically, and in a new and spiritual way by us (*Kerygma Petrou*: Clement's *Stromata* 6.5).

> For we say, that he is a worshipper of God, who does the will of God, and observes the precepts of his law. For in God's estimation he is not a Jew who is called a Jew among men (nor is he a Gentile who is called a Gentile), but he who, believing in God, fulfils his law and does his will, though he be not circumcised. He is the true worshipper of God, who not only is himself free from passions, but also sets others free from them (*Kerygmata Petrou*: *Recognitions* 5.34).

It has often been suggested that the *Kerygmata* was composed in the region of Coele Syria where there were many Jewish-Christians who spoke Greek, the original language of this work. Here also, it is claimed, the basic document must have been compiled sometime during the third century, with subsequent Ebionite and Gnostic redaction over the course of the next century. Perhaps this is close to the truth. We have ventured a link, however, between the *Kerygmata* of the Pseudo-Clementines, and the *Kerygma* known to Clement of Alexandria: and it is quite feasible that this *Book of Peter's Preaching* (or Teaching) could have originated much further south—perhaps at Caesarea. Here, in this Greek-speaking city, according to both the *Acts of Peter* and the Clementine *Recognitions*, Peter made the headquarters of his mission. Moreover, it was a city with very strong academic associations with Alexandria.[1]

It is important to note that the introductory epistles, discussed earlier, are of later date than the *Kerygmata* itself, being affixed to the basic document sometime during the third century. There is, however, one more distinct source document that has clear associations with the Judaean Church, and we must now briefly examine its contents.

4. *The Ascents of James*

From the beginning of Pseudo-Clementine research it has been recognized that a substantial part of the first book of the *Recognitions* (chs. 27–71) differs both in content and form from the rest of the work. It would certainly appear that the compiler has added to the basic document at least three distinct pieces of material, whether by his own hand, or by some other. The first of these (chs. 27–42) is an account of creation and a history of Israel to the coming of the True Prophet (Jesus). This section serves an apologetic purpose, compiled between 130 and 135 (if the reference in ch. 39 is to Hadrian's expulsion of the Jews from Jerusalem), and clearly before the final separation of the Church from its Judaic forebear, to demonstrate the divinely appointed progression from Abraham, through Moses, to Christ. Salvation (for Jews and Gentiles alike) was no longer to be attained through sacrifice, however necessary this may once have been, but by the wisdom of God mediated to the world by the True Prophet.

A second section (chs. 44–52) deals with the root problem of whether Jesus should be understood as 'the eternal Christ', and traces the history of his priestly and salvatory role. It concludes that: 'Him, therefore, has God appointed in the end of the world; because it was impossible that the evils of men could be removed by any other, provided that the nature of the human race were to remain entire.' The passage shows particular concern for the pious saints who have died before the coming of Christ, echoing the anxiety of the early Church about the implications of the imminent parousia. Its theme has much in common with some of the earlier canonical Epistles (Hebrews and 1 Thessalonians), yet it reflects a situation in which the final separation between Christians and Jews has already taken place (cf. ch. 50).

---

1.   One important connection was Origen, who taught successively in both these prominent centres of learning.

The third section comprises the passage which is thought by many to correspond to the *Ascents of James* cited by Epiphanius. The Greek word which we translate 'Ascents' comes from a verb meaning 'to mount or ascend'; and, of course, in this context it refers not only to the steps of the Temple which James is said to have climbed in order to answer the Jews' questions about Jesus, but also to the upward course of James's spirit at the moment of his martyr's death. As to the date of this section, there are indications that it could not be early. It refers to Christ as the 'only begotten Son', to a 'baptism of threefold invocation', and to the 'Eucharist of the Lord', though these intimations of later theology might easily represent a recension of an earlier source. If the account of the death of James on the steps is dependent upon that of Hegessipus, as some have suggested, it could not have been written before the beginning of the second century. On the other hand, the story in the *Ascents of James* has a certain raciness and immediacy in the telling; and it may well be that both its author and Hegessipus used a common early source which puts us in touch with the most primitive tradition of James's martyrdom.

With so complicated a process of transmission and redaction as these several documents present, it would be unwise to make too firm assertions about the date and provenance of the Pseudo-Clementine writings. We do need, however, to devise a working hypothesis which will help not only to set these several works within a historical context, but which will also assist us to relate them to other writings. It is more than likely that a collection of Petrine teachings, and a book of Peter's journeys, independently circulated in the Palestinian and Syrian regions during the early second century, and were brought together to form the base document of the *Homilies*. Another 'Romance' telling of Peter's acquaintance and journeys with Clement of Rome, and of Peter's struggle with Simon Magus—the so-called *Recognitions*[2]—would attract early popularity; and it may be that each of these two works, though remaining separate, contributed something to the other. Ebionite and Gnostic redaction of the base document over the course of the next century or so, particularly of the *Homilies*, produced these complex works in their present form.

---

2. This recension survives only in a Latin version, being a fourth-century translation of an earlier common source made by the scholar Rufinus. For a study of the Clementine *Homilies* and *Recognitions*, see Chapter 3, section 2.

5. *The Apocryphon of James*

The only extant copy of this short document is a Coptic translation of a probable Greek original which is generally thought to have been written during the first half of the second century. It forms part of the Nag Hammadi collection (usually known as the Nag Hammadi Library), and is the second tractate of Codex I. The place of origin is not obvious from the content, but since the text features Peter and James (the Just), in dialogue with the risen (but not yet ascended) Lord, its association with primitive Jewish Christianity has to be assumed. A Palestinian or Coele-Syrian location is a distinct possibility. However, the antithetical link between this document and the *Epistula Apostolorum* (which we shall examine in a later chapter) suggests that both these writings may have originated either in Asia Minor, or in Egypt, composed, it is often suggested, to support one side or the other, respectively, of the controversy surrounding the teachings of the 'heretic' Cerinthus. This is a hypothesis which will require testing in due course; but our first task will be to explore the content and purpose of the *Apocryphon*.

The *Apocryphon of James* derives its title from its opening words, couched in the form of a letter from James, for it purports to contain a 'secret teaching' (or a 'secret book') which the Lord had revealed to himself and Peter. Interestingly, James sends the teaching with the same degree of caution with which, as we saw earlier, Peter had entrusted his teaching to James in the *Epistula Petri*:

> You asked me to send you a secret teaching revealed to me and Peter. I
> could not turn you away, nor, however, speak with you, so I have written it
> down in Hebrew characters. I send it to you, and to you only, but because
> you are a servant of the salvation of the saints. Be careful and take heed not
> to rehearse to many this writing, which the Saviour did not wish to divulge
> even to all of us, his twelve disciples (*Apocryphon of James*, p. 1).[3]

From the start of this work, then, we are reminded of the special revelatory gifts of Peter and James who are accorded equal status above the Twelve. We cannot avoid the impression, as with other early Judaeo-Christian writings, that there is here a perceived need to emphasize Peter's conformity to the primitive Jerusalem *kerygma*, as well as to enlist both leaders in support of the author's particular Gnostic stance. How far in fact Petrine Christianity had moved away from that of the Jerusalem tradition by the end of

---

3.   Page nos. refer to Codex I of the Nag Hammadi Library.

the second century, and the significance of any such division, we shall discuss in a later chapter. We will have difficulty understanding this document at all, however, unless we interpret its often very paradoxical teaching in the light of the divergent and conflicting theological beliefs within the Church that, throughout the second century, strove for predominance.

The *Apocryphon* seems to present itself in two parts which may, or may not, be the work of the same author—first a letter; and then an account of a revelatory dialogue. The letter is contained in the first two pages of the manuscript, with a postscript in the final page. In between there lies a post-Resurrection dialogue between the Saviour and his disciples, in which, by means of revelation, James and Peter receive the Lord's teaching in the form of dominical 'Sayings'. One possible explanation for this format is that the entire work is a compilation, the revelatory material being added to the letter (or vice versa) by some later redactor. Another equally plausible hypothesis is that the letter originally *accompanied* the 'Secret Book' as a separate document, becoming integrated in the course of translation and transmission. Unfortunately, the name of the intended recipient of the letter remains itself a mystery, for the papyrus leaf of the first page is damaged. Attempts at a reconstruction of the text tend to point to the letter being addressed to Cerinthus, some of whose teachings certainly seem to be reflected in the *Apocryphon*; and while not all scholars would wish to be quite so positive, we might make some progress if we first considered who Cerinthus was, and in what respects his doctrine differed from that of more orthodox Jewish Christianity.

The name of Cerinthus is very much associated, as was mentioned earlier, with Ephesus and Asia Minor at the turn of the first century; and there is little doubt that his particular Christology enjoyed some popularity in these regions from this time onwards. Cerinthus, however, hailed from Egypt at the close of the first century, and was educated, so Irenaeus informs us, in the wisdom of the Egyptians. No work of his is extant; but we are once again indebted to Irenaeus (our chief source about Cerinthus) for some insight into his beliefs. Like both Carpocrates (also of the Alexandrian School) and the Ebionites, Cerinthus rejected the notion of the virgin birth of Jesus. He was the son of Joseph and Mary, in the ordinary course of human generation, albeit a wiser and more righteous human being than others; but after his baptism the heavenly Christ entered into Jesus in the form of a dove, departing from him just prior to the Crucifixion. Thus, Jesus suffered, died and rose from the dead; but the eternal and pre-existent Christ had returned to the supreme deity.

Although Irenaeus makes little distinction between the teachings of Cerinthus, Carpocrates and the Ebionites on the question of the nature of Jesus, he actually tells us very little about Cerinthus's views on the Law, prophecy or the Scriptures. We know that the Ebionites held decidedly different beliefs on the matter of the Jewish Law, reckoning its observance to be a prerequisite for Christians as for Jews. Carpocrates, in contrast, seems to have believed that Jesus, though disciplined in the Law, came to despise it, and taught his disciples to rise above it, and attain to his own spirituality. This idea, common enough in Gnostic thought, is certainly well represented in the *Apocryphon*. Those who will be saved will save themselves; for just as Jesus himself was endowed with faculties and powers to destroy assailing passions, so his disciples are called upon not to avoid temptation or persecution, but to relish and overcome it—and in the process become the Lord's equals. We must suppose that Cerinthus and Carpocrates did indeed share a number of core ideas; and this letter of James, whomever it addresses, echoes some of them. What we do not find in the text, however, are any of the extravagant theories concerning the creation, the transmigration of souls, the practice of magic or the promotion of licentiousness, which Irenaeus imputes to the Carpocratians; and we might infer that the sect for whom the document was written had developed a form of Christianity that is fundamentally (though not sophisticatedly) Gnostic, influenced by Judaic Wisdom literature as well as by the Egyptian *Hermetica*, while at the same time wanting to maintain the individual's responsibility for his or her own salvation through compliance with the will of God. We will look in vain for any doctrine of Atonement in this book. Christ is portrayed in terms of the suffering righteous one who is thereby vindicated (Wis. 2.10-24), and exalted to the right hand of his Father, as those will be who follow him.

The main body of the text (pp. 3-15) bears all the characteristics of a Farewell Discourse, and clearly owes much to the Fourth Gospel (Jn 13–16). The major difference, of course, is that the Johannine discourse takes place before Gethsemane, whereas here, in the *Apocryphon*, it takes the form of a post-Resurrection meeting immediately prior to a much-delayed Ascension. In some respects, the Lord's teaching is identical in both discourses: as Jesus suffered persecution on the cross, so would they, if they would follow him to salvation (p. 6; cf. Jn 15.20); he himself is about to ascend to the Father, and so will they—but not yet (pp. 13, 14; cf. Jn 13.33, 36, 37); the disciples had been slow to perceive while he was with them. Blessed are those who have not seen, yet have believed (p. 12; cf. Jn 14.9;

20.29); in their supplications to the Father for mercy, Christ would be their Advocate (pp. 10, 11; Jn 14.15).

Yet despite this apparent consensus with the Fourth Gospel, there are some obvious differences in the interpretation of these dominical Sayings. The ultimate salvation of the disciples is clearly dependent upon their own efforts; and their need for an Advocate, and for spiritual support through prayer and intercession, are signs that they are not yet ready to follow him to the promised life beyond the world:

> Woe to you who need an advocate! Woe to you who stand in need of grace! Blessed are they who have spoken out and obtained grace for themselves!... Do you perhaps think that the Father is a lover of mankind, or that he is won over by means of prayers, or that he bestows grace on someone because of another, or that he listens to someone who asks. For he knows the will and also that of which the flesh is in need (*Apocryphon of James*, p. 11).

A fundamental theme of the work is the concept of the disciples having their spiritual deficiency filled before they can attain to perfection. When Peter complains that they are already filled (echoes, perhaps, of 1 Cor. 4.8), and are thus ready to accompany him into the kingdom, the Saviour warns him of the continuing necessity to ensure they are not found wanting. 'Being filled' is of necessity an ongoing process; and they need constantly to be on their guard. The essential dualism of flesh and spirit, wholly characteristic of Gnostic writings (though by no means confined to them) is dominant in the work:

> If the soul is saved from evil, and the spirit is saved as well, then the body becomes free from sin. For the spirit makes the soul alive. But the body kills it. That is, it kills itself. Truly I tell you he will not forgive any soul its sin, nor the body its guilt. For none of those who have worn the flesh will be saved. For do you think that many have found the kingdom of heaven? (*Apocryphon of James*, p. 12).

Those who have 'worn the flesh' are they, presumably, who have not contended for freedom from the flesh, but rather gloried in it, seeking earthly things. The Gnostic's primary aim is to escape from the body, to find freedom from the demands of the flesh, and to return to his or her spiritual home. The symbolism of 'stripping off' the body, as if a garment, is a particularly potent one, used in many of the Apocryphal Gnostic works;[4] but it is also a concept that is firmly rooted in the New Testament itself (cf. 2 Pet. 1.14).

4. Cf. *Gos. Phil.* 23; *Epistle of Peter to Philip* 137.

The *Apocryphon* ends with James and Peter being permitted to glimpse something of the heavenly glory and splendour that await the elect. The vision, however, is short-lived; for they are recalled to earth by the remainder of the Twelve who are anxious to hear what had been revealed. James sends the disciples to their appointed tasks, while he himself, prayerfully, goes back to Jerusalem. There is little doubt that the author of this early document orientates to Jerusalem and the primitive Jewish Church, yet is clearly influenced by the nascent Gnosticism of Alexandria as typified in what we know of the teachings of Cerinthus. Whether the paradoxical Sayings incorporated into the text have any claim to authenticity is questionable. Rather more probably they represent an attempt to demonstrate the confused and erroneous beliefs of more orthodox Christianity which fails to understand the true nature of Christ. We shall encounter this theme often, and with even greater emphasis, in the Gnostic writings yet to be considered.

6. *The First Apocalypse of James*

Until the discoveries at Nag Hammadi, no document seems to have been known—certainly none had been attested—with the title of the *Apocalypse of James*. It is all the more remarkable, then, that Codex V of the Nag Hammadi Library was found to contain not one, but two, apparently unrelated documents bearing that title. For convenience the two texts are designated the First and Second Apocalypses of James; but while they appear successively in this fourth-century Codex, there is no indication that they were composed by the same author, and no certainty about the provenance and date of the works. Both appear to look back to the primitive Jerusalem Church, however, corroborating traditions associated with James the Just. We may speculate that the original documents were composed in Greek during the early part of the second century, and translated into Coptic a century or so later. Although they are called Apocalypses, because of the 'question and answer' character of the texts they may more appropriately be described as Dialogues.

The *First Apocalypse of James* is unequivocally Gnostic. In the guise of a discourse between Jesus and James, it seeks to impart Gnostic instruction to the true disciples on the question of how they are to return to 'the one who is'. Salvation is its main theme. What is fundamental to the teaching is that redemption is not to be achieved without suffering. The work is set in two acts, the first taking place just two days before the Crucifixion, and the second sometime after the Resurrection. At the start of the work,

Jesus tells James his brother (here 'brother' is used in a spiritual, rather than a material, sense) that he is about to be arrested, and that James will be exposed to the same kind of sufferings as he himself is shortly to experience. In the first revelation, Jesus warns James to escape persecution and flee Jerusalem until he learns about the nature of his adversaries, and is given the means spiritually to combat them. In the post-Resurrection revelation, the Lord calms James's troubled spirit, reveals to him the manner of his redemption, and reminds him that whatever might happen to the flesh, the important thing is the liberation of his real spiritual self:

> Do not be afraid, James! You too will be arrested. But depart from Jerusalem! For this city always gives the cup of bitterness to the children of light; it is a dwelling-place for many archons. But your deliverance will deliver you from them. That you may know who they are and of what kind they are, you should flee... (*First Apocalypse of James*, p. 25).

> James, thus you will be exposed to these sufferings. But do not be sad! For the flesh is weak—it will receive what is appointed for it. But as for you, do not be timid, neither be afraid... Cast away from you the cup, which is the bitterness! For none of the archons will be able to stand against you. For you have begun to understand their roots from beginning to end (*First Apocalypse of James*, pp. 32 and 40).[5]

There is here a clue about the Saviour's role in the redemption of his disciples. It is because he himself has passed through the sufferings, victorious and unscathed, that he is able to provide for them the formulae to make their own escape from the flesh, through the suffering which they must also endure. No longer are they to flee; but they must be equipped to answer those who would deter their progress to the world of light. Such enemies the author describes as archons, as we have seen—a term which literally means a magistrate or ruler of a synagogue, and is used extensively by the sect known as the Valentinians with this special connotation. Before we proceed, then, we need to say something about this sect whose developed and systematic teachings are discernible in so many of the Gnostic writings of the second and third centuries.

So few of Valentinus's writings have been preserved in any form that it is impossible to be certain of how much of the sophisticated and mystical symbolism which has come down to us as Valentinian Gnosticism derives from the man himself, and how much from his later followers. Though an Alexandrian, Valentinus taught chiefly in Rome during the first half of the second century, and may well have established schools in Ephesus, Antioch

5. Page nos. refer to Codex V of the Nag Hammadi Library.

and even Cyprus. He certainly knew and used the Gospels, and in many respects he was evidently content to follow the teachings of orthodoxy— even to the point of offering himself (so the story goes) as a serious candidate for episcopal appointment.

His aim was to devise a philosophical or theological system that avoided any causal relationship between the perfect, supreme and unknowable deity and the imperfect material cosmos. The 'Creator God'—that is, the God of the Jews—had to be an inferior deity, at some evolutionary distance from the ultimate and highest God. In order to demonstrate this principle, Valentinus imagined a series of genealogical steps to distance the supreme being from the manifestly corrupt and evil world. The Godhead comprised thirty aeons (emanations from the fulness of deity), grouped as a series of eight divine powers (ogdoads) ranged in pairs of opposites (male and female syzygies), each pair begetting the next. The lowest of the aeons was Achamoth ('Wisdom') whose Greek form is Sophia. She fell from grace into the void outside the fulness (or Pleroma) of the deity, and there, in liaison with other heavenly powers, she gave birth to Ialdabaoth, the Creator Spirit. The restoration of order and harmony in the Pleroma is brought about by the creation of two new aeons, Christ and the Holy Spirit, who, together, produced their perfect offspring, Jesus, born of a virgin. His return to the Pleroma, so the Valentinians believed, would be the means whereby those whose nature was 'pneumatic' (that is, the Gnostics) will themselves return to the world of light, whence they came.

Many of the foregoing heavenly personalities we shall meet from time to time in the Gnostic writings, and some familiarity with the names is clearly necessary if we are to make sense of the texts. What is more important, however, is an appreciation of the underlying principles that are common to all Gnostic works, and which Valentinus chose to clothe in such mythological and poetic dress. Matter and spirit are essentially opposed. Yet, while the created world and most of its inhabitants are tainted and corrupted by evil, some have the possibility of at least a limited redemption. These are the ordinary Christians (called 'psychics') who have souls capable of salvation through following the teachings of the earthly Jesus. The Gnostics themselves ('pneumatics'), having within them the spark of divinity and the seeds of eternal life, are predestined to salvation by means of their union with the eternal and real Christ whom they alone are able to perceive and know. All other human beings, being by nature carnal, are destined for inevitable and eternal destruction.

It will be obvious that the *First Apocalypse of James* contains Valentinian ideas. We are able to go further, however, for its language and thought seem to reflect exactly Irenaeus's description of the teaching of some followers of one Marcus, an early Asian disciple of Valentinus. So close are the parallels between Irenaeus's description of this sect and the *Apocalypse* that it is inconceivable that the heresiologist did not have before him a copy of the very work. Especially close are those passages that relate to the answers the disciples must give to the principalities and powers who check their souls' movement towards their heavenly destiny. We might compare, for example, the following passages:

> You are to say to him: 'I am a son, and I am from the Father.' He will say to you: 'What kind of son are you, and to what Father do you belong?' You are to say to him: 'I am from the pre-existent Father, and am a son in the pre-existent.' He will say to you: 'And with what charge have you come?' You will say to him: 'I have come at the behest of the pre-existent, that I may see those who are ours, those who have become aliens.' He will say to you: 'And of what kind are these aliens?' You are to say to him: 'They are not altogether aliens, but they are from Achamoth, which is the female...' (*First Apocalypse of James*, pp. 33, 34).

> They instruct them, on their reaching the principalities and powers, to make use of these words: 'I am a son from the Father—the Father who had a pre-existence, and a son who is pre-existent. I have come to behold all things, both those which belong to myself and others, although, strictly speaking, they do not belong to others, but to Achamoth, who is female in nature, and made these things for herself' (Irenaeus, *Adv. Haer.* 1.21.5).

Of particular importance for our understanding of the development of Gnosticism in the early centuries are the final sections of the work (pp. 36-44). Unfortunately, these concluding pages have not survived without damage, and the many lacunae will not permit a definitive interpretation of the text. Throughout the work, however, James is commended by the Lord for the profundity of his understanding—in contrast to the Twelve who are reproved either for their lack of perception, or possibly for their antagonism towards James (p. 42). To him, then, is entrusted the transmission of Gnosis, first to Addai,[6] who, after some ten years, would write down these mysteries and pass them on to one Levi. Levi was to marry and produce

---

6.   Addai, the traditional founder of Christianity in Edessa, is often identified with the Apostle Thaddaeus (Mk 3.18). His appearance in this James tradition is sometimes thought to support the idea that Christianity came to Edessa from Jerusalem, rather than from Syria.

two sons, the younger of whom, on reaching the age of 17 years, would proclaim and promulgate the insights he had inherited (p. 37). With such fascinating detail does the author of the *Apocalypse* trace the gradual progression of Gnostic ideology over the course of generations, beginning at Jerusalem, and moving into the wider world. He testifies that James (rather than any of the Twelve) was the prime agent of Gnostic revelation; and he assures his readers that, providing they adhere to the rites of passage herein described, they would find, as James himself was now to do, that suffering and martyrdom is in fact the way to salvation.

7. *The Second Apocalypse of James*

Several missing words and lines in the early sections of this document, beginning as it does on the middle pages of Codex V, do nothing to facilitate the translation and interpretation of this important text. What is clear, however, is that this so-called *Second Apocalypse of James* comprises substantially a report of James's address, from the steps of the Temple in Jerusalem, to a multitude of hearers, and then goes on to relate his subsequent martyrdom. The account seems to have been delivered to one Theudas by one of the priests who witnessed the incident, and written down by James's relative Mareim:

> This is [the] discourse which James [the] Just delivered in Jerusalem and which Mareim wrote down. One of the priests told it to Theudas, the father of this just man, since he was a relative of his. He said, 'hasten and come with [Mary] your wife and your relatives! …[…]…[…]…[…] Hasten then! Perhaps [if] you yourself will guide us to him [he will] come to his senses. For see, there are many who are disturbed at his [slander?]. They are extremely angry [at him. For he has said (?)]: 'They [do not (?)] pray […]' For [he has said] these words many times… (*Second Apocalypse of James*, pp. 44-45).[7]

Theudas (rather than Joseph) is identified as the father of the just man (James) and husband of Mary; and James is claimed in a later passage (p. 50) to be either a half-brother of Jesus, sharing the same mother, or else a more distant relation through James's father.[8] We must allow the possi-

---

7.   This translation and interpretation, as generally throughout this book, unless otherwise stated, is from Schneemelcher (ed.), *New Testament Apocrypha*. The long square brackets indicate missing lines in the poorly preserved text.
8.   No definitive solution to this strange anomaly readily presents itself. Whoever

bility that the lacunae in the text may only partly account for the confusion about the exact relationship between Jesus and James, for the very inclusion of these passages would seem to suggest some uncertainty in the mind of the author. Whatever uncertainty there might have been is used to good advantage, for, in a later passage still, the question of the relationship between Jesus and James is once again raised; and James learns from the Saviour that 'your father is not my father. But my father has become a father to you' (p. 51).

The speech itself, delivered apparently over a period of at least two days, contains intimations of hidden teaching revealed especially to James by the Redeemer. At one point in the discourse, James appears to quote the actual words of the risen and exalted Lord as he reveals to him the mysteries of his nature and his appearing. James himself is to become the 'illuminator and Redeemer' to those who belong to Christ:

> Through you those who wish to enter in (the heavenly place) will open the good door. And they turn about (on the path they have so far followed?), that they may (henceforth) walk in the way which (leads) before this door, and follow you and enter, [and you] accompany them inside and give to each one the reward that falls to his share. For you are not the redeemer or helper of strangers. You are an illuminator and redeemer of those who are mine—but now they are yours. You are to give revelation, and you are to bring good among them all (*Second Apocalypse of James*, p. 55).

James explains to the listening crowd how his understanding of the risen Lord had been transformed. Bidden to reach out and embrace Jesus, he had been surprised to find that the Lord was other than he had expected (p. 55); and in the same kind of Docetic imagery the Apostle Peter uses to describe this enigmatic Christ (cf. *Acts Pet.* 20), James begs his hearers to throw off the materialistic fetters that hinder their own appreciation of the nature of the Redeemer, and come to know the freedom which the Spirit brings (p. 59). His final appeal is couched in terms of the overthrow of the Temple and all that it stands for, a threat which, according to this version of the martyrdom, provokes the crowd to violence.

If Luke had obliged with a third historical treatise to follow his Gospel and Acts, it would doubtless have included an account of the death of James the Just. As it is, we must make what we can of the varying reports of Josephus, Hegesippus and Clement of Alexandria, and the narrative embedded in the Pseudo-Clementine *Recognitions* (see Chapter 1, section

was James's father, it may be said that some traditions regard James as the cousin or step-brother (rather than the brother) of Jesus.

2 above). Josephus, whose presence in Jerusalem at the time tends to lend verisimilitude to his account, claims that a hastily convened Sanhedrin, summoned by the ruthless Sadducean High Priest Ananus in 62, condemned James to death by stoning. The charge levelled against the 'brother of Jesus who is called Christ' was that he had transgressed the Law.[9]

Neither the somewhat later account of Hegesippus,[10] nor the brief summary of the incident by Clement of Alexandria,[11] corroborates the cause of James's death to be his contravention of the Law. Indeed, both seem at pains to stress his 'righteousness'. What appears to have angered the Pharisees (not, in this account, the Sadducees) was James's intransigence in insisting on the divinity of Christ. While Clement omits any reference to the stoning, he follows Hegesippus in adding to Josephus's report the fact that James was thrown down from the pinnacle of the Temple, and then (since the fall did not end the matter) was beaten to death by a fuller's club. Hegesippus concludes his story of James's martyrdom with the statement that immediately there followed Vespasian's siege of the city, thus placing the incident in 67, in contrast to the date given by Josephus.

The story is rather different in the Pseudo-Clementine *Ascents of James*.[12] Here, the Pharisees (in the person of the tolerant and accommodating Gamaliel) seek to placate the crowd, and to give James the benefit of any doubt. He was, after all, a highly popular figure in the city. Despite the efforts of Caiaphas and the Sadducees, he successfully turns the priests and people in James's favour—until one of the enemies of the Christians (clearly Saul of Tarsus, though he is unnamed) deliberately stirs up a tumultuous riot. James is cast headlong from the top of the Temple steps. He is taken for dead, but he somehow survives—though, strangely, we hear no more of him.

Something of all these accounts has found its way into the *Second Apocalypse of James*:

> And they rose up saying: 'Well then, let us kill this man, that he may be removed from our midst! For he will be of no use to us at all.' And they were there, and they found him standing by the pinnacle of the Temple, beside the mighty cornerstone. And they decided to cast him down from the height, and they cast him down. But [when] they [looked upon him], they

9. Josephus, *Ant.* 20.197-203.
10. Hegesippus, *Hypomnemata* Bk 5—recorded by Eusebius, *HE* 2.23.4-18.
11. Clement, *Hypotyposes* Bk 7—recorded by Eusebius, *HE* 2.1.5.
12. *Recognitions* 1.

observed [that he was still alive (?). Then] they arose (?) [and went down,] seized him and [abused] him, dragging him on the ground. They stretched him out, rolled a stone on his abdomen, and trampled him with their feet, saying: '(O you) who have gone astray!' Again they raised him up, since he was (still) alive, made him dig a hole, and made him stand in it. When they had covered him up to his abdomen, they stoned him in this manner (*Second Apocalypse of James*, pp. 61-62).

In such a position of humiliation, James utters his final prayer—a prayer unlike 'the one which he was accustomed to say' (p. 62). What that 'accustomed' prayer might have been, we can only surmise. Prominent in the prayer are those pleas for deliverance that might have their root in the prayer which Jesus taught his disciples (Mt. 6.13). Where it differs fundamentally from the Lord's Prayer, however, is the Gnostic renunciation of the world as the sphere of evil. Release from this earthly sojourn to the place of salvation is James's only hope and earnest aspiration.

At the heart of this Apocalypse is the theme of James's special role as the redeemer of those (Gnostic souls) who 'have come into being', as he himself has come into being. In his speech from the steps he gives elated expression to his discovery of the true nature of the Saviour, and of how he himself was 'kissed on the mouth and embraced' in token of his new status as the beloved one. He was to become the first to divest himself of his fleshly clothes, and the heavenly Father's instrument in returning those who belong to him to their heavenly reward. James's final appeal to the Jews assures them that the Father will not judge them for their former deeds; but if they will break free from the evil dominion that holds them, he will mercifully forgive their misguided ways. If they persist, however, in refusing to listen to his words, he says to them in the name of the Lord:

See, I have given you your house—this of which you say that God made it, (and) in which he who dwells in it has promised to give you an inheritance. This I will tear down, to the ruin and derision of those who are in ignorance (*Second Apocalypse of James*, p. 60).

That the document should be classified as Gnostic cannot be questioned. Its fundamental aim is to show how spiritual insights have been accorded to James to which others have not yet attained. Gnostic concepts abound: 'the Pleroma of Imperishability' (p. 46), 'the revealing of that which was hidden' (p. 47), among others. Yet nowhere is there to be found the developed mythology characteristic of later Gnosticism, a fact that suggests an earlier date for this Apocalypse (perhaps early second century) than that of the previously considered *First Apocalypse of James*.

8. *The Protevangelium of James*

Early interest in the circumstances of the birth and infancy of Jesus was bound to be stimulated, rather than satisfied, by the brief accounts of his nativity and childhood in two of the canonical Gospels. Whatever oral or written sources might have been used by Matthew and Luke in the compilation of their accounts, it was inevitable that popular and primitive traditions would begin to circulate in a succession of what have come to be known as 'Infancy Gospels'. The *Protevangelium of James* is one of the earliest of these. Like other such Gospels, this work owes much to the canonical texts; but it expands and embellishes these, and adds material which is to be found nowhere else, concerning the miraculous birth, and the early years, of Mary herself.

Clearly, these documents were intended to give answers to important christological questions, as well as to satisfy the natural curiosity of the faithful about the 'hidden years' of the Saviour. If Jesus were in some sense the Son of God, how was it possible for him to be naturally conceived? How might the virginal status of Mary be verified? In what way did the realm of nature mark this uniquely mysterious happening? The book as we now have it begins with a detailed account of the marvellous birth and early years of Mary, and how her parents (Joachim and Anna)[13] resolved to offer their child, male or female, as a gift to the Lord. The story bears strong resemblance to the nativity story of Jesus, particularly in the angelic annunciation of the birth (4.1), and in the song that Anna sings on the child's first birthday:

> I will sing a [holy] song to the Lord my God, for he has visited me and taken away from me the reproach of my enemies. And the Lord gave me the fruit of righteousness (*Protevangelium* 6.2).

When Mary was three years old, she was placed 'on the third step of the altar', and given to the Lord; and here in the Temple she happily remained until puberty, at which time the council of the priests decided she ought to leave the Temple and be given in marriage to a widower of Judaea whom the Lord would choose. The choice was made by the use of rods (cf. Num. 17), and the lot fell to an apprehensive and fearful Joseph. The story continues with the Annunciation when Mary was sixteen, her visit to Elizabeth her kinswoman, and Joseph's consternation at hearing the news, all told in

---

13. The genealogy of Jesus on his mother's side is not recorded in the New Testament, and the names of her parents are to be found only here.

the familiar words of Luke's account, with only minor alteration. There follows a tradition unknown to the canonical evangelists (or at least unused by them) of the priestly condemnation of Joseph for consummating his marriage to one who had been set aside as a Temple virgin, and of his subsequent exoneration. The journey to Bethlehem for the enrolment (according to the decree of Augustus) includes another tradition found (in this form) nowhere else—the legendary story of the Hebrew midwife who delivers the child in a cave at Bethlehem,[14] and how Mary is certified to be pure and undefiled.

A short extraneous passage in the narrative (18.2), in which Joseph takes up the story in the first person, tells of the miraculous cessation of nature at the moment of Mary's delivery. Although the passage does not appear in some early versions of the text, and no doubt derives from a separate source, it speaks more powerfully of the sacredness and mystery of Christ's birth than does the crude account of Salome's witness of Mary's unsullied condition:

> Now I Joseph was walking about, and (yet) I did not walk. And I looked up to the vault of heaven and saw it standing still, and I looked up to the air and saw the air in amazement, and the birds of heaven remain motionless. And I looked at the earth and saw a dish placed there, and workmen lying round it, with their hands in the dish: and those who chewed did not chew, and those who lifted up anything lifted up nothing, and those who put something to their mouth put nothing (to their mouth), but all had their faces turned upwards. And behold sheep were being driven, and yet they did not come forward, but stood still; and the shepherd raised his hand to strike them [with his staff], but his hand remained up. And I looked at the flow of the river and saw the mouths of the kids over it and they did not drink. And then all at once everything went on its course (again) (*Protevangelium* 18.2).

The book concludes with the story of the visit of the Wise Men, largely based on the Matthaean account (though truncated in one of the versions), followed, strangely enough, by the report of the murder of Zacharias (father of John the Baptist) by King Herod, and the appointment of Simeon as Temple priest in his stead. It has long been suspected that the story of Zacharias (22.1–25.1) is a later addition to the original narrative; and certainly it seems to have little connection to the main story. There are, however, more fundamental doubts about the work's integrity. It is not inconceivable that the book was originally intended to recount only the

---

14. Justin Martyr witnesses to the tradition that Jesus was born in a cave near Bethlehem because Joseph 'could not find lodging in that village' (*Dial*. 78).

circumstances of Mary's wondrous birth, and that at some later stage the nativity of Jesus (17.1–21.3) was added.[15] There is no textual evidence for such a conclusion, but the work does exhibit the signs of compilation, one legend being added to another in the course of the book's transmission.

The only claim of authorship in the text occurs at the end of the work. James (the Lord's brother) writes of the tumult that arose upon the death of Herod, and how he withdrew into the wilderness, and wrote the history that now bears his name. None, it would seem, could be better placed than he, the natural son of Joseph, to undertake such a chronicle.[16] It is hardly likely, however, that the original work was composed earlier than the second century, for its author was manifestly dependent upon the canonical Gospels, and in all probability wrote in Greek. The book was certainly known to Origen who refers to it as the Book of James; but no unequivocal earlier citation is to be found. The place of writing is said to be Jerusalem (25.1), and there is no compelling reason to challenge this—though some have doubted that the author was wholly conversant with Jewish customs.

The *Protevangelium* contributes largely to the James tradition, but its chief import concerns the insight it affords into the early development of the tradition of Mary. Already, in the second century, the notion of the immaculate nature of the mother of Jesus is being promulgated, reinforced by this record of her miraculous birth; and while the theory of her perpetual virginity is not expressly stated, there is no doubt that the entire tenor of the book leads to such an assumption, as the following passage illustrates:

> When the child (Mary) was three years old, Joachim said: 'Let us call the undefiled daughters of the Hebrews, and let each one take a lamp, and let these be burning, in order that the child may not turn back and her heart be enticed away from the Temple of the Lord.' And he did so until they went up to the Temple of the Lord. And the priest took her and kissed her and blessed her, saying: 'The Lord has magnified your name among all generations; because of you the Lord at the end of the days will manifest his redemption to the children of Israel' (*Protevangelium* 7.2).

15.   It should be noted that the original title of the work was probably 'The Birth of Mary', some manuscripts adding the name of James as its author. One early version (the Syriac), however, has 'Birth of our Lord and our Lady Mary'.

16.   Joseph, in the text, is said to be old, and to have sons by a previous marriage (James, presumably, being one of them). Jesus, then, is thus perceived not as the brother or cousin of James, but as his step-brother.

In the eastern Church, the *Protevangelium of James* was guaranteed an avid readership, for celibacy and chastity were highly prized, especially among encratite and Ebionite communities. In the west, however, the book failed to find favour, though there is little doubt that it made a significant contribution to mariological thought and the *theotokos* controversy of later centuries.[17]

17. The Greek term *theotokos* literally means 'God-bearer', but is usually interpreted to mean that Mary was the 'mother of God'. It reflects the idea, prominent in the *Protevangelium*, of the miraculous conception and birth of Mary.

Chapter 3

THE CHURCH IN SAMARIA

The Acts of Peter
The Pseudo-Clementine Homilies and Recognitions
The Epistle of Peter to Philip
The Gospel of the Nazaraeans
The Gospel of the Ebionites

Attention was drawn in the brief historical survey (Chapter 1) to the immense importance of the clash, recorded in Acts 8, between the Apostles and the Samaritan sorcerer Simon Magus. Whatever might be said about the authenticity of the Lukan story, the ramifications of the traditions associated with this charismatic figure simply cannot be ignored. Two major early works—the *Acts of Peter* and the Pseudo-Clementine *Homilies* and *Recognitions*—are constructed around the ongoing struggle between Peter and Simon, fundamentally illustrative of the perceived need to show Christianity's superiority over magic and superstition, and to proclaim Peter's God as the one true and only power. We shall begin this chapter with an examination of these two works, noticing particularly how the author of the Clementine Romances uses the contest to symbolize the burgeoning conflict between Jewish and Gentile Christianity, Simon representing the 'enemy' Paul.

The other figure plainly associated with the Samaritan Church, and, of course, with Simon Magus, is Philip the Deacon, the first among the followers of Jesus to emulate his mission in this region. We referred earlier to the confusion found in early literature (and which persists today) between Philip the Apostle (Jn 1.43) and Philip the Deacon (Acts 6.5). The comparatively late *Acts of Philip* records Philip's activity in Asia, and has no association with Samaria. Two other documents are pseudonymously attributed to or associated with Philip—the *Gospel of Philip* and the *Epistle of Peter to Philip*. Of these works, the former is accredited to Philip the Apostle on the sole basis that he is the one Apostle mentioned by name in the text. Since it has stronger associations with East Syria than with Samaria, we shall reserve examination of this important book until Chapter 4. The *Epistle of Peter to Philip*, on the other hand, might well relate to Philip the Deacon, and we shall consider this work in the present chapter.

Although only fragmentary quotations remain of the so-called *Gospel of the Nazaraeans* and the *Gospel of the Ebionites*, these two works, wherever they were compiled, were certainly much used in the Palestinian regions where these Jewish forms of Christianity were in evidence. It will be convenient, then, to discuss them in this chapter.

1. *The Acts of Peter*

There is no certain earlier witness to the *Acts of Peter* than that of Eusebius at the beginning of the fourth century.[1] Eusebius refers to an 'Acts bearing his [Peter's] name', a book which, together with the *Gospel of Peter* and the so-called Revelation, he maintains to be of doubtful authenticity. In this same passage he does refer to Origen's assertion in his *Commentary on Genesis* that Peter was crucified head-downwards—a detail which is recorded in the Martyrdom section of the *Acts of Peter*. We cannot be absolutely sure, however, whether Origen's information came from these Acts, or from some other tradition. Eusebius's comment must therefore stand as the earliest certain citation. It should be noted, however, that several fourth-century works seem to have been familiar with the text of the *Acts of Peter*, notably the *Acts of Philip* and the work known as the *Life of Abercius*.[2]

The *Acts of Peter* is extant in only one (almost complete) sixth-century Latin manuscript discovered at Vercelli (and designated the *Actus Vercellenses*). The final chapters dealing with the martyrdom of Peter are also separately extant in Greek, however, and it is likely that this section circulated independently of the earlier narrative, such was the popular appeal of martyrdom texts in the early centuries. Two other fragmentary 'Acts' of Peter—the one concerning Peter's daughter,[3] and the other a Gardener's daughter[4]—have generally been assumed to have belonged originally to

---

1. *HE* 3.3.2.
2. Several verbatim passages from the *Actus Vercellenses* appear in the fourth-century *Life of Abercius*.
3. The Coptic papyrus fragment that contains this story was discovered in the late nineteenth century.
4. This story appears in the so-called *Epistle of Titus* (or *Pseudo-Titus*), a document which came to light at the close of the nineteenth century.

the *Acts of Peter*, and to have become separated from the work. I discuss below the reasons why such an assumption should be questioned.

The first four chapters of the *Actus Vercellenses*, which are set in Rome, are, in fact, not about Peter, but about Paul, who is on the point of leaving for Spain, thus opening the way for Simon Magus to enter the city and enchant the people with his powerful magic. Peter himself does not appear until ch. 5, prompted to sail from Caesarea to Rome because he hears of Simon's successes among Paul's converts. Because of this it has been thought that the early chapters concerning Paul may not have been part of the original text; and since the Stichometry of Nicephorus[5] suggests that the work was once at least a third longer than it now is, the commonly accepted explanation is that the work originally began with deeds of Peter in Jerusalem before sailing for Rome. Among these lost or misplaced 'Acts' were the two stories of the daughters of Peter and the Gardener. The four chapters concerning Paul, it is then suggested, borrowed from some 'Acts of Paul', were added at some later date to replace the lost section, to form a suitable introduction to Peter's work in Rome.

Such a hypothesis is certainly attractive. Yet it is hardly necessary to invent a Judaean beginning for these Acts, unless we make the assumption that we are dealing with a complete 'history' of Peter's involvement with Simon, both in Palestine and in Rome. It may rather be the case that the *Acts of Peter* (in Rome) was originally intended to show this Apostle's part in the establishing of the Church at the centre of the empire—in which case, the story of Paul's absence from the city would provide the necessary *raison d'être* for Peter's journey. Furthermore, there would seem to be no adequate explanation why the two daughter stories should become isolated from an assumed Judaean portion of the work, as well as from each other, only to turn up centuries later in two separate documents of very different character. Because the stories of Peter's daughter and the Gardener's daughter are usually included in the *Acts of Peter*, however, it will be convenient to discuss them at this point.

---

5.   Stichometry (from the Greek *stikos*, meaning a row or file) is the study of the number of lines in a document. Sometimes, when sections of the work are missing, an estimate is made according to the number of pages which the codex would originally have had. Nicephorus, Patriarch of Constantinople in the ninth century, produced a catalogue of the Scriptures—Old Testament, New Testament and the Apocryphal books. His important list of book lengths is still in use today.

a. *The Story of Peter's Daughter*

The aim of this strange story is to demonstrate the superiority of God's wisdom, and the constancy of his providence, even when most incomprehensible. While Peter was healing a crowd that had gathered on the Lord's Day, his own crippled daughter lay neglected in a corner. Peter is prevailed upon to cure his daughter, but then immediately returns her to her former crippled state. He explains to the disappointed onlookers that the girl's beauty had once been the cause of temptation to many, and a danger to herself. When she was only ten years old, a certain Ptolemaeus had lusted after her, and sought to make her his wife. No sooner had he taken the young girl to his house than she was visited with this terrible infirmity, and Ptolemaeus returned the girl to her father's house. The story goes on to record the subsequent remorse and penitence of Ptolemaeus, and his recompense for his evil intent. When he died, he bequeathed a piece of land to Peter's daughter which the Apostle is at pains to aver was sold, with the proceeds being given to the poor. Peter concludes by reminding his audience that not always are we able to understand the ways of God, though we need never doubt his providence:

> Know then, O servant of Jesus Christ, that God cares for his own and prepares good for every one of them, although we think that God has forgotten us. But now, brethren, let us be sorrowful and watch and pray, and God's goodness shall look upon us, and we wait for it ('Peter's Daughter', pp. 139-40).[6]

While the story, as it stands, may be taken quite literally, it would be a mistake to dismiss or ignore an allegorical interpretation. We might see a parallel, for instance, between the process of Ptolemaeus's conversion, on the one hand, and that of Saul, on the other, as he journeyed to Damascus (Acts 9). When afterwards he was alone in his bedroom, Ptolemaeus, blinded by tears of remorse, sees a great light, and hears an admonishing voice. He is bidden to go to Peter's house where all would be revealed to him:

> Ptolemaeus, God has not given the vessels for corruption and shame; nor is it right for you, a believer in me, to defile my virgin, one whom you are to know as your sister, since I have become for both of you one spirit. But get up and go quickly to the house of the apostle Peter, and you shall behold my glory; he will explain this matter to you. But Ptolemaeus made no

---

6. All page references to the story of Peter's Daughter are from the Berlin Coptic Papyrus 8502. The story is generally associated with the *Acts of Peter*.

delay, and told his servants to show him the way and bring him to me. And coming to me he told me all that had happened to him in the power of the Lord Jesus Christ. Then he did see with the eyes of his flesh and with the eyes of his soul, and many people set their hopes on Christ ('Peter's Daughter', p. 138).

The relative complexities of the Ptolemaeus element of the story, as well as its clear allegorical overtones, suggest that it may not have formed part of the original story at all. An alternative hypothesis would be that it constitutes an embellishment of an earlier and simpler text, composed for a Christian community that still remembered the persecution of Paul, and his subsequent conversion and mission. If this were indeed the case, the story, as a whole, demonstrably illustrates the truth that 'God cares for his own'.

The Peter's Daughter story is clearly of Palestinian origin, but whether it looks back to Jerusalem, Caesarea or Galilee for its setting cannot be positively asserted. Wherever it was, Peter and his family dwelt there (p. 141). The tradition itself, doubtless, goes back to early times—perhaps to the first century, and in one of the more ascetic communities of the eastern regions of Palestine. Its subsequent redaction and transmission are questions that admit of less certainty, though the story, as we now have it, is not likely to have been composed much earlier than 160, nor later than 220.

b. *The Story of the Gardener's Daughter*
Although there are obvious major differences between this story and the one we have just considered, there is sufficient evidence to show that the two stories were once used in association to illustrate an assumed common teaching—the supreme desirability of chaste living. Augustine, in his treatise against the Manichaean Adimantus,[7] cites the two stories together, but we cannot by any means be sure that he assumed that they were necessarily from the same Petrine (or Pseudo-Petrine) work. Indeed, a careful comparison of the two stories will show that, while it is very probable that the author of the Gardener's Daughter story knew and used the earlier Petrine tradition, the stories cannot be regarded as parallel narratives. It will become plain, as we examine the story, that its purpose was to promulgate a completely celibate way of life within an encratite community.

An old peasant begs Peter to offer a prayer for his only daughter, a virgin. Peter obliges, and tells the man that God would do what was best for the girl. To the old man's great consternation, his daughter immediately drops down dead. The man pleads for his daughter's restoration, and again

7.   Augustine, *Contra Adimantum* 17.

Peter complies. In the course of the days, an unscrupulous guest of the man, pretending to be a believer, seduced his daughter, and carried her off. The moral of the story, of course, like that of the Peter's Daughter story, was that God always knows best. The tradition is used by the author of the so-called *Epistle of Pseudo-Titus*[8] to persuade of the truth of the encratite belief that no eventuality, not even death itself, can be worse than sexual pollution.

Comparisons are often drawn between the ascetic nature of the two Daughter stories and the general tenor of the *Actus Vercellenses*, the greater part of the *Acts of Peter*, shortly to be considered. The inference is that since the virtues of chastity and sexual continence predominate in all these writings, they were probably constituent parts of one work. It should be noted, however, that all the early Apocryphal *Acta* are characteristically ascetic, displaying in varying degrees this same preoccupation with sexual purity. It will be remembered that it was for this reason that the Manichaean sect collected and used these documents in preference to the more ortho-dox Lukan Acts. Whatever date may be assigned to the several major Apoc-ryphal Acts, or their relationship to each other, it would seem reasonable to suppose that the Daughter tradition is very primitive, arising, no doubt, somewhere in the more easterly parts of that region which looked back to Peter as their founding Apostle.

A fragment of a thirteenth-century codex which contains part of an address by Peter to a bereaved father might, as some have suggested, reflect the Gardener's Daughter tradition, for it illustrates the same bold tendency to enlist Petrine support for the encratite cause:

> Peter speaking to a (man) who bitterly complained at the death of his daughter, said 'So many assaults of the devil, so many struggles with the body, so many disasters of the world she has escaped; and you shed tears, as if you did not know what you yourself have undergone'.[9]

c. *The Actus Vercellenses*

It is certainly feasible, as some have been at pains to demonstrate, that the foregoing stories were once part of an extended *Acts of Peter*—though, if this were so, we should need to ask what became of the remainder of the

---

8.   This extremely ascetic work, of uncertain provenance and date, survives in one eighth-century Latin version only. The text of the manuscript was published by D. de Bruyne in 1925.

9.   From p. 153 of the Codex Cambrai 254 fragment, first edited by D. de Bruyne in *Revue Bénédictine* 25 (1908), p. 152.

Judaean material which must surely have accompanied them. A much more likely hypothesis is that the *Acts of Peter*, as this has come down to us, was from the start concerned only with Peter's activity in Rome, and that the introductory chapters concerning Paul's departure to Spain serve merely to set the scene for Peter's arrival in the city. The Stichometry of Nicephorus suggests, however, that the original document was considerably longer than its present form. If the 'Roman' hypothesis is to be allowed, then, the missing portion of the work—perhaps further exploits of Peter and Simon in Rome—would need to be accounted for; and we shall consider this problem as we proceed.

The *Actus Vercellenses* is a seventh-century Latin text which purports to record Peter's encounters with Simon Magus in Rome. It begins, as we have seen, with Paul's departure from Rome, and Peter's voyage from Caesarea to reclaim those converts of Paul who had succumbed to Simon's persuasive magic. Throughout the work, Peter and Simon trade miracle for miracle, each striving to outdo the other, and prove the superiority of his God-given power. Some of the episodes border on the bizarre—indicative, perhaps, of folk origin. One such story tells of the restoration of life to a smoked tunny fish which was seen hanging in a window. Peter throws the dried fish into a nearby fish-pond, and the onlookers are able to watch it swim and eat—and, of course, are persuaded. Other wonders are more in keeping with those of the canonical writings. Acts of supernatural healing, exorcisms and raising dead people to life abound throughout, and clearly the purpose of all these wonders is to make conversions among the people. Yet argument and reasoned discussion has its place. At one point, Peter recalls for his Roman audience his early clashes with Simon in Judaea when this unprincipled charlatan had taken advantage of the hospitality of an honourable and over-trusting woman named Eubula, stealing her gold. The incident is made the occasion for Simon's flight to Italy, and of Peter's consequent chase. The fact that this story is told here in retrospect (ch. 17) and referred to again (ch. 23) lends weight to the hypothesis that these Acts originally contained no Judaean section.

In the Arena, and in the presence of senators and people, Simon is challenged to one final contest, the raising to life of a young man who had been slain at the behest of the Prefect. Once again, Peter's supremacy is upheld. In desperation, Simon summons all the people of Rome to witness the spectacle of his casting himself off from a high place, and flying up to God, whence he came. Peter, witnessing this incredible sight, cried out to the Lord Jesus:

'Let this man do what he undertook, and all who have believed on thee shall now be overthrown, and the signs and wonders which thou gavest them through me shall be disbelieved. Make haste, Lord, with thy grace; and let him fall down from this height, and be crippled, but not die; but let him be disabled and break his leg in three places!' And he fell down from that height and broke his leg in three places. Then they stoned him and went to their own homes; but from that time they all believed in Peter (*Acts of Peter* 32).

Simon now plays no further part in the Acts; but this episode marks the beginning of Peter's martyrdom. This final section (chs. 30–41) circulated separately from the rest of the Acts from an early date (as, because of their popularity, martyrdom texts were prone to do). The *Martyrdom of Peter*, almost complete in its Latin version, is preserved in three Greek manuscripts of about the tenth or eleventh centuries, as well as in a few later eastern versions. It describes the events leading up to, and including, the crucifixion of the Apostle in Rome. Peter was charged with irreligion (or 'atheism'),[10] the one indictment that would be certain to incur the death penalty. It should be noted, however, that Peter was not put to death 'for the Name', nor even for insurrection, but because he insisted on interfering in the domestic affairs of powerful and influential men in the city. When the four concubines of the Prefect Agrippa heeded Peter's warning that they should no longer live in impurity, the Prefect threatened to burn him alive. Matters came to head when Xanthippe, the beautiful wife of Albinus, the friend of Caesar, also decided to separate from her husband, and Agrippa was constrained to deal with the situation.

The first of two well-known early traditions occurs at this point. Xanthippe informs Peter of a plot to take him, and he plans to leave Rome. On the road he encounters the risen Christ making his way into the city, and Peter asks the Lord where he is going (Quo Vadis, *Acts of Peter* 35). The Lord replies that he is going to Rome to be crucified again; and Peter 'came to himself', and returns to face his ordeal. The vexed question of the necessity of suffering and persecution loomed large in the early centuries of the Church; and here, in this tradition, the definitive apostolic teaching finds expression—that the Christian ought not to *seek* martyrdom, but to accept it gladly if it should come.

The other tradition, unrelated to the first, and quite distinct from it, concerns the story of Peter's crucifixion upside down, in accordance with his

10. Christians, unlike Jews, were not exempt from Emperor-worship. Those unwilling to acknowledge the deity of the emperor were charged with atheism.

own request. We noted earlier that Origen was familiar with such a tradition, and may well have known and used the *Acts of Peter* as his source. The Gnostic character and mystical tone of this passage would seem to suggest that it had no part in the original work. In a wonderful peroration addressed to his cross, Peter witnesses to man's fallen and distorted state, symbolized by his own upside-down cross, and to the salvatory reversal which only Christ's cross can accomplish:

> Concerning this the Lord says in a mystery, 'Unless you make what is on the right hand as what is on the left and what is on the left as what is on the right and what is above as what is below and what is behind as what is before, you will not recognise the kingdom' (*Acts of Peter* 38).

This is clearly a passage with very strong Gnostic overtones, and it may be that the entire section (chs. 37–39) represents a later addition to the original text. In view of Origen's apparent familiarity with the tradition itself, the more likely scenario is that the original martyrdom section, with a simpler motive for the 'upside-down' tradition, attracted Gnostic embellishment during the course of its independent transmission.

The textual relationship between the *Acts of Peter* and other Apocryphal Acts, particularly those of Paul and John (see Chapter 6), is problematic, and present scholarship does not provide a definitive solution. That being the case, all we may say for certain about the date of the *Acts of Peter* is that it appears to be one of the earliest works of this genre, its original form being compiled towards the end of the second century.

2. *The Pseudo-Clementine Homilies and Recognitions*

So closely related are these documents contextually with the *Acts of Peter* that attempts have been made from time to time to show that the author of their underlying basic document knew the earlier *Acts*. All these works, it is true, have Peter's spiritual contest with Simon Magus as their central theme; yet neither the course of events, nor the places visited, in the Pseudo-Clementines bear much relationship to those of the *Acts of Peter*, and the general consensus of opinion tends to reject the idea. Of the writings that have come to be associated pseudepigraphically with Clement, the third (or fourth) Bishop of Rome,[11] the two Romances known as the

11.   Clemens Romanus, according to Irenaeus, was the third Bishop of Rome after Peter, following Linus and Anencletus. Other lists and documents suggest that he followed Linus.

Homilies and the *Recognitions*, though of little intrinsic historical value, are theologically the most valuable. We shall see that the history of the transmission of these third-century writings, which are clearly related, is extremely complicated. Our plan here will be first to examine their content and purpose, and only then to consider their relationship to each other.

The framework of these romantic novels focuses on Clement's fortuitous meeting with Peter at Caesarea Maritima, and his subsequent journeys up the Phoenician coast with the Apostle towards Antioch. At the beginning of the story, Clement's older twin brothers and their mother had left home to travel abroad in the east; and when no news of them had been received for some time, his father decided to follow, leaving the young Clement alone in Rome. Some years later, when Clement had developed an interest in religious matters, and having heard of an appearance of the Son of God in Judaea, he journeyed to the Holy Land. There he was introduced to Peter—and in the course of their travels together, Clement is joyfully reunited with his family, who, like himself, had been attracted to the new faith. The narrative of the journey is descriptive of Peter's preaching and healing in the towns and cities they visited, and is enlivened considerably by their encounters with Simon Magus, which often take the form of a theological dialogue. Peter, of course, always has the better of the argument, and Simon finds an excuse to move on to another town. The storyline is skilfully constructed to maintain the interest of the reader, as well as to introduce the teaching of the 'True Prophet'—Jesus.

It will be recalled that one of the introductory documents accompanying the Pseudo-Clementine literature was the letter from Peter to James purporting to introduce a compendium of his teaching or preaching. Many have sought to identify that teaching within the *Homilies* and *Recognitions* in the light of that introductory letter, and in conjunction with a Table of Contents of Peter's Teaching which appears at the end of the first book of the *Recognitions* (1.75). If the Table of Contents did indeed form part of the basic Clementine document, this would certainly have provided a reasonable approach to the identification of an early *Kerygmata Petrou* used as a source document by the compiler of the Pseudo-Clementines. That such a document did once exist is, at the very least, conceivable, for several early writers, including Origen, claimed to have knowledge of a book fitting that title and description, though often regarding it as spurious. Furthermore, as we discussed in Chapter 2, Clement of Alexandria actually quotes from a work he calls the *Kerygma Petrou*, clearly attributing the work to Peter himself. Attempts to show parallels between Clement's quotations and pericopes from the *Homilies* and *Recognitions* have not always found favour. Yet there is little doubt that close comparisons can be drawn; and if we allow (what must surely be the case) that the source documents would inevitably have been shaped by the compiler of the basic document, and then undergone further redaction in the course of the years that followed, the parallels are remarkably close.

Another probable source document of the Pseudo-Clementines, no longer discretely extant, is what the fourth-century writer Epiphanius called the *Itinerary of Peter*.[12] Although Epiphanius considered the work to have been produced by Ebionites in order to claim Petrine authority for their doctrines, his citation does demonstrate that a work describing the missionary journeys of Peter was once in popular circulation. Epiphanius also mentions in the same passage a work entitled the *Ascents of James*—presumably a document that described the events leading up to the martyrdom of James, the Lord's brother, in Jerusalem. The *Ascents of James* was discussed in the previous chapter, and we need here merely to reiterate that, while it is no longer discretely extant, it survives in the first book of the *Recognitions*.

While there remain huge differences of scholarly opinion on the question of the composition of the Clementine *Homilies* and *Recognitions*, there is no disagreement on the hypothesis that at some point the various sources mentioned above were woven together to form what is usually referred to as the basic document, or *Grundschrift*. At what precise point the enigmatic figure of Simon Magus came to represent, following Ebionite reconstruction, the hated figure of Paul, is not easy to determine. There is no doubt, however, that such Ebionite adaptation was introduced, making Paul the chief 'enemy' of Jewish-Christian 'orthodoxy'. Paul's 'apostolicity' is repudiated, and his dissolution of the Law is soundly condemned. The polemic against him is most clearly expressed, perhaps, in the following passage from the *Homilies*, in which Peter challenges Simon's (= Paul's) authority:

> If, then, our Jesus appeared to you in a vision, made Himself known to you, and spoke to you, it was as one who is enraged with an adversary; and this is the reason why it was through visions and dreams, or through revelations that were from without, that He spoke to you. But can any one be rendered fit for instruction through apparitions? And if you will say, 'It is possible,' then I ask, Why did our teacher abide and discourse a whole year to those who were awake? And how are we to believe your word, when you tell us that He appeared to you? And how did He appear to you, when you enter-

12. Epiphanius, *Panarion* 30.15-16.

tain opinions contrary to His teaching? But if you were seen and taught by Him, and became His apostle for a single hour, proclaim His utterances, interpret His sayings, love His apostles, contend not with me who companied with Him. For in direct opposition to me, who am a firm rock, the foundation of the Church, you now stand (*Homilies* 17.19).

The anti-Paulinism of the *Homilies* is considerably diminished in the *Recognitions*, produced as this was for a westernized readership. Nevertheless, we have here two closely related Jewish-Christian works; and the questions that have dominated critical debate for the century and more since they were discovered in the early years of the nineteenth century have chiefly concerned matters of textual priority and dependency. Has one compiler used the other's, and if so, which? And if both are dependent on a common *Grundschrift*, which of them more nearly represents the original? Once again, there is no consensus. In some respects, the *Recognitions* seem to contain the more primitive concepts and teaching—though the Latin version is unlikely to reflect the original basic document very closely. We must also allow that the extant Greek *Homilies* presents a very much altered edition from that of the original compilation, the Homilist promoting his own Ebionite interpretation of the nature and work of Christ, with the occasional Gnostic overtone. We considered the introductory writings to the Pseudo-Clementine literature—the *Epistle of Peter to James* and the *Contestatio of James*—in the chapter on the Judaean Church, for these Jewish-Christian writings do seem to look back to James and the Jerusalem tradition. We might, then, imagine, by the same token, that the Homilist redactor of the basic document could just as reasonably be placed within the same Judaean tradition. The earlier *Grundschrift*, however, most certainly originates from further north—northern Samaria, perhaps, if not Coele Syria—and it is for this reason that we have examined the Clementine *Homilies* and *Recognitions* in this present chapter.

We might hazard that the basic work underlying both the later Latin and Greek versions might have been compiled during the early to middle part of the third century, somewhere within that region where Elchasaite Gnostic Christianity met Ebionite Judaic Christianity, and where folk memories of the apostolic clash with Simon Magus were still strong.

3. *The Epistle of Peter to Philip*

One of the most intriguing manuscripts that came to light at Nag Hammadi is this composite document which does indeed begin with the record of a letter from Peter to his apostolic colleague Philip. The entire letter, so far as we have it, may be quoted here:

> Peter, the apostle of Jesus Christ, to Philip our beloved brother and our fellow apostle and to the brethren who are with you: greetings! Now I want you to know, our brother, that we received orders from our Lord and the Saviour of the whole world that we should come together and give instruction and preach in the salvation which was promised us by our Lord Jesus Christ. But as for you, you were separate from us, and you did not desire us to come together and to know how to organise ourselves in order that we might tell the good news. Therefore would it be agreeable to you, our brother, to come according to the orders of our God Jesus? (*Epistle of Peter to Philip*, p. 133).

We must infer from the letter that at some point between the Resurrection of Jesus and the final parting of his risen presence from the disciples, Philip had undertaken a sole missionary enterprise, and was, for some reason, reluctant to return to the rest of the Apostles. Peter, as the undisputed leader and spokesman, writes a firm but tactful letter requesting Philip to join his colleagues, so that, together, the missionary planning might proceed. Such sentiments are wholly in line with one of the most firmly established of apostolic traditions—that to each of the Twelve was given some specific missionary charge; and that before individuals went each to their allotted sphere, they were first to come together to be empowered by the Spirit of the Lord. Philip gladly acquiesces. Yet we cannot but sense a note of disapproval and tension, in Peter's choice of words, at Philip's unilateral and almost pre-emptive mission; and it is tempting to see here the first intimation of that fundamental divergence on the question of spiritual authority which has bedevilled Christian orthodoxy ever since.

The *Epistle of Peter to Philip* presents the modern reader with a number of problems, first among which concerns the identity of its recipient. There can be no doubt that the circumstances reflected in the letter are best understood in terms of Philip the Deacon's missionary excursion into Samaria (Acts 8). Yet the writer is at pains to show that it is Philip the Apostle, one of the Twelve, who is addressed. The fact that the episode appears to describe a pre-Pentecostal occurrence tends to add weight to the claim of the Epistle itself, and argue for Philip the Apostle. He figures only slightly, however, in either the Gospels or the Acts, though early tradition, confirmed by several writers of the second century, places him in Phrygia for the whole of his ministry and later life.[13] He is said to have settled in

---

13. Polycrates' *Letter to Victor*, Bishop of Rome towards the end of the second century; see *HE* 5.24.

Hierapolis, where the cult of the goddess Cybele originated, and where the Christian ecstatic sect of Montanism took firm root, and there produced four daughters with charismatic gifts of prophecy. Philip the Deacon, on the other hand, is given by Luke a leading role in bringing the gospel to Samaria; and having left his converts to the good offices of Peter and John, he was carried off by the Spirit to the Gaza road to bring enlightenment to the Ethiopian, and thence made his home in Caesarea. To add to the confusion between the two Philips, we are given to understand that he also had four prophetic daughters (Acts 21.9). It is clear that there has been some conflation of traditions; and it may be that the author of the *Epistle of Peter to Philip* himself shared in the confusion, conferring apostolic status on the Evangelist and Deacon, while crediting the Apostle with the evangelistic achievements of the Deacon. We shall encounter the same confusion in other early works either attributed to or associated with Philip as we proceed.

In the narrative that follows the letter, Peter now assembles all the Apostles on the Mount of Olives ('where they were accustomed to gather with the blessed Christ when he was in the body') for prayer, enlightenment and power. The scene is reminiscent of the gathering on Olivet (Acts 1) when, according to Luke, the Eleven were commissioned to preach the gospel to the ends of the earth. What follows this scene, however, seems to have little ostensible connection with the narrative. Indeed, the entire section from this point to almost the end of the document appears to be a Gnostic inclusion within the narrative, which resumes again on the final page. The closing text of the document reads like a conflation of Ascension-type commissioning and Pentecostal empowerment, with hints of a Resurrection epiphany:

> Peter gathered together the others also, saying, 'O, Lord Jesus Christ, author of our rest, give us a spirit of understanding in order that we also may perform wonders.' Then Peter and the other apostles saw him, and they were filled with a holy spirit, And each one performed healings. And they parted in order to preach the Lord Jesus. And they came together and greeted each other saying, 'Amen.' Then Jesus appeared saying to them, 'Peace to you all and everyone who believes in my name. And when you depart, joy be to you and grace and power. And be not afraid; behold, I am with you forever!' Then the apostles parted from each other into four words in order to preach. And they went by the power of Jesus, in peace (*Epistle of Peter to Philip*, p. 140).

It would seem reasonable, then, to divide the document broadly into two parts: first, the record of how the Apostles were brought together to be given understanding and enlightenment, and to be empowered for their common mission; and within this narrative setting, a Gnostic dialogue between the risen Christ and his disciples has later been inserted, followed by a series of interpretative speeches by Peter to prepare the Apostles for the inevitability of suffering. It is clear from this central section that the Gnostic Christians for whom the document was compiled were facing imminent persecution, and their anxieties focus on how they are to confront their enemies, and how they might be delivered from the evils of the world in which, unaccountably, they find themselves trapped.

An introductory prayer on the Mount of Olives, after the Eleven had 'fallen to their knees', calls to mind Jesus' own prayer for deliverance in Gethsemane. This prayer is followed by a series of eight questions addressed to the risen Christ, as he appears to them on the mountain, questions designed to explicate the nature and necessity of the suffering which he promises them. The passage illustrates the fundamental Gnostic dilemma: how can those who belong to Christ, and whose spiritual destiny in the heavens is assured, be persecuted and detained in this earthly prison? The dilemma has its roots in the incomprehension of the disciples, recorded in the Gospel, at Jesus' own suffering; but for these Christians who have now recognized within themselves that element of divinity which ought, surely, to protect them from all evil, the idea of suffering was bound to perplex. So the questions are relevant indeed:

> Then the apostles answered, and said, 'Lord, we would like to know the deficiency of the aeons and their pleroma, and how are we detained in this dwelling place, or how we came to this place, and in what manner shall we depart.' Again: 'How do we have authority of boldness, and why do the powers fight against us?...' Then the apostles worshipped again saying, 'Lord, tell us: In what way shall we fight against the archons, since the archons are above us?' (*Epistle of Peter to Philip*, pp. 134 and 137).

Jesus reminds the disciples that they had already been given his instruction while he was with them in the flesh, but they had neither understood nor received it. Now he explains again, in terms contrived to give dominical support to the Gnostic myth. If the questions themselves seem completely devoid of Christian content, the answers reveal a conscious effort to fuse canonical teaching with Gnostic ideas. Christ himself is the Pleroma, the fulness of being—a concept that finds full expression in the canonical Epistles to the Colossians and Ephesians.[14] The return to the Father of those who belong to Christ, imprisoned as they must be for a time in this evil sphere,

14. Cf. Col. 1.19; Eph. 1.22; 3.19.

can be accomplished only through a true understanding of the teaching of Christ. Their enemies are not only of this world, but also of a higher sphere; for there are evil powers above them who seek to thwart their escape— 'spiritual hosts of wickedness in the heavenly places', as the author of the Epistle to the Ephesians describes them (6.12). It is precisely because they belong to Christ that they, like him before them, must suffer; but when they 'strip off what is devoted to corruption' they will become 'luminaries in the midst of mortal men'.[15] In Peter's (Pentecost) address to the disciples, what appears to be an ancient credal formula which very evidently follows orthodox lines, shows the influence of early Church kerygma on the Gnostic compiler:

> Our illuminator, Jesus, came down and was crucified. And he bore a crown of thorns. And he put on a purple garment. And he was crucified on a tree and he was buried in a tomb. And he rose from the dead (*Epistle of Peter to Philip*, p. 139).

The theme of mission clearly forms an essential part of the *Epistle of Peter to Philip*. The whole question of the relevance of evangelism to Gnostic belief is one which would require a chapter of its own, for at the centre of the Gnostic understanding of salvation is the belief that some are inherently capable of salvation, possessing the spark of divinity within them, while others are not. We need, of course, to recognize that there is no single, closed, and all-embracing Gnostic system, but that communities developed in very different ways. Nevertheless, so far at least as the Gnostic interpolations are concerned, we must interpret the call to be luminaries in terms of seeking out and saving those who *already* belong to Christ, but whose awareness of their divine destiny has not yet been recognized. In other Gnostic documents, this idea is expressed by the simile of sleep or drunkenness, the subject having been beguiled or led astray by the temptations of the world. There is also in this document the idea that witnessing to the truth is one of the weapons they must wield to combat the forces, both earthly and heavenly, which are arrayed against them.

It is sometimes suggested that the outer sections of this work were originally part of an extended 'Acts of Philip' or an alternative 'Acts of Apostles', used by the compiler of the Epistle to lend authority to his Gnosticized

---

15. *Epistle of Peter to Philip*, p. 137; cf. Col. 3.8-10. The concept of 'stripping off' the garment of the flesh is important for Gnostic thought (cf. *Gospel of Philip* 23; *Dialogue of the Saviour*, Codex III, p. 143), but is also rooted in the New Testament; cf. 2 Pet. 1.14.

interpolations. While there is no evidence to show that such an extended document ever existed, it may well be the case that a localized Philip tradition was introduced here to reinforce the true (Gnostic) teaching of Christ, and to explicate the real nature and mission of his followers. Although clearly Valentinian in its teaching, the document cannot be said to exemplify the excessive mythology of later and more developed forms of this Gnostic system. For this reason, the work may be considered to have been compiled in the second half of the second century, or early in the third. Written originally in Greek, it was later translated into Coptic, in which form it appears in the fourth-century Codex from Nag Hammadi.

4. *The Gospel of the Nazaraeans*

The *Gospel of the Nazaraeans* and the *Gospel of the Ebionites* are two of the so-called Jewish-Christian Gospels generally associated with early Palestinian Christianity. Because these several documents survive only in fragmentary citations by the patristic writers and early ecclesiastical historians, they are sometimes referred to as the Lost Gospels. A third such work, given the title of the *Gospel of the Hebrews*, is usually linked with Egyptian Christianity, and we shall therefore leave consideration of this work until a later chapter.

We must be clear at the outset that what one authority identifies as a passage from the *Gospel of the Nazaraeans*, for instance, may by another be claimed to come from the 'Hebrew' Gospel, and vice versa. Consequently, in some instances there is a need to make a judgment on the context and tone of the passage quoted, as to which of the three Jewish Gospels is meant. Furthermore, there is no absolute certainty that what are variously called the *Gospel of the Nazaraeans* and the *Gospel of the Hebrews* were not in fact the same work—though it must be said that the majority opinion leans towards the theory that there were three distinct and separate 'Jewish' Gospels.

That a Gospel written in either the Aramaic or the Hebrew language was in use by Christians living in the region of Coele-Syria is attested by several early writers; and many are convinced that it was closely linked with the Gospel of Matthew, being either a version of Matthew, or perhaps even its original form. According to Papias, Matthew had written his Gospel in 'the Hebrew tongue';[16] and if this may be assumed to have been the case, it is difficult to determine whether the Nazaraean Gospel was an edition of

16. See Eusebius, *HE* 3.39.16.

this original Matthaean Gospel, an Aramaic or Hebrew translation of a later Greek version of Matthew, or, indeed, the original itself. What cannot be disputed is that many of the passages quoted or cited from the *Gospel of the Nazaraeans* (sometimes confusedly referred to as the Hebrew or Jewish Gospel) are indeed closely paralleled in Matthew's Gospel.

Of the many fragments of this Gospel which have survived through the writings of Origen, Eusebius, Jerome, Epiphanius and others, we might instance here just two, whose identification is generally accepted today, in order to illustrate the kind of variations we might expect to find between the Nazaraean Gospel and the canonical (Greek) Matthew, as well as the confusions mentioned above.

(From Jerome's *Commentary on Matthew*; cf. Mt. 12.13):

> In the Gospel which the Nazaraeans and Ebionites use, which we have recently translated out of Hebrew into Greek, and which is called by most people the authentic (Gospel) of Matthew, the man who had the withered hand is described as a mason who pleaded for help in the following words: I was a mason and earned my living with my hands; I beseech thee, Jesus, to restore to me my health that I may not with ignominy have to beg for my bread.

(Again, from Jerome's *Commentary on Matthew*; cf. Mt. 6.11):

> In the so-called Gospel according to the Hebrews instead of 'essential to existence' I found 'mahar', which means 'of tomorrow', so that the sense is: Our bread of tomorrow—that is, of the future—give us this day.

Another passage, whose identification is often disputed, occurs in Jerome's *Commentary on Isaiah*, and refers to the Gospel account of the baptism of Jesus. Because some of the terminology of the quotation expresses ideas which are akin to Alexandrian mystical Wisdom literature, the citation is often assigned to the *Gospel of the Hebrews*. There are equally good reasons, however, for believing that the passage originates in the *Gospel of the Nazaraeans*, not least the fact that Jerome himself is quite explicit about it:

> According to the Gospel written in the Hebrew speech, which the Naza-raeans read, the whole fount of the Holy Spirit shall descend upon him… Further in the Gospel which we have just mentioned we find the following written: And it came to pass when the Lord was come up out of the water, the whole fount of the Holy Spirit descended upon him and rested on him and said to him: My Son, in all the prophets was I waiting for thee that thou shouldest come and I might rest in thee (Jerome, *Commentary on Isaiah* 4).

This is an important fragment because its implied Christology is in accord, so far as can be ascertained, with that of the Nazaraean sect. One of the key characteristics of all forms of Jewish Christianity was the insistence on the observance of the Law as a prerequisite for Christian membership; and for most Christians of Jewish origin neither the notion of Christ's pre-existent divinity nor that of his virgin birth was acceptable. The status of Sonship was conferred upon the human Jesus at his baptism in the Jordan; and this 'Adoptionist' Christology, while proving attractive to many Christians in every age, has nevertheless been responsible for much theological controversy through the centuries. The Nazaraeans, however, while insisting on the requirements of the Law, seem to have leaned towards a more orthodox or catholic Christology, believing that in some way Jesus' pre-existently divine status was *affirmed*, rather than *conferred*, at his baptism. It should be recognized, however, that it is impossible to be categorical about the theological beliefs of the Nazaraeans; and it may be that Nazaraean communities varied considerably in their ideas of the nature of Christ. The passage quoted above seems to reflect these uncertainties. It first appears to represent an Adoptionist view of Christ, the whole fount of the Holy Spirit descending upon Jesus at his baptism; but later in the passage the text suggests his pre-existent Sonship. We might reflect that the same inexactitude occurs in the canonical texts.[17]

The earliest mention of a Gospel written in the language of the Hebrews is to be found in the *Memoirs* of Hegesippus quoted by Eusebius.[18] In that work, Hegesippus is said to have made extracts from a Gospel which the Hebrews used, written in the Syriac tongue (which would undoubtedly be Aramaic). By the middle of the second century, then, there seems to be no doubt that in the regions of northern Palestine and southern Syria the form of the Gospel in use by many Christians of Jewish origin was being read in their own language. It had clear and close affinities with the Gospel of Matthew; and its use by Christians of the Nazaraean sect led to its being referred to as the *Gospel of the Nazaraeans*.

5. *The Gospel of the Ebionites*

Not until the time of Epiphanius is there a witness of a Gospel in use by the Jewish-Christian sect known as the Ebionites. To compound the con-

---

17. Lk. 3.22; Acts 2.22.
18. *HE* 4.22.8. Hegesippus, Book 5 of his *Commentary on the Acts of the Church*, c. 180 CE.

fusion of titles already mentioned, Epiphanius actually refers to it as the *Gospel of the Hebrews*, and claims it to be a mutilated version of Matthew's Gospel.[19] The question now arises: how are we to distinguish between the passages quoted by Epiphanius, on the one hand, and the quotations by Jerome from what he also calls the Hebrew Gospel, but which we earlier identified as the *Gospel of the Nazaraeans*? Our only expedient is to be found in the *content* of the passages themselves. Other writers before Epiphanius, from Irenaeus to Origen, have described the Ebionite sect, adumbrating their teaching and lifestyle—their Cerinthian form of Adoptionist Christology, their obsessive zeal for circumcision and the Law, their use only of the Matthaean Gospel. How accurate were these early insights we cannot tell; but at the least they provide valuable clues towards a reasoned identification of the sources of the quotations.

Epiphanius himself records that the form of Matthew used by the Ebionites specifically excluded the birth and infancy stories, and began with the account of John's ministry of baptism:

> It came to pass that John was baptising; and there went out to him Pharisees and were baptised, and all Jerusalem. And John had a garment of camel's hair and a leathern girdle about his loins, and his food, as it saith, was wild honey, the taste of which was that of manna, as a cake dipped in oil.

> Thus they were resolved to pervert the word of truth into a lie and to put a cake in the place of locusts (*Panarion* 30.13).

The deviation in the description of John's food is doubtless an indication of the vegetarian customs of the Ebionites—though there is little direct evidence of this manner of life. We may certainly assume that the name of the sect, whatever its origin, was intended to reflect the idea of poverty; and simplicity of life, as befitting Christ's 'little ones', must have included at least frugality. A play on two Greek words in this passage[20] is sufficient evidence for many scholars to show that this passage was written in Greek (unlike the Aramaic *Gospel of the Nazaraeans*), and was therefore a quotation from the Greek translation of the original Aramaic Matthew. If this were the case, important questions now present themselves: who were these Ebionites, and what was their relationship, if any, to other Jewish-Christian groups such as the Nazaraeans; and in what geographical location did the

19. Epiphanius, *Panarion* 30.3.
20. The Greek *akris* ('locust') is similar in sound to the word *enkris* (meaning a cake dipped in oil and honey). The similarity does not occur in the Syriac or Hebrew languages.

Gospel of the Ebionites originate and circulate? Epiphanius's belief that the Ebionite sect arose from the Nazaraeans is generally rejected today, because, apart from their common attitude to the law, there is little to link the two groups. That the Ebionites appeared considerably later than the Nazaraeans is not often questioned; but few would now claim that the one group was an offshoot of the other, or that the Ebionites represent a continuous development from Jerusalem or Pella Christianity.

By the middle of the second century, however, several important factors were exercising considerable formative influences on the course of Palestinian Christianity. As the Pauline liberal and inclusive form of the faith began to spread east of Antioch, as well as west, so the more legalistic of Jewish-Christians were increasingly forced either to conform to Pauline 'orthodoxy', or to revert to Judaism. At the same time, in the years between the fall of Jerusalem in 70 and its final demise following the Bar Kochba debacle in 135, the task of reshaping and reformulating the Judaic national identity and cultus, begun at Jamnia, proceeded apace; and again Jewish converts to Christianity were faced with real choices about whether to consolidate their break with their Jewish heritage, or throw in their lot with the new rabbinic Judaism. Yet another factor was the emergence during the second century of forms of Gnostic belief which found ready syncretic partners among Jews searching for some new belief. Hegesippus records an extensive list of such heretical groups, though most of the leaders he mentions by name are otherwise unknown.[21] Among his record is the sect known as the Carpocratians, whom Irenaeus lists, along with the Cerinthians, as having the same christological beliefs as the Ebionites[22]—the Gnostic concept that Christ was no more than a man (albeit the most righteous and wisest of all) upon whom, after his baptism by John, the eternal Christ of the heavens descended and rested upon him until the time of his Passion. This idea is clearly represented in another of Epiphanius's quotations from the Ebionite Gospel:

> When the people were baptised, Jesus also came and was baptised by John. And as he came up from the water, the heavens were opened and he saw the Holy Spirit in the form of a dove that descended and entered into him. And a voice (sounded) from heaven that said: Thou art my beloved Son, in thee I am well pleased. And again: I have this day begotten thee. And immediately a great light shone round about the place (*Panarion* 30.13.7).

21. *HE* 4.22.5-7.
22. *Adv. Haer.* 1.26.2.

Before leaving the *Gospel of the Ebionites*, it will be well to mention a work cited by Origen, in his *Homily on Luke*, and by Jerome, in his *Commentary on Matthew*, which both writers refer to as the *Gospel of the Twelve*. Little is known about this work, but it seems likely, from the brief comments of these early writers, that it was of the Synoptic form, and leaned towards a gnosticizing view of Christ. For this reason, although Jerome identifies it with the Nazaraean Gospel, the majority opinion has tended to associate it with the *Gospel of the Ebionites*. The manifold uncertainties about all these Lost Gospels, however, should make us wary about the attribution of so vague a document. What is without question is that the second century saw the production of numerous 'Gospels', many of which were Gnostic in character, and few of them known to us by anything more than a passing quotation or citation.[23] It would be reasonable to speculate that the *Gospel of the Ebionites* first became known, about the middle of the second century, in the region to the east of Caesarea, that great Greek-speaking seat of learning, and origin and repository of so many early Christian works. Epiphanius, we know, travelled widely in this region, particularly in the Jordanian parts of Samaria; and his citations from this edited version of Matthew's Gospel, translated for Greek-speaking Jewish-Christians of a more conservative outlook than the Nazaraeans, provide clear evidence of how Gospel tradition, both oral and written, was used to authenticate the many differing views of Christ. They also serve as an indication of the syncretic incorporation of Gnostic thought into Gospel tradition during this period of Jewish uncertainty and transition.

23. For instance: the *Gospel of Perfection*; the *Gospel of Truth*; the *Gospel of the Four Heavenly Regions*; the *Gospel of Matthias*; *et al.* Space will not permit the detailed consideration of these works.

Chapter 4

THE CHURCH IN SYRIA

The Gospel of Peter
The Gospel of Philip
The Apocalypses of Peter
The Apocalypses of Paul

It would be a mistake to assume that Christianity first came to the province of Syria solely by way of its chief city, Antioch. Certainly the New Testament testifies to the paramount importance of this Roman city for the early movement of the faith into Asia Minor and Greece; and while no eastern missionary thrust towards Edessa is mentioned in the Acts, clearly we cannot rule out some early apostolic evangelism within this region from Antioch. There would be constant trading movement from Antioch to Edessa along the ancient Silk Road, and we might well expect (though there is little record of it) that the Antiochene faith would find its way along this route. However, it must also be recognized that Christianity was migrating northwards through Samaria to Damascus and beyond; and the forms of the faith as it passed through these regions could be expected to deviate from those Pauline norms which might originate from Antioch. Such divergence is discernible in the writings of the Syrian Church. It is generally accepted that Matthew's Gospel originated in this region, its earliest form in all probability being composed in Aramaic, for Christians of Jewish orientation. Though it exceeds all other Gospels in its representation of the bitter controversy between Jesus and the Jewish religious authorities, it nevertheless sees the 'House of Israel' as the Messiah's chief concern. The *Gospel of Peter*, as we shall see, was distinctly anti-Jewish in tone; and its geographical associations with Antiochene Christianity will doubtless account for both its social and theological divergence from the eastern Syrian Matthaean Christianity.

In this chapter we shall also be concerned to note the influences of Valentinus and his followers on the literature of the region. The so-called *Gospel of Philip*, whatever may be the manner of its composition, is clearly touched with Gnostic ideas which would seem to stem from Valentinian thought; and we shall find that few of the documents of the Syrian second-century Church are entirely free of this Valentinian influence. The apocalyptic literature associated with Peter and Paul, both traditional and Gnostic, is all included in this chapter, partly because Syrian origin is at least as likely as any other, but partly also the better to compare and contrast the different literary forms and doctrinal issues.

1. *The Gospel of Peter*

When Bishop Serapion of Antioch was apprised, towards the end of the second century (c. 180), that a heretical form of the Gospel, in the name of Peter, was being used in the town of Rhossos, some 30 miles north of Antioch, he was concerned enough to investigate. Eusebius has the story, and records it at some length.[1] Serapion's investigations at first gave him no cause for alarm, and he pronounced the use of the book legitimate. A subsequent inspection brought a change of mind, however. Realizing that he had been duped by those who had been 'lurking in some hole of heresy', he recognized the work to be Docetic in character, and forthwith proscribed its use.

Apart from the several references by Eusebius to a *Gospel of Peter*, the only other positive attestation is by Origen,[2] though it is by no means certain that he had first-hand knowledge of the work. Justin Martyr mentions a book which he calls the *Memoirs of Peter*, but this is more likely to refer to the *Preaching of Peter* (*Kerygma Petrou*) which we considered in Chapter 2 than the document discovered at Akhmim. Again, although the fifth-century historian Theodoret states that the Nazaraeans used a Gospel 'according to Peter', this intriguing information finds no support elsewhere. Indeed, one Apocryphal scholar has suggested that what is known about the Nazaraean sect seems to preclude any link with this Gospel.[3] Nevertheless, we might want to speculate that Jewish-Christians of the Greek-speaking regions around Antioch, for whom traditionally Peter had been allotted pastoral charge,[4] would want to use a Gospel that not only maintained continuity with their Jewish heritage, but which was also representative of the high

---

1. *HE* 6.12.2-6.
2. *Commentary on Matthew* 10.17.
3. M.R. James, *Apocryphal New Testament* (Oxford: Clarendon Press, 1924), p. 14.
4. See Eusebius, *HE* 3.1.2; 1 Pet. 1.1.

Christology of the mainstream western Church. The *Gospel of Peter*, it seems, was such a work. Its roots were firmly established in Jewish tradition, yet its tone was highly critical of Jewish obduracy and intransigence; and its portrayal of Christ could not have been too far removed from that of the Nazaraeans.

Neither Origen nor Eusebius offers any clues about the content of the Gospel, except that it leant towards Docetism. In 1884, however, in a burial ground at Akhmim in Upper Egypt, a codex was unearthed that contained several early and important manuscripts, one of which seemed to match Serapion's description of this Gospel. Separated by three blank pages in the same codex was another document, transcribed by the same hand, entitled the *Apocalypse of Peter*, a work which we shall examine later in this chapter. The untitled document that has come to be known as the *Gospel of Peter*[5] is in fact merely a fragment of a larger whole. It begins at a point during the trial of Jesus before Pilate, and ends with an extraordinary account of the Resurrection. We are left to assume that neither the earlier parts of the Gospel, nor its conclusion, have survived— though there is naturally no proof that the original work comprised anything more than a Passion–Resurrection narrative.

The Gospel seems to be of the Synoptic type, and parallels with all four traditional Gospels are scattered throughout the fragment. Inevitably, then, the primary scholarly concern has revolved around the relationship between the *Gospel of Peter* and the canonical four. Does it represent a primitive source from which, among other early sources, the traditional evangelists have compiled their Gospels? Is it rather a later work than any of the canonical Gospels, its author constructing a kind of 'diatessaron', perhaps even before Tatian's celebrated work of the same kind? Some have attempted to show that there are underlying elements in this Gospel that are independent of the traditional Gospels, actually going so far as to identify an early Passion narrative—a 'Cross Gospel' or 'epiphany story'—embedded in the text. What is certain is that there is little exact verbal identity between this Gospel and the New Testament Gospels; so the most probable hypothesis is that the compiler, during the middle years of the second century, created his Gospel using both oral and remembered written sources. Of special interest are those elements of the Gospel that diverge from the canonical norm. In the preliminary stages of the trial, for instance, Joseph

_____

5.   Peter identifies himself as the author in the concluding (unfinished) verse of the fragment.

of Arimathea begs Pilate for the body of Jesus, instead of at the customary place of this episode following the Lord's death:

> Now there stood there Joseph, the friend of Pilate and of the Lord, and knowing that they were about to crucify him he came to Pilate and begged the body of the Lord for burial. And Pilate sent to Herod and begged his body. And Herod said, 'Brother Pilate, even if no one had begged him, we should bury him, since the Sabbath is drawing on. For it stands written in the law: The sun should not set on one that has been put to death' (*Gospel of Peter* 2.3).

This passage, like others that follow, may well contain traditions which the other evangelists either did not know, or chose not to use; and it would be to go beyond the evidence to assert that every divergence from the canonical norm must be late and inaccurate. Mention has already been made of the anti-Jewish character of the *Gospel of Peter*. In the passage quoted above, and in several places in the narrative, emphasis is placed on the callousness and cruelty of the Jews. Here, for instance, it is shown that the demands of the Law take precedence over any humane considerations. The decencies of burial are accorded to the body of Jesus because the Law demands that 'the sun should not set upon one that had been murdered' (2.5 and 5.15). Repeatedly the Jews are represented as unfeeling and cruel, as several non-canonical features of the Gospel illustrate: Jesus is pushed and hustled by the running crowd; it is the Jews, not the Romans, who buffet and scourge Jesus, and mock him with the crown of thorns; and throughout the trial narrative, the chief aim of the compiler of the Gospel seems to be to shift blame for the death of Jesus from the Roman authority to the Jews themselves.

Whether Bishop Serapion was in possession of a more extended Gospel than we now have, as is generally assumed, we cannot know. It is possible that his considered judgment concerning the Docetism of the book was based on earlier sections of a larger work. There are, however, three points in the extant fragment which are just capable of Docetic interpretation, and we might consider these now:

1.   At the point of crucifixion, Jesus 'held his peace, as having no pain' (4.10). His silence here is taken, by those who wish to interpret the Gospel Docetically, to indicate that Christ was essentially impervious to suffering. There is, in fact, no suggestion in the text that the two thieves were less stoic or more vociferous, but the implication is certainly that Jesus' silence was unusual and spiritually engendered. There is no need to deduce from this

pericope, however, that Jesus was not truly and fully human. The text simply draws attention to his quiet acceptance of pain, and is best translated by the illustrative phrase '*as if* he had no pain'.

2.   The Cry from the Cross—'My power, power has abandoned me' (5.19). Unlike the canonical version, we have here a statement, not a question. Until recent years, the usual interpretation of this saying from the cross has been, if not Docetic, at least Cerinthian, Jesus recognizing that the divine power which had descended upon him at his baptism was now returning to the heavens. The Greek word translated 'power' (*dunamis*), however, is sometimes used in patristic literature as a circumlocutory term for 'God'; and, for this reason, the *Gospel of Peter*'s version of the saying is now generally understood to have the same sense as the canonical version. It must be conceded, however, that the rather strange substitution of the word 'power' for 'God' suggests some Gnostic influence, the heavenly Christ abandoning his human and fleshly image at the moment of Jesus' death.

3.   The third passage that could conceivably imply a Docetic Christology focuses on the use of the Greek verb *analambano*, which has the general meaning of 'to go up'. When Jesus had uttered the great cry from the cross, 'he was taken up' (5.19). Did the compiler mean to imply that Christ ascended to the heavens immediately upon death, or was the word used (as it sometimes has been) simply to mean that he died? If the former interpretation was intended, of course we must infer a Docetic view of Christ. It may be the case that the phrase simply means (as it does in the Synoptic Gospels) that Jesus 'yielded up his spirit'; but there is little doubt that it is the spirituality and exalted nature of Christ, rather than his humanity and suffering, that is here emphasized.

When we come to the Resurrection narrative, we find that it is this same emphasis on the other-worldly Christ that is paramount. Clearly the general populace of Jerusalem, as well as the fearful and apprehensive Scribes and Pharisees, were expecting spectacular repercussions following the powerful signs that had accompanied the Crucifixion, for crowds made their way, early on the Sabbath day, to the sealed sepulchre. If they had waited there with the guard until the next morning, they would not have been disappointed:

> Now in the night in which the Lord's day dawned, when the soldiers, two by two in every watch, were keeping guard, there rang out a loud voice in heaven, and they saw the heavens opened and two men come down from there in a great brightness and draw nigh to the sepulchre. That stone which had been laid against the entrance to the sepulchre started of itself to roll and gave way to the side, and the sepulchre was opened, and both the young men entered in (*Gospel of Peter* 9.35-37).

If it may be said that in earlier sections of the *Gospel of Peter* it is the *form* and *order* of the various episodes that diverge from the canonical norm, in the Resurrection narrative it is rather the *content* of the story. Long before the visit of Mary Magdalene and her friends, early on the Lord's day, the stone had rolled aside (by itself), and, witnessed by the soldiers on watch, 'three men came out from the sepulchre, two of them sustaining the other, and a cross following'. Whatever other additions or embellishments to the 'true' Gospel might have concerned Serapion in the *Gospel of Peter*, this passage must surely have been one—particularly as he read the extraordinary end of the passage:

> and the heads of the two reaching to heaven, but that of him who was led of them by the hand overpassing the heavens. And they heard a voice out of the heavens crying, 'Hast thou preached to them that sleep?', and from the cross there was heard the answer, 'Yea' (*Gospel of Peter* 10.40-42).

The image of a heightened and exalted Christ is by no means confined to this Gospel. We encounter the same image, for example, in the Apocryphal *Acts of John*,[6] where the head of the transfigured Christ appears to Peter, James and John to stretch up to the heavens. The Revelation of John the Divine also contains the description of a mighty, cloud-wrapped angel coming down from heaven, with one foot on the land and one on the sea (Rev. 10.1). The whole Resurrection passage in the *Gospel of Peter* is imbued with apocalyptic ideas, with the triumphant and glorified Christ coming forth from the tomb, and the inference of the voice from the heavens that 'them that sleep' should also rise. A strong parallel could be found in the second-century *Ascension of Isaiah*, an early Christian work fashioned in the manner of a Jewish Apocalypse:

> The angel of the Holy Spirit and Michael, the chief of the holy angels, would open his (the Beloved's) grave on the third day, and that the Beloved, sitting on their shoulders, will come forth and send out his twelve disciples... and those who believe on his cross will be saved (*Asc. Isa.* 3.16-18).

---

6. *Acts of John* 90. The same image is found also in Hermas's *Shepherd* (*Sim.* 9.6), where the Lord was so tall that he 'overtopped the tower'.

The most interesting example of the exaltation imagery of the Gospel occurs in the testimony of a certain Alcibiades of Apamea concerning the origin of the Elchasaite sect. He claimed that the prophet Elchasai had received the so-called *Book of Elchasai* from an angel whose height was 96 miles. We might also note that the writings of Mani, who may have spent his early years in an Elchasaite community in this area, contain quotations from the *Gospel of Peter*. If such a link can be established, as certainly seems to be more than likely, we might reasonably conjecture that the *Gospel of Peter* was in use in the regions of Syria that lie between the Orontes River and the Euphrates, where Antiochene 'orthodoxy' met and mingled with Jewish apocalypticism and Mesopotamian mysticism. We must assume that the Gospel was composed, no later than the middle of the second century, by one who was familiar not only with all four traditional Gospels (which he used from memory), but also with early traditions some of which were in contradiction to those Gospels. To what extent these divergent sources represented and reflected the earliest *kerygma* is presently impossible to say; but clearly the *Gospel of Peter* deserves more than to be dismissed as a spurious and inconsequential work.

2. *The Gospel of Philip*

In an important third-century Gnostic work known as the *Pistis Sophia*, the Apostle Philip is entrusted by the Saviour, along with Thomas and Matthew, to witness and record his teachings:

> It happened now when Jesus heard these words which Philip said, he said to him: 'Excellent, Philip, thou beloved one. Come now at this time, sit and write thy part of every word which I shall say, and what I shall do, and everything which thou shalt see.' And immediately Philip sat down and wrote (*Pistis Sophia* 44).

And Mary Magdalene expresses her recognition and appreciation of this commission:

> Concerning the word which thou didst say to Philip: 'Thou and Thomas and Matthew are the three to whom it has been given, through the First Mystery, to write every word of the Kingdom of the Light, and to bear witness to them'; hear now that I give the interpretation of these words. It is this which thy light-power once prophesied through Moses: 'Through two and three witnesses everything will be established. The three witnesses are Philip and Thomas and Matthew.' (*Pistis Sophia* 43).

Whether these passages constitute a reliable witness to a 'Gospel of Philip' continues to be a matter of debate; but they certainly point in this direction. Epiphanius actually refers to such a work by name, and quotes a short passage from it.[7] Unfortunately, there is no exact textual counterpart of this passage in the extant *Gospel of Philip*, the only copy of which came to light in the discoveries at Nag Hammadi. The general theme of Epiphanius's quotation is certainly to be found in the Gospel, for it refers to the soul's ascent to its eventual destiny through the spheres controlled by the higher powers, the archons. If there is no precise textual correlation, the *substance* of the quotation is often expressed; and many confidently postulate that Epiphanius, like the author of the *Pistis Sophia*, was acquainted with a Gospel-type work which purported to be written by Philip.

We must note, however, that there is no claim to authorship in the text of this Nag Hammadi document. The work seemingly derives its name from the one and only apostolic reference in the text: Philip the Apostle is attributed with a somewhat cryptic remark about Joseph's garden, and the wood of the cross of Jesus coming from one of the trees he had planted (91). This passing mention of Philip in the text is hardly sufficient evidence to assume that the work was attributed to Philip from the start. Indeed, the use of the third person would seem to suggest the opposite conclusion; and the title of the work, appearing only in the colophon, might indicate that its earliest use was by the fourth-century Coptic translator himself. We cannot, of course, rule out the possibility that the few early witnesses to a 'Gospel of Philip' were, in fact, referring to the text we have before us; but nor are we able positively to identify the so-called *Gospel of Philip* with the document they clearly knew.

Like the *Gospel of Thomas* (see Chapter 5), which appears immediately before it in the same codex, the *Gospel of Philip* divides itself by paragraphs into a series of unrelated or loosely connected aphorisms. The *Gospel of Thomas*, as we shall see, purports to be a collection of dominical sayings, each one of the 114 Logia beginning with the words, 'Jesus said'. Here, in the Gospel of Philip, on the other hand, we are presented with what may best be described as a *florilegium* or anthology of theological statements, rather than 'sayings', which are intended to represent an interpretation of the teachings of Jesus. That this interpretation is broadly Gnostic, and of the Valentinian kind, is generally recognized,[8] though much of the material is not specifically Gnostic at all. Occasionally the language of Valentinian mythology is employed, especially with the themes

7.   *Panarion* 26.13.
8.   See Chapter 2, section 6, for a description of Valentinian theology.

of creation and redemption. More generally, the statements *allow* a Gnostic interpretation of fundamentally Christian themes, emphasizing the essential dichotomy between this world and the world of light:

> My God, my God, why have you forsaken me? The Lord spoke these words on the cross. For there he was separated... The Lord is risen from the dead. He did not come as he was, but his body was wholly perfect. It consists of flesh. But this flesh was true flesh. Our flesh, however, is not true flesh, but an image of the true (*Gos. Phil.* 72).[9]

The *Gospel of Philip* clearly shares the same distaste for material and fleshly things as the *Gospel of Thomas* and other Gnostic works, portraying the world as a deceitful and insidious force for evil which seeks to distort the truth, and pervert the children of light. By mistake the world was created by an inferior power who himself is as corruptible as his creation. Only those who are children, and who put on the light, will be able to cast off the restraints of the world and achieve incorruptibility. This theme runs throughout the Gospel, never too far from any of the excerpts or aphorisms. Yet the compiler frequently links the idea of salvation with the sacramental mysteries of baptism, chrism, the Eucharist and what he calls the Bridal Chamber. This association is so prominent a feature, in fact, that many commentators of the text have surmised that the Gospel might originally have been a kind of catechism for new initiates to the Gnostic community. Whether or not this might be so, there can be no disputing the fact that this preoccupation with the sacraments of salvation brings us to the heart of the work, and needs to be examined.

At several points in the Gospel, the compiler is anxious to differentiate between the nominal and the real. Because an entity has a good name does not necessarily make it good; for the archons use names to deceive (13). If this is true in general terms, it is especially true of those mysteries that pertain to the soul's rise to the highest realms. Baptism is a sacrament of the mainstream Church; yet it is meaningless and ineffectual unless it conveys the Holy Spirit:

> If anyone goes down into the water and comes up again without having received anything, and says 'I am a Christian', he has borrowed the name at interest. But if he receives the Holy Spirit, he possesses the name as a gift. He who has received a gift does not have it taken away. But he who has

---

9.   Damage to the codex is particularly extensive at this point, and several words may only be surmised. The lacunae in the text have been filled by the translator (Hans Martin Schenke), and these insertions are included to make sense of the passage.

received something at interest, it will be demanded back from him. So it happens with us, when anyone submits to a mystery (*Gos. Phil.* 59).

That a Gnostic work should seem to recognize those outward forms of Christian initiation which customarily belonged to catholic orthodoxy—baptism, chrism and the Eucharist—will seem paradoxical, prompting the speculation, perhaps, that the *Gospel of Philip* derives from a comparatively early and unsophisticated Valentinian period. The frequent references to these sacraments is certainly a clear indication that their initiatory role was as significant to this sectarian community as it was to the mainstream Church. We will completely fail to appreciate the sacramental theology of the *Gospel of Philip*, however, unless we consider it in conjunction with another recurring theme of the work—the nature of begetting, and of creation. The compiler is anxious to show that the true people of God are his creation, born of the Spirit. Christians are a new and different race, descended not from the Jews, nor from the Greeks, but begotten of God (102). By the same token, the sacraments of water and oil, important though they are as signs of that new beginning of the Spirit, are not the progenitors of the Christian soul. The Christian soul is born of God, brought into being by that union of the Father and the Holy Spirit which is symbolized by the Bridal Chamber.

The concept of the Bridal Chamber, which also figures (though to a lesser degree) in the *Gospel of Thomas*, is still something of an enigma. It is just possible, as some believe, that the term describes an actual ritual reserved for those who have attained to higher knowledge, or who are entering the life of celibacy. Again, the concept may have funerary connotations, signifying the soul's reunion with Christ in death, for several references to it include the idea of the world which is to come. In essence, however—since it clearly must have its origin in the canonical imagery of the 'bridegroom'[10]—it probably symbolizes that longed-for reunion with Christ for which the faithful soul must wait while the bridegroom is absent. We might imagine a solemn rite of dedication and commitment in which those who have recognized their divine origin solemnly join themselves (as in a marriage) to Christ. Whether such a rite would involve prayer and fasting, and how far it might entail an encratic way of life, is, of course, impossible to say; but that the sacrament of the Bridal Chamber was seen by these and other Gnostics as, perhaps, the greatest and most wondrous mystery of all is obvious from the prominence that is given to it in this Gospel.

10. See Mt. 9.15 and parallels.

Associated with the mystery of the Bridal Chamber, though inferior to it in importance, is what is termed the 'redemption'. The compiler explains in terms analogous to the Temple in Jerusalem:

> There were three buildings as places of offering in Jerusalem: the one which opens to the west was called 'the holy'; another which opens to the south was called 'the holy of holies', where only the high priest might enter. Baptism is the 'holy' house. The redemption is 'the holy of the holy'. 'The holy of the holies' is the bridal chamber. Baptism has after it the resurrection and the redemption. The redemption is in the bridal chamber. But the bridal chamber is in what is superior to them (*Gos. Phil.* 76).

It needs to be remembered that in Gnostic writings the cross of Christ is rarely seen in terms of a redemptive act. Although the cross is occasionally mentioned in this Gospel, it has no obvious part in that process of salvation which is the basic theme of the work. The mystery of 'redemption', which is clearly associated here with the Bridal Chamber, seemingly constitutes a cognitive act of recognition, on the part of the baptized, of his or her already redeemed status as a child of God, and a true inheritor of the kingdom. It would appear to be a stage in the Gnostic's upward rise to his or her destined place with God.

The sacrament of the Eucharist is more than once included in the list of 'the Lord's mysteries' (68), though it is clearly not regarded intrinsically as an initiatory rite. It is evident that in this Gnostic community there are priests who consecrate the bread and the cup to bring the sustaining spiritual food of Christ to his people. In a passage that delineates the notion of incorruptibility, and the means of achieving perfection, we are given an insight into the significance of the sacrament:

> The cup of prayer for which thanks is given contains wine as well as water. It represents the blood and fills with the Holy Spirit. And this is all that constitutes the perfect man. When we drink this cup, we shall receive for ourselves the perfect man (*Gos. Phil.* 100).

The author or compiler of the Gospel is emphatic that the sacraments of water, oil or wine are not of the same high order as the greatest mystery of all—presumably that of the Bridal Chamber (76 and 98). That they still played an important part of the life of this community, however, is indicative of a group which had not completely repudiated mainstream ecclesiastical practice. This perhaps tells us something about the date of the work. It also undoubtedly provides some clue as to its geographical provenance. The more highly developed Gnostic systems, and those 'heretical' groups situated at some distance from the main centres of orthodox Christianity, had, by the third century, rejected not only the hierarchical structures, but also the liturgical forms of the institutionalized Church. By its very nature, Gnosticism was philosophically orientated towards the individual, not the group; and the mediation of liturgical forms came to be considered as unnecessary as the orthodox movement towards an ordered priesthood was unwelcome. We may with some confidence, then, place the composition of the *Gospel of Philip* not too distant from Antioch, compiled during the early decades of the third century, if not up to half a century earlier.

3. *The Apocalypse of Peter*

The concept of 'apocalyptic' is arguably the most difficult of all religious ideas to define, for it encompasses many different forms and literary styles. Strictly, the word itself has to do with the divine revealing of hidden truth concerning either things as they are, or of things as they will be. The pseudonymous authors of apocalyptic literature, whether of Jewish or Christian orientation, claim that by revelatory or visionary experience they have been granted insights into eternal reality. The chief emphasis of apocalyptic was to show, within the historical process, how God would bring final justice and judgment upon his world. In this sense we may say that apocalyptic is an aspect of eschatology.

   Herein, of course, lies our difficulty; for the Gnostics were by and large unconcerned about the end time of this present world. They recognized, as clearly they must, that in the world they would be subject to danger, temptation and persecution—powers which could hinder the individual's rise to his or her eternal destiny. But while the idea of a cosmological judgment does, somewhat incongruously, find a place in some Gnostic works, it is the *realized* eschatology of John's Gospel, not the signs and portents of the Synoptics or of the Johannine Apocalypse, that provides the true Gnostic rationale. The traditional *Apocalypse of Peter*—our present concern—differs markedly from the Coptic work of the same title discovered at Nag Hammadi. Unlike its Gnostic counterpart, it describes in vivid terms the sufferings of the wicked, and the blessings of the righteous, in the age to come. Although the Coptic document is not at all prophetically interested in these matters, what it does share with the traditional Apocalypse, apart from its pseudonymity, is that both describe visionary experience that interprets events shortly to take place.

   An *Apocalypse of Peter* had been known from as early as the second century. Clement of Alexandria, among others, cited the work, considering it to be (in his phrase) 'an inspired writing'. The second-century Muratorian

Canon[11] also lists the book, but its author adds a caveat which casts some doubt on its apostolic authenticity. The book then disappeared, and did not reappear until excavations at Akhmim in Upper Egypt towards the end of the nineteenth century uncovered a codex which contained a fragment of the Apocalypse, written in Greek, and identifiable by one or two of the patristic quotations. At the beginning of the twentieth century, the discovery of an Ethiopic version of the *Apocalypse of Peter*, embedded in the Clementine collection of writings, brought confirmation of the identity of the work, and supplied additional text which had not survived in the Akhmim fragment. The two versions, Greek and Ethiopic, are manifestly related, though there are considerable textual differences between them; and the fundamental problem for scholars has been to try to decide which of the versions represents the original. The general consensus today makes the Ethiopic version the primary text. This view (which is here challenged) follows M.R. James's hypothesis that the Greek version was a translation of the Ethiopic by the author of the *Gospel of Peter* (with which it was juxtaposed in the same codex, and transcribed by the same hand), for use as the apocalyptic section of his Gospel (see section 1 of this chapter). This hypothesis has undoubtedly a certain logicality. The position of these two Greek documents in the same codex, and in the same scribal hand, however, might simply indicate that the copier mistakenly *thought* the two works were related; and it should also be recognized that the textual similarities between the *Gospel of Peter* and the *Apocalypse of Peter* are less compelling than once was believed. Furthermore, all of the early patristic citations treat them as separate books. For these and other reasons we shall now consider, the hypothesis adopted here will be that not only has the Greek version of the *Apocalypse of Peter* no connection with the *Gospel of Peter*, but that, contrary to the majority opinion, it represents the original version of the work, the Ethiopic version being a development and later extension of it.

Before turning to these matters, however, we must briefly examine the content of the Apocalypse. Looking first at the Ethiopic text, we find an introductory section which describes a meeting of the Lord with his disciples on the Mount of Olives, when in general terms Christ explains to Peter and his companions what will happen when the end comes. An important feature of this section is the parable of the fig tree, by which the Lord

---

11.   The Muratorian Canon is a (probably) second-century catalogue of the books of the New Testament. The fragment of an eighth-century manuscript containing this early work was discovered and published in the eighteenth century by L.A. Muratori.

warns of the imminence of the coming judgment upon the house of Israel. The passage is, in fact, a conflation of two fig tree stories, one from Matthew and one from Luke, with their slightly different teachings (Mt. 24; Lk. 13).

> 'Receive ye the parable of the fig-tree thereon: as soon as its shoots have gone forth and its boughs have sprouted, the end of the world will come.' And I, Peter, answered and said unto him, 'Explain to me concerning the fig-tree…' And the Master answered and said unto me, 'Dost thou not understand that the fig-tree is the house of Israel? Even as a man hath planted a fig-tree in his garden and it brought forth no fruit, and he sought its fruit for many years. When he found it not, he said to the keeper of his garden. "Uproot the fig-tree…"' (Ethiopic *Apocalypse of Peter* 2).

It will be noticed in this section that there are numerous allusions and references to the Synoptic Gospels, especially from Matthew, focusing on the coming parousia of the Lord, and the signs and portents that will precede his coming. This entire introductory section is missing from the Greek version of the Apocalypse, and it is problematical whether it was ever part of this text. Certainly we cannot assume that the Akhmim text was necessarily the same length in its original state as the Ethiopic.

Much the same may be said of the concluding section of the Ethiopic text, also missing from the Akhmim version, in which, following the account of the Transfiguration, the disciples watch as Jesus ascends, with Moses and Elijah, into the heavens. Again, this passage, with its several Matthaean references, is missing from the Greek text. It is, of course, quite possible that the complete Greek version once contained these episodes; and this is the usual explanation for the omissions. Two important points need to be kept in mind, however: first, that the two outer sections of the Ethiopic text are completely different in tone from the inner section which corresponds with the Akhmim text—prompting questions about whether the Ethiopic version is a composite text; and secondly, that the inner section of the Ethiopic text has very few allusions to the canonical Gospels, suggesting again that this section came from a different source.

The inner visionary section of the Ethiopic version, as has been noted, closely parallels the Akhmim text—though the parallels are by no means exact. It constitutes essentially a lurid description of the torments of hell heaped upon the deserving wicked, on the one hand, and on the other, of the blessings that accrue in abundance to those who have lived out their earthly lives in righteousness and purity. The content of this section of the work shows a marked resemblance to Jewish Apocalypses of the first century—notably to the book of Enoch, parts of which, significantly enough, were also contained in the codex found at Akhmim. There are few indications in this section, if any, that the work is specifically Christian, and many to suggest that it follows the lines of Jewish apocalyptic.[12] We might then conjecture that the primary text of the *Apocalypse of Peter* was written in Greek (the Akhmim text), and was probably itself dependent on a Jewish Apocalypse as its source.

In the *visionary* descriptions of heaven and hell, the two versions have much in common, both being uncompromisingly severe, as the following representative passage will show:

> And in another place were glowing pebbles, sharper than swords or any spit, and men and women, clad in filthy rags, rolled upon them in torment. These were they who were rich and trusted in their riches and had no mercy on orphans and widows, but despised the commandment of God (Akhmim *Apocalypse of Peter* 30; cf. Ethiopic version 9).

It is in the few *narrative* passages which both share in common, however, that huge differences of outlook and tone occur. Though both focus on the eschatological day of judgment, the Ethiopic compiler wants to associate the end of the ages with the awaited parousia of Christ. The same kind of differences might be observed in a comparison of the canonical Epistles of 2 Peter and Jude, where the latter book may be seen (like the Akhmim document) to be orientated towards a Jewish eschatology, and the former being a Christianized redaction of Jude, with an emphasis on the return of Christ in glory.

If we may postulate that the author of the Ethiopic text of the *Apocalypse of Peter* borrowed an already existing Apocalypse that had its roots within Judaism, we must now ask what his purpose might have been. That Christian eschatological ideas devolved from an amalgam of Jewish Prophetic, Messianic and Dualistic traditions, with their preoccupation with the imminence of the end, and a new beginning, is beyond reasonable doubt. The first Christians clearly understood themselves, and were so understood, to be a reforming sect within Judaism; and the idea of the Messianic deliverance of the faithful (centred now on the person of Jesus) was carried over into the new faith. Jesus' own emphasis on the inauguration of the kingdom, and the promise of his return in glory, modified and developed these Jewish concepts. Inevitably, during the first and second

12. The complexities of the argument for this are beyond the scope of this book. Readers who wish to go further may wish to consult my book *Peter: The Myth, the Man and the Writings* (Sheffield: Sheffield Academic Press, 2002).

centuries, Jewish Apocalypses would form the basis of Christian literature designed to strengthen, warn and encourage the faithful as they awaited the parousia, while living in a dangerous pagan world. Sometimes these warnings were couched in the form of prophecies of the Greek or Eastern Sibyl.[13] More often the Christian author would use the language and form of Jewish apocalyptic, often simply Christianizing the earlier work, as in the case of the later portions of the book of Ezra.[14]

While it is impossible to be precise about the date and provenance of the *Apocalypse of Peter*, there are several textual clues in the Ethiopic version to suggest that this work was composed in Egypt (Alexandria) during the early decades of the second century. A date around 135 is often proposed, largely because the references to 'false Christs' and a 'false Messiah' in the fig tree stories reflect the circumstances surrounding the time of the Bar Kochba revolt. The final severance of Christianity from Judaism was not yet irrevocable; but Israel had received its final warning, and the axe was ready to strike. The Greek version, on the other hand, is more difficult to date. It might be of help to consider the differing use, by the two author-compilers, of the Synoptic Transfiguration tradition (Mt. 17 and Lk. 9). The Ethiopic version follows the canonical story quite closely, though making the Ascension of Jesus a concomitant event:

> Two men…their faces shone more than the sun and their raiment also was glistening… And I approached God Jesus Christ and said to him, 'My Lord, who is this?' And he said to me, 'These are Moses and Elias…' And I said to him, 'My Lord, wilt thou that I make here three tabernacles, one for thee, one for Moses, and one for Elias?…' And behold there came suddenly a voice from heaven saying, 'This is my Son, whom I love and in whom I have pleasure, and my commandments…' And there came a great and exceeding white cloud over our heads and bore away our Lord and Moses and Elias (Ethiopic *Apocalypse of Peter* 15–17).

The Greek version, on the other hand, describes only the appearance of two unnamed representatives of the 'righteous brethren who had departed out of the world'. There is no mention of Moses or Elias. It is hardly a Transfiguration story, nor even a deliberately truncated version of it, as

13. The Christian Sibylline writings are Christian poems produced in the late third to fourth centuries. Prophetic and apocalyptic in character, they are concerned largely with eschatological themes.
14. Later added chapters of the book of Ezra (chs. 1–2 and 15–16 of the Fourth Book) are Christian adaptations of Jewish apocalyptic, largely directed against the Jews.

is sometimes suggested. A better solution is that a Christian redactor has attempted to adapt this essentially Jewish vision of the world of departed faithful souls by setting the account within a Transfiguration setting. The conclusion we may draw is that the Akhmim text represents an early (end of the first century) Christian adaptation of a Jewish Apocalypse; and that the later Ethiopic compiler enlarged and extended this work to produce a book suitable for his Christian readers across the Red Sea.

4. *The Coptic Apocalypse of Peter*

Among the discoveries at Nag Hammadi was a fourth-century codex (Codex VII) containing an important Gnostic tract transcribed in Coptic, and given the title, at both the beginning and the end of the text, of the *Apocalypse of Peter*. The work has almost nothing in common with the traditional *Apocalypse of Peter*; and to avoid confusion it is usually referred to as the Coptic Apocalypse. Because it purports to record a vision, vouchsafed to Peter, of events shortly to take place, it may legitimately be classified as apocalyptic. There is no doubt that it does reflect some of the apocalyptic concepts of Mt. 13. Like the two *Apocalypses of James*, examined in Chapter 2, however, it is essentially more revelatory than traditionally apocalyptic. Whether or not we may properly describe the tractate as Gnostic, we will in due course need to decide.

The scene of the vision is the Temple in Jerusalem on the eve of the Crucifixion. Because the Saviour has established Peter as 'a base for the remnant whom I have summoned to knowledge' (71), it is to Peter, and Peter alone, that the vision is granted; for he, first of all, must be given to understand the true meaning of the sacred events that are shortly to come about. Peter's vision—or visions, for there were three—correspond to the trial and arrest of Jesus, the Crucifixion, and the Resurrection. Their purpose is to correct the Apostle's complete misunderstanding of the real nature of Christ, and of his saving work, so that he in turn might enlighten those of God's children who come after. We may consider each of the three visions in turn:

1. The arrest and trial scene is clearly reminiscent of the Matthaean account, the uncomprehending priests and people vociferous in their hatred and condemnation of Jesus. Peter is overcome with fear as the clamouring crowd surges towards them; but the Lord bids him view the scene with the eyes of the mind, and to see that it is the crowd itself that is blind:

Peter, I have said to you many times that they are blind and have no leader. If you wish to know their blindness, lay your hands upon the eyes of your garment[15] and say what you see.

But when I did so I saw nothing. I said, 'No one sees anything in this way.' Again he said to me, 'Do it again!'

And fear and joy came upon me, for I saw a new light, which was brighter than the light of day, and afterwards it came down upon the Saviour (*Apocalypse of Peter* 72).

The first lesson that Peter had to learn was that neither those who had opposed Christ during his time on earth, nor even those who had undiscerningly praised and followed him, had recognized his true nature and being—a fact to which the canonical Gospels themselves bear repeated witness.[16] He himself—the real self—was inviolable, impervious to suffering. Here is the first intimation in the Apocalypse of its Docetic nature. We are, of course, to understand that the fleshly image of Christ is to be taken and led away to trial and crucifixion; but throughout the entire charade, the real Christ, with Peter at his side, remains a spectator of the Jews' blind folly.

The author of the Apocalypse uses this scene to denigrate those many pernicious and lawless groups which claim to be Christian, but which have compromised with the world. The text is an important witness to the syncretic growth of divers Gnostic and esoteric forms of the faith in this region. We can readily envisage a community threatened on all sides by aberrant sects that have perverted the true teaching of Christ. We can only speculate about the identity of these groups, but it is evident from the text that they are at odds with each other. Moral laxity and sexual license would appear to be the hallmark of one sect. Another, which 'thinks good and evil are the same' (77), is castigated for its antinomian behaviour. The author is primarily concerned, however, to denounce the blindness of Christian orthodoxy—those supposed Christians who 'cleave to the name of a dead man' (74), and imitate the hierarchical structures of mundane authority in the vain belief that in their leaders they will find the authority of God:

But there are others of those who are outside your number, who are called 'bishop' or 'deacon', as if they had received authority from God. They recline at table, and thus fall under the judgment of the first places. They are canals without water (*Apocalypse of Peter* 79).

15. Either this means the eyes of his body (his physical eyes), or the text may be corrupt.

16. Cf., e.g., Jn 14.9.

2. The Crucifixion scene is unashamedly Docetic, with the true Christ standing by the cross, watching and laughing as the hands and feet of his fleshly image are nailed to it:

> When he said this, I saw him as if he was laid hold of by them. And I said: 'What is this that I see, O Lord? Is it you alone whom they take, and do you lay hold of me? O who is this who is glad beside the tree and laughs? And another they strike upon his feet and on his hands?'
>
> The saviour said to me: 'He whom you see beside the tree glad and laughing, this is the living Jesus. But he into whose hands and feet they drive the nails is his fleshly likeness, the "ransom", which alone they are able to put to shame' (*Apocalypse of Peter* 81).

The passage is complicated by the polymorphic appearance of no fewer than three 'Christ' figures—the fleshly likeness of Christ, hanging on the cross, the real Christ, close by, watching and laughing, and the living, glorified Saviour who stands with Peter, invisible to the crowd, and explains what Peter sees. A further complication is the close parallel between this presentation of the Crucifixion and the teaching of the early second-century Gnostic writer, Basilides. According to Irenaeus's description, Basilides taught that Simon of Cyrene, who carried Jesus' cross, was transfigured into the outward form of Jesus, and took his place as a surrogate victim on the cross: while Jesus, in the outward form of Simon, stood by, laughing. Such an expedient would certainly avoid what for most Gnostics would be inconceivable, the notion that the perfect Son of God could experience pain and suffering; but deceit and trickery of this kind is far removed from the thought of the author of the *Apocalypse of Peter*. Nevertheless, it should be recognized that what lies behind both accounts is the Docetic principle that the true Christ is essentially inviolable.

3. In the last of the three visions, the glorified Christ, risen, now, and 'woven in the Holy Spirit', approaches Peter from the cross. Swathed in ineffable light, and surrounded by a host of worshipping angels, he brings to Peter words of encouragement and strength—for the Apostle's task is clearly set out before him. He has been a witness to the vain and wholly ineffectual attempts of the powers of darkness to subdue and extinguish the Lord of light; so he must now strengthen Christ's 'little ones' in the knowledge of their own immortal and inviolable status:

> These things, then, which you have seen, you are to hand them on to the 'aliens' who are not of this age. For a gift of such kind has no place among men who are not immortal, but only in those who were chosen because of their immortal nature, which has shown itself to be strong enough to receive that Spirit which imparts its abundance (*Apocalypse of Peter* 83).

The Apocalypse ends with the Saviour's reiterated assurance that his immortal ones need have no fear, for none of their enemies has power over them; and in words reminiscent of a Resurrection appearance, the Lord utters his parting blessing—'Peace be with you. Be strong!' And Peter 'came to himself'.

There is no clear indication in the text of the provenance of the Apocalypse. The fourth-century Coptic manuscript is undoubtedly a translation of an earlier Greek document; and a Palestinian or Syrian homeland has usually been suggested. There are some textual clues, however, that might conceivably point to an Asian origin. The Temple Discourse at the beginning of the Apocalypse (70–71) owes a good deal to the First Epistle of Peter; and there are numerous allusions throughout the work to the Second Epistle of Peter. Wherever these two canonical Epistles were composed, the provinces of Asia Minor were their most likely destination. That the author of the *Apocalypse of Peter* was thoroughly acquainted with both these Petrine Epistles is beyond doubt. Ignatius and Polycarp, among other early Asian witnesses, testify to the rapid establishment in these provinces of a catholic, hierarchical orthodoxy whose determined aim was to eradicate the Gnostic heresy. We may reasonably speculate, then, that the 'little ones' of Peter's Apocalypse were situated in the eastern provinces of Asia Minor, but close enough to Antioch to be threatened by the conforming demands of the monarchical episcopate. The Apocalypse may be assigned to the late second century, at a time when Gnostic Christianity was beginning to encounter fierce opposition from the increasingly institutionalized mainstream Church.

5. *The Apocalypse of Paul*

A fourth-century manuscript, transcribed from a Greek original, is the oldest extant form of a work entitled the *Apocalypse of Paul*. The book seems to have enjoyed wide circulation from about the middle of the third century, for many recensions have come down to us, in Syriac, Coptic, Latin, Greek and Slavonic. There are indications that Origen may have been familiar with the work, though no identifiable quotation has been recorded. Notwithstanding its apparent early popularity, all later writers who mention the book, including Epiphanius and Augustine, believed it to be spurious. Sections of the text are clearly of late origin, but it may be that these have been added by later editors. No complete version of the Apocalypse is extant, but the Latin text, perhaps, is as close to the original form as it is presently possible to attain.

The versions of the text differ extensively, but it is possible to arrive at a fair understanding of the content of the original work. It begins with an account of how the secret revelation which Paul had once received (caught up to the third heaven)[17] came to be published. In the last decade of the fourth century, a certain well-respected man, living in the very house at Tarsus that had once belonged to Paul, was moved by the Spirit to search in the foundations of the house, and make public what he found. His search uncovered an inscribed marble box in which was found a manuscript containing Paul's revelation, and the shoes in which he used to walk on his missionary journeys. A copy of the manuscript was kept by the Emperor Theodosius, to whom it was first sent; but the original was sent to Jerusalem for dissemination.

The revelation is then set out, at considerable length, for all to read. Paul is first given an insight into the twice-daily gathering of guardian angels before God, both to worship him, and to bring him news of their individual charge in the world, whether they have done good or evil. After this, Paul is caught up in the Spirit and carried up to the third heaven where he is permitted to witness the judgment of one recently arrived from the world. He is then conducted through the regions of heaven; and in imagery even more florid than that of the earlier Petrine Apocalypse which this work obviously resembles, Paul's vision is described. Typical is the following:

> And I looked round that land and I saw a river flowing with milk and honey; and at the edge of the river were planted trees full of fruit. And each tree was bearing twelve times twelve fruits in the year, various and different. And I saw the creation of that place and all the work of God (*Apocalypse of Paul* 22).

Paul is then taken to a place where a river flows whose waters streamed, whiter than milk, into the Lake Acherusia. In this water, those permitted to enter the city of Christ across the lake, are first baptized. And the angel of Paul's vision says to him:

> 'Follow me, and I shall lead you into the city of Christ.' And he stood by Lake Acherusia and put me in a golden boat and about three thousand angels were singing a hymn before me until I reached the city of Christ. Now the inhabitants of the city of Christ rejoiced greatly over me, and I entered and saw the city of Christ; and it was completely golden and there were twelve walls around it and twelve towers in it (*Apocalypse of Paul* 23).

---

17. See 2 Cor. 12.1-2; Paul intimates to his converts at Corinth that he was the recipient of a heavenly vision, but was forbidden to disclose its content.

As Paul is escorted through the city, through which flows four rivers, of honey and milk and wine and oil, he is greeted by the great and holy figures of the past: Isaiah and Jeremiah, among the Prophets; Abraham, Isaac and Jacob, among the Patriarchs and Saints; the Psalmists and the Innocents in other places. And in the midst of the city he is shown the great high altar where David sings psalms 'at the time of the offering of the body and blood of Christ'.

Paul's tour of the heavenly places ended, he is led beyond the ocean that encircles the whole earth to the place of darkness and torment. It is in this vivid description of the punishments of the lost and damned that the author of the Apocalypse especially shows his dependence on the *Apocalypse of Peter*:

> And I saw to the north a place of varied and different punishments which was full of men and women, and a river of fire poured over them. And I looked and saw very deep pits and in them were very many souls together; and the depth of that place was about 3,000 cubits, and I saw them sighing and weeping and saying: Lord, have mercy on us. But no one had mercy on them (*Apocalypse of Paul* 32; cf. Ethiopic *Apocalypse of Peter* 8).

Singled out for special penalties are those who have held office in the ministry of the Church—bishops, deacons and lectors; and those also who have reviled and rejected the word of God in the churches suffer equally severe punishment as those who have neglected the orphans and widows, or committed acts of fornication. The close parallels in many of these passages to the Petrine Apocalypse suggest that the author was not merely acquainted with it, but knew it well. His allusions to the established ministry, however, tend to confirm the composition of the work to be considerably later than the *Apocalypse of Peter*, yet still within the period when Christians of this region recognized and treasured their Jewish roots. Assigning a precise date to the work is impossible, largely because we cannot be certain whether the writer of the introductory preface was the author of the entire work. If so, then the Apocalypse cannot be earlier than the last years of the fourth century. If not, it is conceivable that the original writing was produced, perhaps in a region of Syria or Cilicia where the name of Paul was still celebrated above all other, at some point during the late second or early third century.

6. *The Coptic Apocalypse of Paul*

This work, one of four so-called Apocalypses appearing sequentially in Codex V in the Nag Hammadi discoveries,[18] describes the revelatory ascent of Paul through the heavens, journeying from the third heaven to the tenth, where he 'greets his fellow spirits'. No work of precisely this description seems to have been known before it came to light at Nag Hammadi, though it may be of some significance that Epiphanius mentions an 'Ascension of Paul'[19]—noteworthy, perhaps, in that, unlike the other Apocalypses considered in this present chapter, the recipient of the vision seems not to have returned to the world. In this respect, at least, the Apocalypse shows some conceptual affinities with the second-century *Ascension of Isaiah*.

There are a few lines missing from the beginning of the manuscript, but the narrative setting is clear enough. Paul is on his way to Jerusalem, and stops to ask the way from a child he encounters on the road. The child—his Spirit-guide—takes his hand and leads him on until they reach the Mount of Jericho. Here, Paul sees a vision of the Twelve Apostles who greet him; and after this he is carried up to the third heaven. It would be impossible to read this account of Paul's upward journey into paradise without recognizing its correlation with the visionary experience recorded in 2 Corinthians. 'Fourteen years ago', he tells his Corinthian friends, he was 'caught up to the third heaven', being privileged to see and hear things that could not be told. Now he finds himself transported beyond this transitional abode of departed souls to the higher regions beyond, at times looking down to the created sphere below, with the Twelve clearly visible, and at other times being accompanied by them on his celestial journey. Paul's object in 'boasting' to the Corinthians about his heavenly vision was to justify his authority as an Apostle of Christ. By the same token, the frequent mention of his close partnership with the Twelve in this apocalyptic vision would seem to have much the same aim of seeking to confirm and establish his apostolic position alongside them.

There are indications in the text of this Apocalypse, however, that might lead us to doubt whether its present form accurately reflects the original. The most obvious clue is that the work is not consistently written in the same person, its early passages being presented in the first person, while

---

18. The others being the two *Apocalypses of James*, and the *Apocalypse of Adam*.
19. *Panarion* 38.2.

the major concluding part is in the third. Such variations of literary style in the same work are by no means conclusive evidence, in themselves, of either redaction or different authorships; but supported by other indications, they may well influence us to examine the work further. The first section of the Apocalypse appears to be based on Paul's account in his Epistle to the Galatians of his journey 'by revelation' to Jerusalem to meet with the Twelve (Gal. 2). It is also reminiscent of Paul's earlier claim that he had been 'set apart before he was born', and been granted a special revelation of Christ for the work to which he had been called (Gal. 1.15). This same theme undoubtedly lies behind the early sections of the Apocalypse:

> The little child answered and said: 'I know who you are, Paul. For it is you who are blessed from his mother's womb. Since now I saw that you were about to go up to Jerusalem to your fellow apostles, [I have…]. That is why you were called. I am the Spirit who accompanies you. Give me therefore your hand…' (Coptic *Apocalypse of Paul* 18).

Thus far, there is little of traditional apocalyptic in the writing, and no hint of Gnosticism. The content and form of the work change radically, however, after Paul is assured that he will be welcomed by the Twelve. From this point on, Paul is carried up to the heavens; and the revelatory visions of judgment and of celestial bliss much more closely resemble the Jewish literary form—though by no means as vivid in its portrayal as, for instance, the traditional *Apocalypse of Paul*. Now, it is not the comments of Paul to the Galatians that form the basis of the writing, but those to the Corinthians, where the Apostle reckons that his 'in or out of the body' experience confirms a place of at least equal standing with the so-called 'superior' Apostles. Like the traditional Apocalypses, this entire section is couched in the first person, and explores the regions of hell and heaven from the point of view of individual eschatology. Unlike them it employs what must be considered to be ideas derived from nascent Gnosticism. The Gnostic influence is shown, certainly, in the progressive stages of the heavens, and notably in the mention of the Ogdoad (the Eighth Heaven), and the idea of 'the old man' (23)—the Creator—who seeks to hinder the soul's passage into the eternal places. More especially it is shown in the concept of 'the sign' by which the true Gnostic may pass by all obstacles, and reach his or her destined goal. In the *First Apocalypse of James* (see Chapter 2), the Lord tells James what he must say, and how he must answer, in order to escape the 'watcher' and 'controllers' of souls. In similar vein, Paul is challenged by the 'old man' at the gate of the Ogdoad:

> The old man answered me, saying: 'How will you be able to escape me? Look here and see these rulers and authorities!' The Spirit answered and said, 'Give him the sign which you have, and he will open for you.' Then I gave him the sign. He turned his face downwards to his creation and to those that were his own of the authorities. Then the way out of the seventh heaven opened, and we went up to the Ogdoad. And I saw the twelve apostles; they greeted me (Coptic *Apocalypse of Paul* 23).

To assign a date to a work which at the very least displays some degree of redaction, and which may possibly represent not one, but two, different original compositions, skilfully woven together, is not a simple task. The Gnostic character of the main section does certainly bring us to the late second or early third centuries—perhaps to a period when Valentinian theology was beginning to have its impact on traditional Jewish-Christian theology, and when the incipient Gnosticism of some of Paul's writings was being exploited. The inferior 'creator God' of Judaism—represented in this Apocalypse by the 'old man'[20]—is unequivocally Valentinian; yet the highly developed mythology that we have come to expect from later Valentinianism is not here present. The story of Paul's encounter with the child at the start of the Apocalypse, on the other hand, and the tradition surrounding his vision at Jericho, could well have come from an earlier period—even as early as the end of the first century—and used here to give a historical setting to the later apocalyptic vision.

20. This concept may have its roots in the 'Ancient of days' of Dan. 7.9.

Chapter 5

THE CHURCH IN MESOPOTAMIA

The Gospel of Thomas
The Acts of Thomas
The Book of Thomas the Contender
The Infancy Gospel of Thomas

The land between the Tigris and the Euphrates is the home of the Thomasine literature we shall examine in this chapter—not, of course, in the sense
that each or any of the books necessarily originates from Mesopotamia,
but because the Judas-Thomas tradition, with all its Gnostic and encratite
tendencies, belongs to Edessa, Edessa to Parthia, and Parthia to the East.
Syrian Christianity, as we have seen, is never without its Antiochene and
Petrine influence; but Thomas, from the literary viewpoint, is as far
removed from Peter as Peter is from Paul. In the same sense that Tatian's
ascetic writings belong to his Mesopotamian homeland, though some may
have been written in or around Antioch, or perhaps even in Rome, so we
cannot mention Thomas without thinking of India and the East—though
the works that bear his name enjoyed wide circulation throughout the
Christian world.

The name Judas-Thomas, firmly rooted though it is in Thomasine tradition, is not easily explained. The word 'Thomas', as we observed in an
earlier chapter, is not a proper name, but from an Aramaic word meaning
'twin'; and we will be familiar with the use of its Greek equivalent
'Didymus' in the Fourth Gospel. Who among the Apostles was affection-
ately known as 'the twin' we cannot be certain; for the name Judas appears
more than once in the several and varying lists of the Twelve in the Gospels. Furthermore, whose twin 'Thomas' may have been is also problematical. If Judas the brother of James (Lk. 6.16) was also called Thaddaeus,[1]

1.   The Apostle Thaddaeus does not appear in Luke's list. He is replaced by Judas
the brother of James. Cf. Mt. 10.3 and Mk 3.18.

as Jerome seemed to believe, we are led back immediately to the Abgar tradition of the founding of Christianity in Edessa; and Judas, in this case, could be identified as the twin brother of James the Lord's brother. We must allow that the 'Judas of James' in the Lukan passage could mean that Judas was the son, not the brother, of James—but in either case Judas is seen to be closely related, through James the Lord's brother, to Jesus himself. We must reckon, however, with the perplexing fact that both 'Judas of James' and 'Thomas' are listed by Luke among the Twelve.[2] It may be that the Evangelists themselves were uncertain, or that subsequent attempts to harmonize the Gospel lists are responsible for the confusion; and perhaps the true relationship of Judas to Jesus, or the precise nature of his 'twinship' within the 'brethren' of Jesus, can never be known. What is certain, however, is that, within the tradition and the writings, Thomas (or Judas-Thomas) is portrayed as being so closely bound up with Jesus that at times he appears to *become* him.

1. *The Gospel of Thomas*

Arguably the most exciting discovery of recent times has been the Coptic version of the *Gospel of Thomas*, which purports to be 'the secret words which the Lord spoke, and which Didymus Judas Thomas wrote down'. Until the appearance of this document at Nag Hammadi, nothing was known of the content of a work by this name, though the Gospel had been mentioned as being heretical by Hippolytus and Origen, and by Eusebius in his *Ecclesiastical History*. A few fragments of papyrus written in Greek had been unearthed at Oxyrhynchus at the turn of the twentieth century, and the Nag Hammadi discovery now enabled these to be identified as part of this ancient work; but the Coptic version is presently the only complete extant copy of the Gospel. It is interesting to note that, according to the early Gnostic work entitled *Pistis Sophia*, Thomas was commissioned by the Lord, along with Matthew and Philip, to write down his words. Here, in the *Gospel of Thomas*, it would seem, we are given what might best be described as a compendium of those words and 'sayings'.

Clearly the *Gospel of Thomas* is not of the same genre as the traditional Gospels. It is a collection of isolated and largely unconnected sayings with little or no narrative linkage between them. For convenience, the text is usually divided into about 114 different sayings, some of which are direct parallels of the familiar canonical texts, others being intriguing deviations

2.   See Lk. 6.16 and Acts 1.13.

from those texts, and some found nowhere else. Among the many important questions the document presents is the relationship of the text to the canonical Gospels. Is the *Gospel of Thomas* in some way textually dependent on the writings that came to form the New Testament? It has to be admitted that there is yet no consensus on this question, though the trend may be towards recognizing that some of the sayings (or Logia) may represent a primitive source which contained traditions that were either unknown to the four Evangelists, or rejected by them. Before we examine the arguments for and against dependency, however, it will be useful to illustrate the distinction between those sayings that have clear canonical parallels, and those that either deviate or embellish, or are absolutely new. It will be understood, of course, that it is this very strange mix and variety of sayings which not only complicates the issue of dependency, but also raises the question of the work's integrity.

At least half of the 114 sayings have direct parallels in the canonical Gospels. Some of these are found in only one of the Synoptic Gospels, while others, such as the parable of the sower, are contained in all:

> Jesus said: Look, the sower went out, he filled his hand and cast the seed. Some fell upon the road; the birds came, they gathered them. Others fell upon the rock, and struck no root in the ground, nor did they produce any ears. And others fell on the thorns; they choked the seed and the worm ate them. And others fell on the good earth, and it produced good fruit; it yielded sixty per measure and a hundred and twenty per measure (*Gos. Thom.* 9; cf. Mk 4.3-8 and parallels).

It will be seen that this version of the parable is somewhat shorter than its Synoptic counterpart, and manifestly does not exactly replicate it. The simplified text is thus seen by some as evidence of its primitive character, on the basis of the general critical rule that later redactors of a text tend to expand, rather than simplify. While this general rule may be a valuable critical tool, there are many instances in early literature where an editor, for a variety of reasons, has decided to abbreviate the text. If we may assume the Markan Gospel to be the earliest of the Synoptics, for instance, it can be shown that there are times when Luke chooses to abbreviate his primary source. On the basis of simplicity, then, we would be hard put to demonstrate the primacy of the *Gospel of Thomas*. Inconsequential variations in text, however, would seem to point not only to the fact that 'Thomas' was not slavishly following the Synoptic text, but also that his Gospel was dependent either upon remembered Synoptic text, or upon an early tradition (written or oral) which the Synoptic writers also knew. If the latter alternative were nearer the truth, it would leave the question of the date and originality of the Gospel without a definitive solution, though it would tend to argue for its independence from the canonical Gospels.

The second group of sayings in the *Gospel of Thomas* is more problematical, for while the passages show obvious associations with the Synoptic sayings, they also embody consequential deviations or glosses in the text. One such saying concerns the question of fasting, prayer and the giving of alms:

> Jesus said to them: If you fast, you will put a sin to your charge; and if you pray, you will be condemned; and if you give alms, you will do harm to your spirits. And if you go into any land and walk about in the regions, if they receive you, eat what is set before you; heal the sick among them. For what goes into your mouth will not defile you; but what comes out of your mouth, that is what will defile you (*Gos. Thom.* 14; cf. Mt. 6.16; Lk. 10; Mt. 15.11).

Although the closeness of the parallels here has convinced some of the dependency of the *Gospel of Thomas* on the Synoptic Gospels, the fact that there is no exactitude might argue in the opposite direction. An alternative possibility might be (as for the previous example) that the author was relying either on remembered texts (either from the canonical Gospels or some other), or on some earlier tradition based on those texts. The important thing here is the conceptual deviation from the canonical norm. With one interpretation of the text, the saying simply echoes Jesus' canonical warnings that outward show cannot lead to salvation. At another level, however, the author may want to emphasize that the old Jewish religious practices no longer have significance for the Christian, and could even be said to be positively harmful. Taken together with other Logia in the Gospel which concern matters of Jewish regulation such as Sabbath observance (27), dietary rules (89) and circumcision (53) as well as fasting, prayer and almsgiving (6, 27, 104), this passage does seem to condemn the old legalistic approach to salvation as being deleterious to the Christian's spiritual advance. Whatever the meaning of these passages, it is abundantly clear that the author has deliberately and radically reinterpreted the original source material to suit a changed viewpoint; for it is inconceivable that Jesus' warnings against hypocritical piety found in the canonical Gospels were less authentic than the utter rejection of these outward practices in the *Gospel of Thomas*. Such deviations would seem to represent an early stage in the Church's (or this particular church's) changing relationship with Judaism, as it seeks to find an appropriate interpretation of Jesus' teachings. If this is indeed the case, there is no need to see this group of deviant Synoptic parallels as evidence of a later redactionary stage in the composition of the *Gospel of Thomas*. Some sayings in the Synoptic tradition were clearly in need of reinterpretation (according to 'Thomas'), while others were not.

There is a relatively large number of sayings, however, that have little or no association with the New Testament Gospels; and many of these are unmistakably Gnostic:

> Jesus said: If they say to you: Whence have you come?, say to them: We have come from the light, the place where the light came into being of itself. It established itself, and it revealed itself in their image. If they say to you: Who are you?, say: We are his sons, and we are the elect of the living Father. If they ask what is the sign of your Father in you?, say to them: It is movement and rest (*Gospel of Thomas* 50).

This passage, very reminiscent of the *First Apocalypse of James* (see Chapter 2), refers to the secret passwords by which the Gnostic souls escape from the clutches of those (archons or watchers) who would detain them in their earthly prison. So uncharacteristic is this saying of the Gospel as a whole, and a few others like it, that some have postulated a second (Gnostic) strand or stratum in the compositional process of the Gospel—a number of new sayings being added to an original early collection by a later compiler. This is certainly one possible solution to the problem. It is important, however, to avoid circularity here. We should not assume that only those sayings with which we are familiar from the New Testament were part of the original and authentic teaching of Christ. Certainly, this particular passage is so representative of later Gnostic thought that it is hardly conceivable that it came from Jesus; but there are sayings in this Gospel that are capable of a Gnostic interpretation, but which, despite their non-appearance in the canonical Gospels, might well have had a place in the original *kerygma*.

One of the most telling arguments against the theory that the *Gospel of Thomas* is an independent work concerns its use of material that is unique to Matthew, Luke or John. If this special and unique material represents different traditions, or distinct Christian communities, it is considerably less likely that 'Thomas' garnered his material from these separate traditions than that he was dependent on the finished Gospels themselves. We might instance two sayings, the first which clearly takes its origin from special Matthew, and the second from John:

> Jesus said: I speak mysteries to those who are worthy of my mysteries. What your right hand does, let not your left hand know what it does (*Gos. Thom.* 62; cf. Mt. 6.3).

> Jesus said: I am the light that is above them all. I am the all; the all came forth from me, and the all attained to me. Cleave a piece of wood, I am there. Raise up a stone and you will find me there (*Gos. Thom.* 77; cf. Jn 8.12).

Furthermore, some of the sayings in the Gospel may be shown to reflect the redactionary form of Matthew or Luke, rather than the original Markan form, strongly suggesting that the author was using the final version of the text.[3] Clearly, if this were proved, the case for the originality and independence of the *Gospel of Thomas* would be considerably weakened. What needs to be taken into account, however, is the whole question of what has been called 'secondary orality'. It is now beginning to be realized that we cannot make a hard distinction between written and oral traditions, as though there were no interaction between them. Written material has a habit of reflecting itself back into oral tradition which in turn becomes the source material for later transcription. Many of the sayings in the *Gospel of Thomas* that show variations from the canonical norm might well derive from oral 'feedback' from written traditions, and coloured by independent local oral tradition.

If the question of the originality of the *Gospel of Thomas* is complex, questions of its Gnosticism and its encratism are no less so. It will be recognized that if the Gospel could be shown to be unequivocally Gnostic in character, this fact alone would tend to suggest a comparatively late date for the work. Those who want to find in the *Gospel of Thomas* a primary source for the teachings of Jesus are understandably anxious to stress the work's non-Gnostic character; and this question continues to be one of crucial critical importance. The first difficulty, of course, is the definition of Gnosticism itself. Few would claim that there is in this Gospel anything approaching the developed Valentinianism of the *Gospel of Philip*. The creation of the world is not seen as a huge mistake, or as the handiwork of a malevolent second-order God; and there is nothing of the usual mythology we find in avowedly Gnostic works to illustrate how the elect find themselves imprisoned in an evil world. Yet there are many sayings that do denigrate the world, and warn of the deadening effects of the flesh. Family ties, the procreation of children, and the possession of worldly riches, are all seen as hindrances to the solitary soul's rise to the place

---

3.　Examples of this may be found in Logia 33, 40 and 99.

whence it came. Many of the sayings emphasize the Gnostic dichotomy between the flesh and the spirit, and that is well-exemplified in the analogy of stripping off and discarding the worthless garment of the flesh:

> His disciples said: On what day will you be revealed to us, and on what day shall we see you? Jesus said: When you unclothe yourselves and are not ashamed, and take your garments and lay them beneath your feet like little children and trample on them, then you will see the Son of the Living One, and you will not be afraid (*Gos. Thom.* 37).

From the textual evidence, then, it would be difficult to claim that the *Gospel of Thomas* is not essentially Gnostic in tone and character—though (depending on our definitions of Gnosticism) we might say the same of the Gospel of John, and other New Testament writings. The real test of Gnosticism in the *Gospel of Thomas*, however, is to be found not so much in what the Gospel actually *says*, but rather what is *omitted*. We find no evidence of an orthodox belief in the salvatory or redemptive role of Christ, a theme which is central to normative doctrine. Rather the inference of many sayings is that the elect are to achieve their own salvation by searching within themselves. Jesus is the illuminator, the one who guides the elect to the light, and opens up the secret knowledge that alone will lead to salvation. There is no place, however, for the cross; and the concept of vicarious sacrifice is completely foreign to this Gospel. Nor, indeed, is the idea of the incarnation of the Christ at all to be found. It is true that one saying seems to refer to the fleshly coming of Christ into the world:

> Jesus said: I stood in the midst of the world, and I appeared to them in the flesh. I found them all drunk; I found none of them thirsting, and my soul was afflicted for the sons of men; for they are blind in their heart, and they do not see that they came empty into the world, and empty they seek to leave the world again. But now they are drunk. When they have thrown off their wine, they will repent (*Gos. Thom.* 28).

While there are numerous Johannine allusions in the Gospel, 'Thomas' here parts company with the Fourth Evangelist. For John, the Word *became* flesh, Christ being truly incarnate in the world. Here, in *Gos. Thom.* 28, it is merely the semblance of the eternal (and Docetic) Christ who appears among humankind, and whom they fail to comprehend because of their blindness and 'drunkenness'. Such concepts are characteristic of Gnostic Christology, and must in no way be mistaken for the incarnational teaching of the mainstream Church.

That the *Gospel of Thomas* leans towards an ascetic ideal is beyond question, though it would be a mistake to label it encratite. The debate that focuses on whether the *Gospel of Thomas* is Gnostic or encratite tends to miss the important point that this work clearly originated in an environment in which extremes of asceticism found a ready partnership with eastern esotericism and Gnosticism; and while it is far from the case that all Gnostics were ascetics, this was a very natural marriage in those regions east of Antioch where this Gospel was doubtless compiled. Certainly there are not a few sayings in *Gospel of Thomas* that seem to encourage sexual abstinence, and might indeed imply that the state of celibacy is preferable to that of marriage. The concept of 'solitariness' occurs frequently in the Gospel,[4] the inference being that only those who have cast off all worldly ties, including familial ones, may enter the kingdom:

> Jesus said: Blessed are the solitary and the elect, for you will find the kingdom, for you came forth from it, and you will return to it again (*Gos. Thom.* 49).

> Jesus said: There are many standing at the door, but it is the solitary who will enter the bridal chamber (*Gos. Thom.* 75).[5]

It must be emphasized, however, that nowhere in this Gospel is the world considered to be intrinsically evil, nor worldly appetites absolutely condemned. What it does say is that fleshly pursuits, and inordinate love of wealth, power and passion, must inevitably hinder the elect from their ultimate spiritual goal.

Does the *Gospel of Thomas*, then, bring us closer than we had been without it to the actual teaching of Jesus? We have to say that no definitive answer can yet be given to this question. It is most unlikely that its author or compiler did not have some acquaintance with the four Gospels themselves. Moreover it seems highly probable that sayings with Gnostic overtones, or additions and amendments to canonical sayings, were the result of later redaction. That being admitted, we cannot rule out the possibility that some of the sayings, including those which hitherto had been unknown in any form, may have their roots in very early oral tradition. Since the work seems to have been known at least by the end of the second century, we may assign a date for its composition around the middle of that century —though some sections may well have been added later. Of its eastern Syrian or Mesopotamian provenance there is little doubt, the work being composed, perhaps, to bring the true teachings of Christ the luminary to a loose confederation of ascetically and spiritually minded Christians, who

4. The word 'solitary' (Greek *monachos*) later came to be used for a 'monk'.

5. See Chapter 4, section 2, for an explanation of the concept of the 'Bridal Chamber'.

lacked any formal organizational structure, and whose sole aim was to enter the kingdom prepared for them in heaven.

2. *The Acts of Thomas*

The *Acts of Thomas* presents us with a wondrous account of the Apostle's missionary activity in India. As such, it takes its place among the five major non-canonical Acts[6] whose popularity in the east guaranteed their survival as a collection (if not exactly a corpus) despite the sustained attacks of the heresiologists of the early centuries. There is abundant evidence of the rejection of the Lukan Acts by Manichaean Christians in favour of this later collection of apostolic Acts, and we shall need to enquire to what extent an original *Vorlage* of the *Acts of Thomas* was revised, extended or embellished, in the course of its transmission, by the Christian groups it served. Before we come to matters of textual transmission, however, we must briefly summarize the contents of the work, and then to say something of its origin.

The narrative begins, in Jerusalem, with the division of missionary responsibility among the Apostles, and Judas-Thomas's refusal to go to the Indians. He acquiesces, however, when the ascended Lord meets him in the marketplace, and sells him as a slave to the merchant Habban, whose master, King Güdnaphorus, needed a carpenter to build him a palace. Habban and Thomas set sail,[7] and with a steady breeze they soon put in at Sandarük (Greek, Andrapolis). Here Habban and Thomas are invited to attend the marriage of the ruler's daughter, an occasion which gave Thomas his first opportunity to preach his encratite gospel. To the chagrin of the bride's father, he sets about persuading the young couple that marriage would bring them neither present happiness nor ultimate salvation. A prudent and hasty departure brings the Apostle to the realm of India proper, where he at last meets Güdnaphorus, and commences the building of his palace—though, to the king's initial disappointment, it turns out to be a heavenly dwelling rather than an earthly one.

From this point on, as Thomas journeys through India, we are given abundant illustrations of the Apostle's power (as the spiritual twin of Jesus), as he preaches chastity, casts out demons, admonishes the wicked,

6. The Acts of John, Peter, Andrew, Thomas and Paul.
7. It is not clear from where! Presumably the journey would include a barge trip down the Euphrates into the Persian Gulf if the destination was south-west India. The location of Sandarük, if such a city existed, is unknown.

performs wondrous deeds, heals and baptizes, and raises the dead—after the manner of Jesus himself. His conversions, particularly among the families of the rich and powerful, bring him into inevitable conflict and persecution. The long and involved narratives concerning Tertia and Mygdonia, the wives respectively of Misdaeus and his kinsman Charisius, reach their conclusion in the imprisonment and death of the Apostle. Despite his manifold tribulations, however, Thomas's efforts are rewarded with eventual success. Not only are Misdaeus's son, Vazan, and his captain Siphor, baptized, becoming deacon and presbyter respectively, but in the end even Misdaeus himself is brought within the fold.

The text of the *Acts of Thomas* is found in several Syriac manuscripts, and in a variety of Greek manuscripts, some of these latter version being considerably shorter than others. There are also extant Latin, Arabic and Armenian versions, as well as translations into Coptic and Ethiopic. Whether the work was originally composed in Syriac or Greek is a matter of continuing debate, and is beyond our present scope. Strong arguments have been adduced for a Greek original, but there is a growing consensus towards the primacy of the Syriac text, largely because of the many Syriasms found in the Greek versions. What is not given sufficient attention, however, is the possibility that the extant *Acts of Thomas* is a composite work which might be traced back to two distinct sources, one Syriac and one Greek, and that subsequent conflation has produced the present versions. Comparison of the two main versions reveals significant differences of outlook, and clear evidence of redaction, the Syriac generally being the more orthodox, perhaps, and the Greek showing signs of Manichaean encratite revision. Despite the complexities of intertextuality, however, we are able to follow the Apocryphal journey of Thomas to the borders of India and beyond.

There is, of course, no historical evidence to show that Thomas ever visited India. The earliest traditions, as we have seen, make Parthia, to the east of Mesopotamia, the allotted missionary area of Thomas; and Eusebius actually records that Bartholomew, not Thomas, was the first evangelist of India, taking with him the Gospel of Matthew.[8] Thomas's legendary links with Edessa may well have encouraged the idea that he went on further east into North India, retracing the route of Alexander. The *Acts of Thomas* seem to imply a journey to the south, however, into the kingdom of Misdaeus—though the earlier stories concerning King Güdnaphorus tend rather

---

8.   Eusebius, *HE* 5.10.3.

to suggest a northern journey.[9] Perhaps the truth of the matter is that we have here two separate sources and traditions, one concerned with northern India, the other with the south, and that these traditions have at some time become interwoven.

The work as it stands is divided into 13 separate acts, with little obvious connection between them. The first six acts concern Thomas's work in the kingdom of Güdnaphorus, while the remaining seven, which include the martyrdom of the Apostle, have to do with his deeds in the court of King Misdaeus. Inserted into the text are two Syrian songs which in their original form would doubtless have circulated separately—the first being a marriage hymn, sung here by Thomas himself at the wedding feast of the daughter of the king of Sandarük, and the second, a Hymn of the Soul (sometimes called the Hymn of the Pearl). Both of these songs appear to have had symbolic meanings in their earliest form, but it is clear that new Christian meanings have been imposed upon them by the compiler of these Acts. Whatever may have been its original purpose in Syrian tradition, the marriage hymn recalls the New Testament parable of the marriage feast (Mt. 21) and the description of the Marriage Supper of the Lamb (Rev. 19). Its deliberate insertion at this point in the story, with Thomas's intervention in the marriage of the king's daughter to save the couple from perdition, served to illustrate the cardinal theme of the *Acts of Thomas*—that only continence and celibacy could assure salvation.

Thomas's principled preoccupation with the encratite ideal was bound inevitably to bring about his downfall, particularly as his interference in the marital affairs of his intended converts was largely confined to rulers and their influential entourage. We should note that Thomas's subsequent trial before Misdaeus is redolent of the trial of Jesus before Pilate:

> After this the king went into the judgment hall and sent for Judas. But when he came, they stripped him and girded him with a girdle, and set him before the king. And Misdaeus said to him: 'Art thou a slave or a free man?' And Judas said: 'I am a slave, but thou hast no authority over me at all' (*Acts of Thomas* 163).

After his summary trial, Judas (Thomas) is commanded to be taken to the mountain, there to be dispatched by four spear-bearing soldiers; and when Judas (Thomas) has offered a short dedicatory prayer, the soldiers perform their duty. Vazan, the king's son, is clearly unhappy with what had taken

9. Ancient records and recent excavations show that a King Güdnaphorus reigned in a region of north-west India.

place, and remains by the tomb in which the body of Judas (Thomas) had been laid, wrapped in fine linen cloths. And after a night and a day, Judas (Thomas) appears to Vazan and Siphor, the captain of the guard. The Resurrection allusions are very evident:

> Judas appeared to them, and said: 'I am not here. Why do you sit here and watch over me? For I have gone up and received what was hoped for. But arise and walk, and after no great time ye shall be gathered to me' (*Acts of Thomas* 169).

The second Syrian song, the Hymn of the Soul, is interposed in the text at the point where Judas is arrested by Charisius, and brought before the king. Once again, we could not fail to recognize the parallels with the trial and Passion of Jesus:

> And they dragged him off and brought him to King Misdaeus. But when the apostle stood before the king, the king said to him: 'Tell me who thou art, and by what power thou dost perform these things.' But the apostle remained silent. And the king commanded his subjects that he should be scourged… (*Acts of Thomas* 106).

Perhaps it was the king's uneasy recognition that Judas possessed a power beyond this world that encouraged the author of the Acts to insert at this point in the narrative the Hymn of the Soul; for this superbly lyrical poem tells the story of the soul's journey into the world to seek and find the pearl, and having recovered it, to return to his heavenly abode. While there is nothing sophisticatedly Gnostic in the *Gospel of Thomas*, it is this spiritualizing theme—that the elect who are trapped in the world must recognize their divine origin and destiny before they can return—that is even more fundamental to the work than its encratic ideal. In the hymn, the son (the soul) is sent out from the kingdom by his father, with adequate provisions for the journey, to retrieve the pearl which is guarded by the serpent, and bring it back. He must leave his splendid robe behind, but is given the assurance that, on his return, his robe will be restored to him in all its glory. In the world he falls prey to temptation, and forgets his mission and his royal nature and destiny. Clad now in the garments of the world, he falls asleep; but his royal father sees the son's plight, and sends to him a letter in the form of an eagle to awaken him and remind him of his task:

> It flew and alighted beside me
> And became all speech.
> At its voice and the sound of its rustling
> I awoke and stood up from my sleep,
> I took it and kissed it,

Broke its seal and read…
I remembered that I was a son of kings
And my noble birth asserted itself (*Acts of Thomas* 111).

The pearl is recovered, the journey back begins, and the son is met by emissaries of his heavenly father bearing the royal robe for him to put on. We may identify a number of allusions to New Testament themes. The story is clearly reminiscent of the story of the Prodigal Son (Lk. 15.22); the royal robe has distinct associations with the 'wedding garment' (Rev. 19.7, 8); and the pearl itself calls to mind the 'pearl of great price' which Jesus likens to the kingdom (Mt. 13.45).

The *Acts of Thomas* is wholly dualistic in outlook. Matter stands in opposition to the spirit, and the present state of humanity is seen as a perversion of their original God-created nature. Entirely corrupt in their bodily state, their eventual restoration can be achieved only by the absolute renunciation of fleshly appetites, the rejection of ignorance and error, and the total adherence to the pure and unadulterated teachings of Christ. Judas-Thomas's great task is to represent and promulgate those teachings. Such encratic ethical concepts found early expression in the writings of the second-century Syrian theologian Tatian, whose *Oratio ad Graecos* displays remarkable ascetic similarities to the *Acts of Thomas*. It is generally recognized, too, that the *Acts of Thomas*, as well as the *Gospel of Thomas* frequently prefer the text of Tatian's *Diatessaron* when quoting from the books of the New Testament.

If the characteristic theological orientation of the work convinces us of an eastern Syrian or Mesopotamian provenance—perhaps Edessa, which was the home of so much early Syrian literature—so indeed do the liturgical practices of the region. Baptism—often referred to in the *Acts of Thomas* as 'the Seal'—has an essentially protective role. Whether with water or by the anointing of oil (chrism), baptism provides an almost magical shield against the powers of darkness and evil, 'sealing' the recipient against all kinds of harm. It is the mark of the baptized's possession by Christ. Thus, when King Güdnaphorus and his brother are eventually brought to the fold, their baptism is expected to convey all-round protection, as Judas-Thomas's invocatory prayer shows:

Now as I beseech and supplicate thee, receive the king and his brother and unite them with thy flock, cleansing them with thy washing, and anointing them with thy oil from the error which surrounds them. Preserve them also from the wolves, leading them in thy pastures. Give them to drink from thine ambrosial spring which is neither turbid nor dries up (*Acts of Thomas* 25).

The variety of practice in the 'sealing' of the convert—whether with water or oil only, or with both—and the different order in which the rite is administered, tends to suggest a comparatively early date before liturgical conventions became fixed; and this in turn argues for an eastern provenance, outside the ambit of orthodox influence. The same may be said of the Eucharist, which is more often than not celebrated with bread only, the 'breaking of the bread' as a mark of unity and fellowship being more prominently expressed than any connection with the death of Christ, or the remission of sins.

3. *The Book of Thomas the Contender*

The third book of the Thomasine tradition—the *Book of Thomas the Contender*[10]—first came to light with its discovery at Nag Hammadi, and has no known witnesses from the early centuries. The single Coptic copy of the work, undoubtedly translated from a Greek original, constitutes the final tractate of Codex II. The manuscript is reasonably well preserved, though there is damage to some of the pages, and some words are altogether missing. Like many others of the Nag Hammadi documents, this codex dates from the fourth century; but this, of course, provides us only with a terminal date for the work's composition. Since it may display some acquaintance with both the *Gospel of Thomas* and the *Acts of Thomas*, however, the book is unlikely to have been written much before the beginning of the third century. In common with the Thomasine Gospel, this work purports to record the secret words of Jesus to his twin brother Thomas:

> The secret words that the Saviour spoke to Judas Thomas and which I, Matthew, wrote down. I was passing by and heard them speak with one another.
>
> The Saviour said: 'Brother Thomas, listen to me, while you still have opportunity in the world, that I may reveal to you what you have pondered in your heart' (*Book of Thomas*, p. 138).[11]

What follows this introduction may best be described as a dialogue between the risen Jesus and the Apostle Judas-Thomas. Thomas is given to understand that, while he is yet far from achieving perfection, he alone, among the Twelve, because he is the Saviour's 'twin and sole true friend',

10. Sometimes referred to as the *Book of Thomas the Athlete* (from the Greek *athletes*, meaning 'one who struggles').

11. Page nos. refer to pages in the Nag Hammadi Codex II.

has begun to comprehend the truth which remains hidden to others. There are veiled allusions, perhaps, in the early stages of the dialogue, to Thomas's incredulity in the upper room on the Resurrection evening. If visible and tangible reality was difficult to comprehend, how would he cope with that which was hidden and spiritual? He was yet a 'beginner'— but one through whom others might come to the truth. The dialogue then takes the form of 'question and answer', concerned largely with the theme of how bestial passion blinds men from the perception of eternal truth, and leads only to death. The very fire of bodily passion which burns hotly within them becomes itself the consuming fire of destruction:

> There are in fact those who have wings as they are chasing after what is visible, that which is far removed from the truth. For that which guides them, which is the fire, will give them an illusion of truth and will shine on them with perishable beauty. And it will imprison them by dark delight and captivate them with stinking pleasure. And it will make them blind with insatiable lust. And it will burn their souls and be for them like a stake stuck in their heart which they never will be able to pull out, and like a bit in a horse's mouth which drags them according to the desire proper to it (*Book of Thomas*, p. 140).

A radical alteration in style begins within p. 142 of the Codex, the dialogue suddenly becoming a monologue in which the Saviour pronounces a series of woes and blessings, after the manner of the Synoptic Beatitudes. The customary explanation of this change is that the *Book of Thomas* is in fact a composite work comprising two quite different texts, joined because of their common ascetic theme. Textual peculiarities in the two sections certainly seem to point to a literary union of this kind—though whether the composition represents a simple joining of one text to the end of the other, or a more complex interweaving of themes and sayings, is still a matter of critical dispute. What is clear is that the second part—the woes and blessings—owes a great deal to the apocalyptic visions of the second-century Judaeo-Christian writings, and especially, perhaps, to the *Apocalypse of Peter*. One possible solution, though not one generally adopted, is that the distinctive literary style of the second part might simply reflect the author's familiarity with these apocalyptic works, and his desire to emulate them in his own. Who could read the following passage, for instance, without becoming conscious of its remarkable parallel in the Petrine Apocalypse?

> Whoever has pursued you will be delivered to the angel Tartarouchos with whom is flaming fire which pursues them, while fiery scourges cast spark upon spark into the face of the one who is pursued. If he flees to the west he

will find the fire. If he turns to the south he will also find it there. If he turns to the north the horror of boiling fire meets him again (*Book of Thomas*, p. 142; cf. *Apocalypse of Peter* 5).

We must reckon with the fact that the concluding title of the work—'The Book of Thomas the Contender writing to the Perfect'—appears to be somewhat at odds with its opening preamble (or proem), which names Matthew (or Matthias) as the recorder and scribe. This perplexing feature might well be an indication of the work's complex compilation, adding weight to the usual hypothesis of its composite nature. The figure of Thomas disappears entirely in the second part of the work; and it may be that the short title 'The Book of Thomas' referred originally to the dialogue section only. We can do little more than theorize at present, however, about how the book (or books) might have appeared originally; and we might feel that such speculation is rather less pressing or profitable than to try to understand the intent and purpose of the author-compiler in his selection of material. It is Thomas's task to propagate abroad the 'secret words' entrusted to him through his dialogue with the Saviour. He is to proclaim the imperative nature of the ascetic way of life in the struggle for perfection. Like the Prophets before him, however, Thomas is concerned that his preaching might fall on deaf ears; and he tells the Saviour of his fear that all who preach such a message will become 'laughing-stocks to the world'. He need have no misgivings! Those who will not heed will pay a severe penalty:

> The Saviour answered and said: 'Truly, I tell you: He who will listen to your word and turn away his face or turn up his nose at it, or smirk in this way—truly I tell you that he will be handed over to the Ruler above, he who rules over all the powers as their king, and he will turn that one away and have him thrown from on high down into the abyss, and he will be locked up in a narrow and dark place' (*Book of Thomas*, p. 142).

The work is clearly intended for the admonition and encouragement of Christian souls and their leaders who were struggling to uphold an ascetic or encratite tradition within an ethos of moral turpitude and sexual laxity. In itself, this tells us little about the date of the work, and even less about its provenance. We might reasonably suggest that both the final compilation and its translation into Coptic took place in Egypt, for the second part of the work does appear to borrow ideas from the Ethiopic version of the Petrine Apocalypse. The Sayings tradition which clearly underlies this woes and blessings section is just as likely to have been known in Egypt as anywhere else; and the community for which this tradition was so eloquently expanded to suit the purpose of the author might well be located in the deserts of Upper Egypt. The Thomasine tradition, however, undoubtedly belongs to Mesopotamia; and the earliest section of the book—the dialogue between Thomas and the Saviour—focuses on that encratite ideal which was the prevailing ethic of these regions during the second century. Notwithstanding a number of New Testament allusions or phrases, particularly in the second part, neither of the sections is specifically Christian. At the same time, it would be an exaggeration to say that that the work is more than marginally Gnostic. We might safely hazard, then, that the dialogue section itself, as well as the underlying traditions of both sections of the book, have their roots in eastern Syria within an area that treasured the 'Thomas' tradition, and at a time (second century rather than third) before the final parting of the ways between mainstream Christianity and fully developed Gnosticism.

4. *The Infancy Gospel of Thomas*

The traditional Gospels provide sparse information about the infant years of Jesus. Apart from the birth stories in Matthew and Luke, and the Lukan story of the twelve-year-old Jesus in the Temple, these early 'hidden years' remain precisely that. It was never the intention of the Evangelists, of course, to write biographies, but to engender faith; and the burgeoning popular interest in the early life of Jesus was met by a ready supply of legendary material which circulated, first as folk-stories, and then gradually in the form of collections. Such a work was the so-called *Infancy Gospel of Thomas*. As a document it has no reliable early attestation. Some believe that this collection of stories was put together no earlier than the fourth or fifth century. The individual stories themselves, however, may derive from the end of the first century—though there is no possibility of proving so early an origin for any of them. That some stories enjoyed wide circulation during the second century is evident from Irenaeus's citation of one of the Thomasine stories, which he alleges to have been incorporated in the spurious scriptures of the Gnostic Marcosian sect.[12] The *Infancy Gospel of Thomas* claims to be a comprehensive account of the childhood work of Jesus, compiled by 'Thomas the Israelite'. Though the emphasis on 'our land' (meaning Israel) in the opening verses might

---

12. Irenaeus, *Adv. Haer.* 1.20.1; the passage quoted was the exchange between the child Jesus and his teacher, Zacchaeus (*Infancy Gospel* 6). Marcus was the leader of a sect or school in the later Valentinian tradition.

suggest a proprietorial claim to authenticity in the face of other contending stories and collections, there is nothing in the work to indicate Jewish origin. In view of the association with the person of Thomas, and of the special prominence of the Syriac versions of the text, we might speculate that the author, perhaps of Jewish Diaspora extraction, was a Christian living in or around Edessa, where Thomasine tradition was persistently robust.

It would be impossible to appreciate this strange composition without first becoming aware of its underlying Gnosticism. The sole purpose of the author was to demonstrate the miraculous power of Jesus from his birth, and that he possessed the same extraordinary wisdom and insight in infancy that he exhibited in later years. When the boy Jesus confounded his teacher with his greater understanding, in exasperation the teacher appealed to Joseph to take the child away:

> Take him away, therefore, I beseech you, brother Joseph. I cannot endure the severity of his look. I cannot make out his speech at all. This child is not earth-born; he can tame even fire. Perhaps he was begotten even before the creation of the world. What belly bore him, what womb nurtured him, I do not know (*Infancy Gospel of Thomas* 7.2).

Throughout, we are presented with a picture of one who is essentially not of this world, a Docetic Christ in whom, from the start, the Spirit of God fully dwelt. Clearly, in the mind of the author, the combination of supernatural ability with the capriciousness of youth would inevitably disturb and dismay; and many of the stories in the earlier part of the work are morally offensive and indefensible, showing the growing Jesus to be cruel, callous and vindictive, and exercising his power without regard for the consequences. The later stories do, in fact, more favourably mirror the miraculous work encountered in the canonical Gospel stories. Indeed, the work ends with a version of the visit of Jesus and his parents to the Temple which diverges only slightly from Luke's account. It is in those stories that are more consonant with the traditional figure of Jesus that we are able to recognize that the *theological* intention of the author is basically no different from that of the Evangelists. In all cases, the miracle stories are told to demonstrate the divine nature of Christ; and here, in this Infancy Gospel, the reaction of the onlookers after each marvel is proof of Jesus' heavenly origin:

> After these things in the neighbourhood of Joseph a little sick child died, and his mother wept bitterly. And Jesus heard that great mourning and tumult arose, and he ran quickly, and finding the child, he touched his breast and said: 'I say to you, do not die but live and be with your mother.'

And immediately he looked up and laughed. And he said to the woman:
'Take him and give him milk and remember me.'

And when the people standing round saw it, they marvelled and said:
'Truly, this child is either a god or an angel of God, for every word of his is
an accomplished deed' (*Infancy Gospel of Thomas* 17.2).

It seems evident that folk-stories and legends about the childhood of
Jesus circulated freely in every region during the early centuries. Some
would surely have local associations. All would be subject to embellishment and exaggeration in the telling; and the favourite stories would find a
place in more than one composition. It is not difficult to identify echoes of
several of the stories in marginally Gnostic Apocryphal works from the
second century. The episode of Jesus and his schoolteacher, for instance,
told three times in this Infancy Gospel, and undoubtedly a legend of considerable popularity, appears also in the *Epistula Apostolorum* (4) (see Chapter
7). It is of some significance that different versions and recensions of the
work vary substantially not only in the length of the text, but also in the
stories they include. Thus, the story of the dyer, contained in one of the
Greek versions, must also have been a favourite tale, finding a place in
variant form in the *Gospel of Philip* (54), as well as in other later Infancy
Gospels. We can hardly fail to notice the parallel with the *Gospel of Thomas*
(77) in the following story of how the boy Jesus healed a man injured by
an axe:

And when a clamour arose and a concourse of people took place, the child
Jesus also ran there, and forced his way through the crowd, and took the
injured foot, and it was healed immediately. And he said to the young
man: 'Arise now, cleave the wood and remember me.' And when the
crowd saw what had happened, they worshipped the child, saying: 'Truly
the spirit of God dwells in this child' (*Infancy Gospel of Thomas* 10.2; cf.
Gos. Thom. 77).

The many allusions to the text of the New Testament, particularly to the
Gospel of Luke, place the composition of this work at the earliest during
the second century. As was noted previously, some of the legends themselves might have been widely known by the end of the first century; but
the document itself, like other less important Infancy texts, will probably
have been produced, at the earliest, towards the end of the second century,
when a Docetic view of Christ predominated in the eastern provinces.

Chapter 6

THE CHURCHES OF ASIA

The Acts of John
The Acts of Paul
The Acts of Andrew
The Acts of Peter and the Twelve Apostles

It would be surprising indeed if, by the close of the fourth century, the various Apocryphal Acts composed to venerate the lives and work of individual Apostles had not been collected to form a body of literature for general reading in the churches. It is well known that the Manichaeans prized such a collection, and used the five Acts of Andrew, John, Peter, Thomas and Paul in preference to the canonical Acts. Indisputable evidence of this is provided by a passage in the Manichaean Psalm-book which refers to episodes contained in all five of these works; and the ninth-century Asian author, Photius, gives a corroborative list, in one of his anti-Manichaean writings, of the heretical doctrines contained in the collection. We are able, however, to delve further back, almost to the presumed time of the composition of these documents. Origen, at the beginning of the third century, may have known one or more of these spurious books, for, in his *Commentary on Genesis* (according to Eusebius) he alludes to Peter's 'head-down' crucifixion, and to Paul's martyrdom in Rome under the Emperor Nero.[1]

The name of Leucius (or Leucius Charinus) has long been associated with one or other of the Apocryphal Acts, and Photius believed that he was the author of all five major works. Whatever connection there may have been, however, it is now generally assumed that no one person was responsible for all the books; for though there are obvious similarities between them, there are also huge differences of style and content. Questions of individual dates and provenance are made more difficult by the extensive cross-fertilization of ideas and traditions that seems to have

---

1.   Eusebius, *HE* 3.1. The earliest witness of these traditions occurs in the *Acts of Peter* and the *Acts of Paul* respectively.

taken place over the course of the transmission of these works. In this chapter we shall examine three of the five major Acts in turn, and, while it is not strictly of the *Actus* genre, the allegorical work, extant only in Coptic, known as the *Acts of Peter and the Twelve Apostles*.

1. *The Acts of John*

Although we begin our survey with the *Acts of John*, this is not to imply its chronological priority over the others. Certainly this was generally claimed at one time; but no definitive consensus on this complex question obtains at present. Since the *Acts of John* displays in abundance those literary and theological characteristics which all have in common, however, it will serve to illustrate the essential elements of the genre. Chief among these, of course, is that the various Acts are primarily records of missionary journeys, after the model of the apostolic journeys of the canonical Acts. The book opens with John travelling to Ephesus via Miletus.[2] Since there seems to be a substantial section at the beginning which has been lost, however, it could be that the earlier section described his exile to Patmos (perhaps from an earlier stay in Ephesus) and his release by the Emperor Domition to return to Asia. One late tradition suggests this,[3] but there is nothing in the *Acts of John* to support it. John's travels are limited to a small area of the western provinces of Asia, using Ephesus as his base. Indeed, only Ephesus itself and Smyrna and Laodicea are actually mentioned, with the statement that he visited 'other cities of the region'. The usual interpretation of this is that he visited the seven churches mentioned in the Revelation.

At Ephesus, John miraculously raises to life Lycomedes, the praetor, and his wife Cleopatra. John takes advantage of the amazement of the Ephesians to collect a crowd to watch a mass healing of old women in the city, and to preach the message of Christ. The content of this preaching is important for our understanding of the Christology of the work, for it deals with ideas concerning the polymorphic and mysterious nature of Christ, and of the meaning of the cross. John then provokes a confrontation with

2.   We hear little of John in the Acts of the Apostles, but Revelation places him (if this is the same John) on the island of Patmos, off the coast of Asia Minor; and later tradition (Polycrates, Bishop of Ephesus, c. 190) says that he lived to a great age in Ephesus, until he had to be carried about by others. Certainly Eusebius has the tradition that to John was given the missionary charge of Asia, and that he died there.

3.   See Eusebius, *HE* 3.20.9.

the priests of the Temple of Artemis on the feast of the dedication of this idol-temple. The temple is destroyed, and the people of Ephesus are converted to the true God. The Apostle then journeys to Smyrna (where he controls the bedbugs in the inn at which he and his party stay the night), thence moving on, perhaps, to the rest of the 'seven' cities of the Apocalypse, preaching and healing as he goes. Having returned to Ephesus, he continues his preaching and healing ministry. As in many of the Apocryphal Acts, that ministry seems to be chiefly conducted among the rich and influential.[4] After making his last act of worship (a Eucharist) he asked for his grave to be dug, made his farewell address, and lay down in the grave and died. Tradition knows no martyrdom for John.

Three passages of special importance in the *Acts of John* shed light on John's Christology, and we shall examine these in more detail in due course. The first of these (in chs. 88–93) teaches the polymorphic nature of Christ, that Jesus is able to reveal himself in different forms at the same time, according to the ability of the beholder to understand. This strongly suggests a Docetic and other-worldly view of Christ, and has its origin, no doubt, in the Gospel story of the Transfiguration. An interesting and unusual account of the Transfiguration is given in this passage of the *Acts of John*. It may be worthy of note that no account occurs in the Fourth Gospel.

The second important passage (chs. 94–96) is usually given the name of 'the Hymn of Christ'. It is indeed a song which describes the dance of Christ, in which (as John recalls it) his disciples are asked to join, just prior to his Crucifixion, in which he manifests his glory. It may well have its Gospel origin in the saying of Jesus about the children's game ('we piped to you and you did not dance'), and the contrast he draws between John the Baptist and the Son of Man (Mt. 11.16-18). In the third passage, which follows on the dance, John speaks of the mystery of the cross. The passage reflects the Gnostic interpretation of the nature of Christ and of his Crucifixion which is revealed only to the elect. It is quite possible that these three passages did not form part of the original *Acts of John*, for their character is quite different from the rest of the book, and there are signs of editing.

It is often confidently asserted that the Apocryphal Acts were composed in the style of the ancient romantic or heroic novel; and it needs to be recognized that there are indeed important literary parallels with such works.

---

4.   Compare the same propensity in the *Acts of Peter* and the *Acts of Thomas*.

In each of the Apocryphal Acts, the apostolic hero is set centre-stage, the epitome of wisdom, grace and power. However, in two respects they differ from the purely aretalogical literature of the ancient world: despite the often bizarre nature of the miracle stories contained in them, the books were intended to be read biographically; and the aim and purpose of the works was not so much to entertain (though no doubt they did), as to convert. The miracles themselves, carefully prepared and staged, present opportunities for the Apostle to preach to the gathered crowd, as in the healing of the old women in the theatre at Ephesus:

> On the next day the crowds came together into the theatre while it was still night, so that the proconsul heard of it and came quickly and took his seat with all the people. And a certain Andronicus who was praetor, and was the leading citizen of Ephesus at that time, spread the story that what John had promised was impossible and incredible... So when John heard this and was disturbed by these words, he commanded the old women to be brought into the theatre. And when they were all brought into the midst, some lying on beds and others in a torpor, and when the city had come running together, a great silence ensued; then John opened his mouth and began to say, 'Men of Ephesus...' (*Acts of John* 31–32).

Again, in the episode of the destruction of the Temple of Artemis, John seizes his moment to change the lives of his hearers by prayer and wondrous deed, so that idolatry in the city is crushed for ever, and bewildered, superstitious and frightened men are brought to the true faith. If at times the miracle stories seem to stray too far across the borders of credibility, it should be remembered that such extravagant excursions are not unknown in the canonical Acts: chains are loosed and prison gates opened, an evangelist is caught up and physically transported in the Spirit, a venomous creature is made harmless. The miracles of the traditional Gospels, of course, furnish the basis of these wonders; but in replicating the mighty works of Jesus, the Apostles themselves necessarily become imitators of Christ, performing 'even greater works' than he. It is this apostolic 'imitation of Christ', especially in the Apocryphal Acts, that is, perhaps, their most significant characteristic. The Apostles become 'divine' beings— 'God-men'.

There is an important difference that we should notice, however, between the content of the apostolic preaching in the New Testament, on the one hand, and that of the Apocryphal books on the other. Throughout the Lukan Acts, the Apostles promulgate the *kerygma*—proclaiming the salvatory cross and Resurrection of Christ, and his subsequent glorification. Rarely do these matters concern the Apocryphal Acts, where the emphasis is

rather to expound the *ethical precepts* of Christ, as the Apostles had come
to understand them. In varying degrees the Apocryphal Acts are ascetic in
tone. We saw this characteristic particularly in the *Acts of Thomas*; but
here in the Johannine Acts, too, the Apostle's preaching focuses on how
Christians must live their lives. His aim is to 'teach the brethren to despise
transitory things' (70); and he catalogues the hindrances to faith and asceti-
cal piety in his address to the assembled mourners of the departed Drusiana:

> Many hindrances assail and cause disturbances to the thoughts of men:
> anxiety, children, parents, reputation, poverty, flattery, youth, beauty, vanity,
> desire, wealth, anger, presumption, indolence, envy, jealousy, negligence,
> violence, lust, deceit, money, pretence, and all such other hindrances as
> there are in this life (*Acts of John* 68).

Reference was made earlier to the three sections of the *Acts of John*
whose Docetic (if not Gnostic) character seems to differentiate them from
the rest of the work. Together they form what is generally called the
'Preaching of John in Ephesus' (chs. 87–105). There is little doubt that
these passages represent separate traditions inserted into the Acts; but
whether they were so inserted by the original compiler of the work, or at
some subsequent time, cannot presently be ascertained. The most persuasive arguments, perhaps, are those which seek to demonstrate that the words
and deeds of John in the narrative sections of the book should be interpreted in the light of these spiritualizing sections, and that they were
therefore an integral part of the original work.

The first passage (chs. 87–93) seeks to explicate the polymorphic mani-
festations of Christ. In a previous section, now missing, Drusiana had
claimed that Christ had appeared to her both in the person of John, and as
a young man. The Apostle now recounts how on many occasions when
Jesus was with them, the Twelve had experienced the Lord's 'other-
worldly' form, and occasionally his ability to reveal himself in different
forms at the same time:

> When he had chosen Peter and Andrew, who were brothers, he came to me
> and to my brother James, saying 'I need you to come to me!' And my
> brother when he heard this said: 'John, what does he want, this child on the
> shore who called us?' And I said, 'Which child?' And he answered me,
> 'The one who is beckoning to us.' And I replied: 'Because of the long
> watch we have kept at sea, you are not seeing well, Brother James. Do you
> not see the man standing there who is handsome, fair and cheerful-
> looking?' (*Acts of John* 89).

True polymorphism—that is, the simultaneous experience of Christ in
different forms—is not encountered at all in the New Testament; and such

polymorphic descriptions as we have in the *Acts of John*, and elsewhere in the Apocryphal Acts, are presumably intended to show that Christ manifests himself according to the ability of each to comprehend. This important concept, which actually finds explicit expression in the *Acts of Peter* (20), illustrates the gradual development of apostolic understanding of the real nature and work of Christ. Elsewhere in this passage John tells of milestones in his own spiritual growth, as Jesus revealed something of his other-worldly self to him. Sometimes when he reached out to Jesus to touch him, he encountered a material, solid body; at other times it was immaterial and incorporeal, 'as if it did not exist at all' (93). Sometimes when he walked with Jesus, the Lord seemed to be raised above the ground, leaving no visible footprints on the earth.

If these representations of Christ point strongly to the Docetic character of the *Acts of John*, the section that immediately follows—the ceremony of the dance, or the Hymn of Christ—is decidedly Gnostic:

> I will pipe,
>> Dance, all of you.—Amen.
> I will mourn,
>> Beat you all your breasts.—Amen.
> The one Ogdoad
>> sings praises with us.—Amen.
> The twelfth number
>> dances on high.—Amen.
> To the All
>> it belongs to dance in the height.—Amen.
> He who does not dance
>> does not know what happens.—Amen. (*Acts of John* 94)

Clearly, the hymn and dance of Christ are intended to demonstrate the meaning of his suffering, and to explain how John, and others with him, are to share in the dance. In a series of cryptic and antithetical statements, the enigma of the cross is laid out, the eternal Christ suffering, and yet not suffering, saving and yet being saved. The Twelve are bidden to join hands in a circle around him, and join in the dance. After the dance is finished, Jesus goes out, and the disciples flee in all directions, John himself to the Mount of Olives, there to weep and lament. The hymn itself refers to Christ's Passion and suffering as a 'mystery' which is revealed only to those who can understand; and John is shown, both here in the dance, and subsequently in a manifestation of the crucified in a cave, that his sufferings could not be measured in terms of physical pain and torment, but was of a different order. They too, as they grew in understanding, would begin

to see the meaning of their own trials and suffering in the light of their true
spiritual nature and eternal destiny:

> What I now am seen to be,
>   that I am not;
> What I am you shall see
>   when you come.
> If you knew how to suffer
>   You would be able not to suffer.
> Learn how to suffer
>   and you shall be able not to suffer.
> What you do not know
>   I myself will teach you. (*Acts of John* 96)

We will recall that several of the Gnostic writings considered in earlier
chapters reflect this notion of Christ's invulnerability. We might compare,
for example, passages in the Coptic *Apocalypse of Peter* and the *First
Apocalypse of James*, in both of which tractates he who suffers the physical torments of the cross is seen to be merely the fleshly image of the true
Christ.[5]

The third passage, following on from the dance, describes John's vision
of the crucified in the cave. The cross itself appears, bathed in light, and
assumes a fixed form; but the Lord above the cross 'has no shape but only
a kind of voice'. Around the cross is a formless multitude representing
those of 'inferior nature' who had not yet been gathered and taken up into
the mystery. The purpose of the vision is to reveal to John (who alone is
ready to hear) the true mystery of the cross, and how these spiritual reali-
ties were perforce expressed for the world in inadequate and deficient
symbols. Though the passage ranks among the most abstruse of all Gnostic texts, we might recognize that its fundamental concept relates to the
inviolability of the eternal and transcendent Christ. The 'mystery' of the
cross, a glimpse of which is here given to John, holds the paradox that
though Christ cannot suffer, yet, in ways quite incomprehensible to the
world, and for its sake, he does:

> You hear that I suffered, yet I suffered not; and that I suffered not, yet I did
> suffer; and that I was pierced, yet I was not lashed; that I was hanged, yet I
> was not hanged; that blood flowed from me, yet it did not flow; and in a
> word, that what they say of me, I did not endure, but what they do not say,
> those things I did suffer (*Acts of John* 101).

5.   *Apocalypse of Peter* 81; *First Apocalypse of James* 31. Cf. also passages in the
Gnostic treatise the *Second Tractate of the Great Seth*. The *Epistle of Peter to Philip*
(Codex VIII, p. 139) represents Jesus as 'a stranger to suffering'.

The end section of the Acts has the story of John's death,[6] a section which must certainly have enjoyed widespread independent circulation, begins (unusually for the *Acts of John*) with a final Eucharist which he shared with his followers and friends. When the grave is dug, John stands within it to make his final commendatory prayer, giving great emphasis to his own avoidance of women, and his celibate and continent life. And 'having sealed himself in every part',[7] he lay down in the trench, blessed his brethren, and 'gave up his spirit rejoicing'. These somewhat surprising liturgical inclusions (the Eucharist and the Seal) may well prove to be precisely that—later redactive additions to the original text. At all events, the absence generally of ecclesiastical interest in the *Acts of John* suggests that the work originates not from Asia Minor, but further to the East, perhaps in Syria. If so, it would be composed for and within an encratite community which clearly knew and treasured Johannine tradition, but which distanced itself from the established centres of Christian orthodoxy. We may also infer a comparatively early date for the work, perhaps as early as the middle decades of the second century.

2. *The Acts of Paul*

It is hardly surprising that the *Acts of Paul* was not subjected to the same universal and speedy condemnation as the *Acts of John*, for it shows no propensity to Gnosticism, and seems in places actually to complement the Pauline tradition of the New Testament. Indeed, it may well have been its acceptance by the Manichaeans, rather than its content, that persuaded the Church at large finally to reject the work. Hippolytus, at the turn of the third century, seems to have known and approved the *Acts of Paul*, referring without demur to the rather strange episode within it concerning Paul's encounter with the lion. Origen was less certain about the book's authenticity, though it appears that even he was not entirely prepared to dismiss it. Tertullian certainly took exception to what he considered to be the book's sanction of women's ministry in the story of Paul and Thecla. He claimed that this spurious work was produced by an Asian presbyter who actually confessed to writing it (with the best of motives), and was removed from

6. Often referred to as the 'Metastasis', from the Greek, meaning 'the departure from life'.

7. The concept of 'the Seal' is more prominent in the *Acts of Thomas*. Refer to Chapter 5, section 2.

office.[8] How true Tertullian's claim is, we cannot know; but it would certainly seem a reasonable possibility. At all events, the book seems to have been in circulation, either wholly or in its parts, at the latest, by the end of the second century.

No complete early manuscript of the *Acts of Paul* is extant. Very many partial papyrus fragments in Greek and Coptic have come to light from the late third century, which, pieced together, provide a reasonably clear indication of the original work. There is yet no certainty, however, about the precise order of the component elements of the Acts, and this leads to some confusion about the route of Paul's journey. Three distinct sections are thought to have had early independent circulation: the so-called *Acts of Paul and Thecla*; items of correspondence between Paul and the Corinthian church, usually known as *3 Corinthians*; and the *Martyrdom of Paul*. Before we consider each of these components at greater length, it will be useful to trace Paul's Apocryphal journey from his conversion to his death.

Two important manuscripts,[9] and a corroborative Coptic parchment fragment from the fourth century,[10] show that these Acts began with the account of Paul's entry into Damascus following his conversion. His stay in Damascus may well have been prolonged in the original text, though nothing of this remains. From Damascus he journeys to Jerusalem, and (according to his later recorded recollection) he met and baptized a lion on the road. No details of his stay in Jerusalem have survived. Paul then travels to Antioch—though it is not clear whether this means the Syrian or Pisidian city. The description of his work in Antioch is meagre, but it appears that Paul here restores to life a dead youth, the son of Anchares and Phila, and is stoned and thrust out of the city for his trouble. At Iconium, his preaching converts Thecla, the fiancée of Thamyris, and persuades her to take up a life of chastity. Thamyris stirs up the crowd against Paul who is promptly imprisoned, while Thecla (for visiting Paul in prison) is sentenced to death at the stake. Rain thwarts this, however; and Paul and Thecla escape to (Pisidian) Antioch. Here again, Thecla finds herself in trouble and is taken to the Arena to be killed by beasts. As the animals attack, she falls into a tank of water—and promptly baptizes herself! The beasts are reluctant to pursue her, and she is freed. Many conversions follow.

8.   Tertullian, *de Baptismo* 17.
9.   The Greek fourth-century Hamburg manuscript and the Coptic fifth-century Heidelberg manuscript.
10.   A fourth-century Coptic fragment held in the John Rylands Library.

From Antioch Paul goes to Myra, a port on the south coast of Asia Minor. In the Lukan Acts Paul changes ship here for Rome. In the *Acts of Paul*, he becomes involved in a family problem after he raises one of the sons from death, and then, for reasons known only to himself, takes ship back to Phoenicia. There is much missing in the papyrus pages, and it is difficult to reconstruct the story. It seems that Paul and his companions were shut up in the Temple of Apollo at Sidon, and fattened up for sacrifice, but the temple collapses. Paul is dragged to the theatre, but escapes and moves on to Tyre, where, after a brief stay, he takes ship for Asia Minor. On his arrival at Ephesus he stays with Aquila and Priscilla. His preaching once again brings him into trouble, and the people (doubtless the same who exploited the Artemis-worship for gain) demand that he be thrown to the beasts. The lion he faces in the Arena is the very animal whom Paul had earlier baptized, and they happily converse together. More beasts are brought in; but a storm of hailstones puts an end to the spectacle, and Paul once again escapes.

He now takes a ship across to Macedonia—probably Philippi. The manuscript is so damaged here that unfortunately we have few details. What we do have is a letter sent by the brethren at Corinth to Paul while he was in Philippi, asking for his intervention in their current problems. This is followed by Paul's reply (*3 Corinthians*). From this letter we learn that Paul has suffered much at Philippi, being 'put in fetters'. We recall that the Acts of the Apostles records that he and his followers were 'beaten with rods' here, and cast into prison for 'disturbing the city' (Acts 16). Arrived at Corinth, Paul stays at the home of Epiphanius, and prepares for his journey to Rome. He remains here for 40 days, preaching and holding services of prayer and the giving of thanks (Eucharist), and then leaves here for Rome, still a free man! The brethren at Corinth pray together as Paul embarks on the ship. The captain is one Artemon, who had previously been baptized by Peter (note the allusion here to the story in the *Acts of Peter*, which the author of the *Acts of Paul* surely knew). On the voyage, Paul has a vision of a gloomy and downcast Christ saying, 'I am about to be crucified afresh' (again, from the *Acts of Peter*). Paul is urged to go to Rome, and admonish the brethren there,[11] and the vision of Christ goes ahead of the ship, walking on the water.

---

11. Was the Church already founded and established in Rome before Paul? Compare the early chapters of the *Acts of Peter* which (unless these chapters are redactive) intimate that Paul was the first missionary in Rome.

Paul is greeted in Rome by Luke and Titus. He hires a barn, and teaches 'the word of truth'. When a cup-bearer to the Emperor Nero hears that Paul is preaching in the barn, he climbs to an upstairs window, and sits on the ledge to listen. He falls, and dies, but Paul restores him (cf. Acts 20.9-12). The popularity of Paul following this miracle concerns Nero who tortures and imprisons him. Nero issues a decree that 'all who were found to be Christians and "Soldiers of Christ" should be put to death'; so Paul is finally beheaded.

It will be noticed that, in contrast to the canonical Acts' version of Paul's travels, there is here only one continuous journey. It is beyond question that the author was influenced by the Lukan Acts and the canonical Epistles of Paul, but it is clear that his intention was not to replace the traditional story with an alternative account. Certainly there is no suggestion that his visits were for the purpose of establishing the churches, for he seems to have been already well known in many of the towns and cities on the journey. When he came to Iconium, a man called Onesiphorus and his family went out on the Lystra road to meet him. Because he knew of Paul only 'in the spirit', his friends at Iconium had furnished him with a description of the Apostle—the only intimation we have of Paul's physical appearance:

> He went along the royal road which leads to Lystra, and stood there waiting for him, and looked at all who came, according to Titus' description. And he saw Paul coming, a man small of stature, with a bald head and crooked legs, in a good state of body, with eyebrows meeting and nose somewhat hooked, full of friendliness; for now he appeared like a man, and now he had the face of an angel (*Acts of Paul and Thecla* 3).

What took place when Paul had entered the house of Onesiphorus is illuminating. There was 'great joy, and bowing of knees and breaking of bread, and the word of God concerning continence and the resurrection' (*Acts of Paul and Thecla* 5). If this is a delightful picture of the warmth and simplicity of early Christian *koinonia*, we can be in no doubt about the fundamental importance of the encratite ethic for the *Acts of Paul*, a characteristic which is shared with other Apocryphal Acts. Salvation begins with continence, and to emphasize the point, Paul begins his address to his assembled hearers with a distinctive version of the Beatitudes:

> Blessed are the pure in heart, for they shall see God.
> Blessed are they who have kept the flesh pure, for they shall become a temple of God.
> Blessed are the continent, for to them will God speak.

> Blessed are they who have renounced this world, for they shall be well
> pleasing to God.
> Blessed are they who have wives as if they had them not, for they shall be
> heirs to God… (*Acts of Paul and Thecla* 5).

Paul's preaching proved to be especially attractive to a virgin named
Thecla; and thus is introduced the *Acts of Paul and Thecla*. Whether the
tradition has any factual basis is quite impossible to say. It is doubtless
true that the widespread popularity of the story would be assured simply
because it was a tale of remarkable Christian piety and sacrifice, courage
and love, told in the characteristic style of classic romance. We may not
dismiss the possibility, however, that the tradition arose from some
remembered conversion by Paul of a high-ranking woman at Antioch or
Iconium (cf. Acts 13.50). Luke's account of the severe opposition that
Paul encountered in these regions from the Synagogue has here been given
a different motive in the *Acts of Paul* to suit the ascetic purpose of its
author. Instead of opposition from the Jews at Paul's preaching of the
Cross and Resurrection, it is the outrage and jealousy of the men of Iconium
at Paul's seductive sorcery that is the cause of the conflict—as the story of
Thecla illustrates. In neither the canonical nor the Apocryphal versions of
what happened at Iconium is the power and will of God thwarted: in the
former, it is the Gentiles who receive the salvation the Jews have forfeited;
in the latter, it is the women who renounce a life of corruption and impurity through marriage who win their eternal freedom.

Some of the oldest and most reliable manuscripts of the *Acts of Paul*
contain the Apostle's Corinthian correspondence. It needs to be emphasized, however, that the marked difference of form and character between
these two letters and the surrounding text suggests that both they and their
introductory material are early additions to the work. The Corinthian brethren have found themselves unable to counter the threat posed by two named
Gnostic interlopers in their midst (Simon and Cleobius), and send an
urgent plea to Paul at Philippi to intervene. What they require is that either
Paul should come to them in person, before his planned journey to Rome,
or else reiterate in writing the truths of the Gospel which he had taught,
and which they had received. The issues, as we might have expected,
include the resurrection of the body, the reality of Christ's humanity, and
the whole question of creation. These are matters which Paul has dealt
with frequently in his genuine letters; but the manner in which the problems are posed in the Corinthian letter requires us to presume a date well
into the second century, when the Gnostic teachings expressed were mak-

ing a significant impact in the churches. The Corinthian letter ends with a summary of those offending teachings:

> What they say and teach is as follows: We must not, they say, appeal to the prophets, and that God is not almighty, and that there is no resurrection of the flesh, and that the creation of man is not God's work, and that the Lord is not come in the flesh, nor was he born of Mary, and that the world is not of God, but of the angels. Wherefore, brother, make all speed to come...
> (*Letter of the Corinthians to Paul* 1.9-16).

Paul's reply (*3 Corinthians*) authoritatively counters the arguments of Simon and Cleobius using ideas and phrases borrowed from previous Pauline correspondence. We can recognize themes from genuine letters as well as from Ephesians and the Pastoral Epistles; and although the letter was long accepted as authentic, especially in the east, we have to say that *3 Corinthians* was almost certainly not part of the original Acts. In the sequence of events as we have them, Paul makes a fleeting visit to Corinth from Philippi, and whatever friction had there ensued, it seems the Apostle's letter has assuaged. Even Cleobius (if this was the same as the Gnostic dissident) has returned to orthodoxy, and being filled with the Spirit, he joins with the brethren in giving thanks that Paul is to glorify God in Rome.

As the voyage to Rome begins, the Lord appears before Paul, and strengthens him for the trials ahead. Like the Quo Vadis scene of the *Acts of Peter*,[12] Jesus states that he is going to Rome to be crucified afresh. 'God forbid, Lord, that I should see this' is Paul's response; and when he arrives in Rome, and greets the brethren there, his sombre mood during the voyage is turned into joy and thanksgiving as he proclaims the great things God has accomplished through Christ. Paul's sermon to the assembled brethren is an important witness to the content of the early preaching of the *kerygma*: the mighty works of God are proclaimed—those first through which God had sought to accomplish his ancient promises to Israel; and then those in these latter days in which he had sent down a 'spirit of power into the flesh of Mary the Galilean according to the prophetic word':

> who was conceived and borne by her as the fruit of her womb until she was delivered and gave birth to Jesus the Christ, our King, of Bethlehem in Judaea, brought up in Nazareth, who went to Jerusalem and taught all Judaea: the kingdom of heaven is at hand (*Acts of Paul*, 'From Corinth to Italy', p. 8).

---

12. *Acts of Peter* 35. This episode was doubtless the model for this incident in the *Acts of Paul*.

Paul then goes on to tell of the wonders that Jesus the Christ had performed—how he chose twelve men of understanding and faith, raised the dead, healed diseases, cleansed lepers, healed the blind, made cripples whole, raised up paralytics and cleansed those possessed by demons.

It was, in fact, such eloquent and powerful preaching, according to the final 'Martyrdom' section of the *Acts of Paul*, that hastened his end. The Apostle had hired a barn in the outskirts of the city, and here he enthralled his crowded audience with his preaching, including one Patroclus, the Emperor Nero's cup-bearer. In an unmistakable adaptation of the episode of Eutychus at Troas (Acts 20.9), this young man falls from a high window, and dies. Paul promptly restores the youth who becomes a 'soldier of Christ'; and Nero begins to fear for his position. All those professing to belong to this king's army are burned with fire; but Paul himself is sentenced to be beheaded:

> Then Paul stood with his face to the east, and lifting up his hands to heaven prayed at length; and after communing in prayer in Hebrew with the fathers he stretched out his neck without speaking further. But when the executioner struck off his head, milk spurted upon the soldier's clothing. And when they saw it, the soldiers and all who stood by were amazed, and glorified God who had given Paul such glory (*Acts of Paul*, 'Martyrdom', ch. 5).

The difficult work of piecing together the various fragmentary strands of Pauline tradition to form a continuous and integrated *Acts of Paul* has certainly succeeded in producing a comprehensible and entertaining narrative of the Apostle's journey from Damascus to Rome. Furthermore, the fact that at least two important manuscripts contain most, if not all, of the constituent parts does tend to indicate at least the possibility that the original work included all of them. We cannot but notice, however, the huge differences of tone and outlook between the component sections. Some passages, like the story of Paul and Thecla, are concerned above all to emphasize the encratite ethic, while others much more closely follow the traditional preaching of the canonical Acts. If the *Acts of Paul* as it stands is indeed a work of composite nature, as would seem to be the case, it is difficult to assign a date for its compilation. No patristic testimony can help us in this task; and the most that may be asserted is that it was composed before 300, the approximate date of the earliest relatively complete manuscript. We must assume, however, that some of the traditions upon which the stories were based may be of early date, treasured especially in the regions of Asia Minor where, in all probability, the work was composed.

3. *The Acts of Andrew*

No complete text of the Apocryphal *Acts of Andrew* has yet been discovered; but a work bearing this title was known to Eusebius, who included it in his list of books heretically composed by the 'wicked and impious'.[13] Gregory of Tours obviously knew these Acts, for he compiled a summary (or epitome) of the complete work.[14] From this summary we derive most of our knowledge about the contents of the original *Acts of Andrew*. A few early papyrus fragments of the text, one dating from the fourth century, provide corroboration of parts of Gregory's summary. Numerous later versions of the Martyrdom of Andrew, in Greek, Latin and Armenian, also help to resolve the original form of the text. The ascetic character of the book appealed to later encratite communities such as the Manichaeans and the fourth-century Spanish Priscillianists.

The original book seems to have been set in two parts. The first part was a description of Andrew's journey from the northern regions of Asia Minor and Thrace to Macedonia and Greece. The second part concerned Andrew's work at Patras, from which headquarters he visited several cities in Achaia such as Corinth, Megara and perhaps Sparta. The summary of Gregory actually begins with the story of Andrew going to Mermidona to save Matthias (or Matthew) from the cannibals, before going on to his allotted area of mission, traditionally, Scythia. This story is so different in character from the rest of the work that it is thought by some to have been added to the original work. The location of Mermidona (if such a place ever existed) is unknown. Gregory does not report the Martyrdom of Andrew at length, believing it to have been adequately recorded by others; and for this long section it is necessary to rely on later manuscripts, of which there are many.

As the summary itself indicates, Gregory was interested to record only the miracles performed by Andrew, and he omits much of the intervening narrative of the original. Evidently the story of Matthew's work among the 'man-eaters', and Andrew's subsequent rescue of Matthew from prison in Mermidona, must have formed part of the work that Gregory knew, for the whole of his first chapter is concerned with this episode. From Mermidona Andrew travels westwards along the southern shore of the Black Sea, exorcizing and healing as he goes. At Amaseia he restores sight to a blind boy

13. Eusebius, *HE* 3.25.6.
14. Gregory was Bishop of Tours towards the end of the sixth century. His summary appears under the title *Liber de Miraculis Beati Andreae Apostoli*.

and raises an Egyptian servant boy from the dead. On another occasion, when Andrew becomes involved in a family dispute, and is imprisoned by the proconsul, his prayers produce an earthquake, he is released, and the proconsul and all his family are converted and baptized. At Sinope he exorcizes an evil spirit from a young man, and cures a penitent adulteress of her dropsy, then 'breaks bread', after which the parents are converted. Rich gifts are offered to Andrew, but he declines them.

Crossing the Hellespont to Byzantium, the ship in which Andrew had embarked encountered a great storm. The Apostle prayed, and the sea was calmed. As they moved through Thrace, he and his party were threatened by armed men. Andrew makes the sign of the cross, and an angel disarms the men. At Perinthus, on the instruction of an angel, Andrew takes ship across the Marmara Sea to Macedonia; and having arrived at Neapolis, he makes his way across hilly country to Philippi. Here he intervenes to prevent the incestuous marriage of two brothers with their cousins. All recognize the Apostle's action to be inspired, and the young people see in Andrew 'the face of an angel'. At Thessalonica many miracles are performed; and so many were his adherents as he continued his journey through the Aegean to Patras, on the west coast of the Peloponnese, that one ship was unable to contain them all. Again, a storm arose, with potentially dire consequences:

> And as he slept a little, one fell overboard. Anthimus roused him, saying: 'Help us, good master; one of thy servants perisheth.' He rebuked the wind, there was a calm, and the man was borne by the waves to the ship. Anthimus helped him on board and all marvelled. On the twelfth day they reached Patrae in Achaia, disembarked, and went to an inn (Gregory, *Liber de miraculis* 21).

The second part of the *Acts of Andrew* begins with the Apostle's arrival at Patras. There is no record of visits to this western and coastal Greek city by any early Evangelist other than Andrew, who, of course, remains today the city's patron saint. Andrew is said to have spent most of his ministry here, using it as a base for his missions to cities in the rest of Achaia; and here he was eventually martyred. According to these Acts, while walking on the shore at Patras he came upon a corpse washed onto the beach. It transpired that the man had been in a ship journeying with 39 others seeking the Apostle when they had capsized. Shortly afterwards, the 39 other corpses washed onto the beach, and Andrew restored them. Using Patras as his base, Andrew visited the cities of Achaia—Corinth and Megara—and perhaps journeyed south to Sparta.

The narrative ends with a detailed account of the circumstances leading to Andrew's death at Patras. The Apostle is summoned to the sickbed of Maximilla, the wife of the proconsul Aegeates. Andrew heals the woman, and her husband offers Andrew a reward of silver (100 pieces) which he refuses. Other miracles occur, and Andrew's standing is high. Even the proconsul's brother Stratocles is converted. But when Maximilla secretly receives instruction from Andrew, and takes a vow of chastity and continence, Aegeates seeks out the Apostle to punish him. The full account of the martyrdom is preserved for us in several Greek and Armenian versions, so we have no need of Gregory's brief summary. After much intrigue and plotting, Andrew is arrested and taken to be crucified. Stratocles attempts to save him. But Andrew now refuses all help, and goes smiling to his cross:

> Do thou, Jesu Christ, whom I have seen, whom I hold, whom I love, in whom I am and shall be, receive me in peace into thine everlasting tabernacles, that by my going out there may be an entering in unto thee of many that are akin to me, and that they may rest in thy majesty. And having so said, and yet more glorified the Lord, he gave up the ghost.[15]

The *Acts of Andrew* is generally categorized as a Gnostic work. Unquestionably, the fundamental dualism of matter and spirit that typifies much of this genre is to be found here in abundance; and its encratism, characteristic of much Gnostic literature, is also prominently in evidence. There is certainly nothing of developed Gnostic mythology in the book, but there are echoes, in Andrew's address to his cross, of that mysticism which we find in the *Acts of John*. We must notice, too, that there is not a single suggestion that salvation is wrought by Christ. Indeed, the name of Jesus is rarely mentioned. Humankind must find rest through the recognition of their own spiritual nature, and by their total renunciation of the flesh. To this extent, at least, the work may be said to reflect the Gnostic ethos of the age. The Apostle's work, following that of Christ, is to reveal the truth, and encourage its acceptance by those who listen to his words. In a moving exhortation to Maximilla he begs her not to return to her former ways, but to reject her husband, and to give herself over wholly to the promptings of her true inner being:

> I beg you, then, wise man (*sic*), that your noble mind continue steadfast; I beg you, the invisible mind, that you may be preserved yourself; I exhort you, love Jesus and do not submit to the worse; help me, you, on whose aid

15. From a translation of the Martyrdom of the Apostle Andrew (*Acts of Andrew*) by Th. Detorakis (1980), p. 351.

as man I call, that I may be perfect; help me, that you may know your own true nature; suffer with my suffering, that you may know what I suffer and you will escape suffering. See what I see and what you see will blind you; see what you ought to see and you will not see what you ought not; hear what I say and what you have not heard reject (*Acts of Andrew*, Codex Vaticanus 808, ch. 9).

It is evident from such of Andrew's speeches as are extant that the *Acts of Andrew* should be read as a work of Christian philosophy, with marked affinities to the contemporary writings of Stoicism, rather than of Gnosticism. It is as the enquirers rationalize their present condition, and ask to what extent it conforms to their spiritual nature that they are given the opportunity to progress to their rest. The choice is the person's; and in order to be helped to choose wisely, each must listen to God's word, mediated by Andrew, his revealer. The *miracles* authenticate Andrew's position; but it is the *words* which effect conversion, for they reveal mysteries beyond the telling.

The individual's freedom to choose life rather than death, despite the attendant cost of such a choice, and thus secure for himself or herself eternal salvation, may be illustrated in an episode which took place at Thessalonica, and is described in a surviving Coptic papyrus fragment. Andrew had cast out a demon from a young soldier who promptly discards his worldly uniform for that of Andrew's army, disdaining the punishment which his action must inevitably incur:

O man of God (the soldier proclaims to Andrew), I have spent twenty pieces of gold to acquire this ephemeral garment for myself; but now I will give all that I possess that I may obtain for myself the uniform of your God (*Acts of Andrew*, Papyrus Coptic Utrecht 1).

The recounting of this brief episode exemplifies the aim of the author of the work which was to set the claims of the kingdom of heaven against those of the world, and to draw out from his readers the conscious realization of their true nature and destiny. This young soldier has recognized that no punishment the emperor might impose for denying the uniform, not even death itself, could begin to match the punishment he ought to have received for despising the garment of the immortal king of the ages. The exorcism that Andrew performed unlocks the soldier's inner mind: 'Do you not see what kind of a man is this?', he asks his companions. 'He has no sword in his hand nor any weapon of war, and yet these great miracles are wrought by him.' It is the convert himself, however, searching his own mind as he listens to Andrew's words, who procures his own enrolment in the heavenly king's army.

There are few clear pointers to the provenance of the *Acts of Andrew*. Syria or Egypt have been suggested, on the grounds of its encratite character, and because of the possibility (no more than that) of common authorship with other major Apocryphal Acts. It is by no means inconceivable, however, that the work was composed somewhere within the regions with which it is associated—Asia and Greece. We must also recognize that, since so much of the original text is lost, it is impossible to be certain about the integrity of the work. It is unlikely to be of earlier date than the middle to late second century.

4. *The Acts of Peter and the Twelve Apostles*

The short Coptic tractate contained in Codex VI of the Nag Hammadi library under the title of *The Acts of Peter and the Twelve Apostles* is, in some ways, the most enigmatic of all of these recently discovered documents. It is, in fact, the only extant copy of a work that hardly fits into the *Actus* genre. Unlike the majority of the documents with which it was found, it does not readily allow a Gnostic interpretation; and, while it is clearly allegorical, it appears to represent a composite work whose explication has not yet found general agreement. Moreover, the text is written sometimes in the third person, and at other times in the first, with Peter himself as the narrator.

The manuscript has sustained some damage in the course of its transmission, particularly in the upper portion of each of its 12 pages. It would appear, however, that the narrative begins with an account of how the Apostles, anxious to commence their appointed ministry, set out together on a missionary voyage to an unknown destination. After sailing for a day and a night, they encounter a storm which drives them to 'a small city which was in the midst of the sea' (Codex VI, p. 1), and they discover that the city is called 'Habitation' (or 'Endurance'). In the city they enquire about lodging, and meet a man whom they mistake for an inhabitant of the city. His description, full of mystic symbolism, is recorded in some detail. He is wearing a linen cloth bound about his waist, and a golden belt about it; and, with unmistakable allusion to the sepulchral linen cloths (cf. Jn 20.7), upon his chest there was tied a napkin extending over his shoulders and covering his head and his hands. Peter takes up the description:

> I was looking at this man, because he was handsome both in form and bearing. There were four parts of his body that I saw: the soles of his feet, a part of his chest, the palms of his hands and his face. There was a book

cover like that of an official in his left hand, and a staff of styrax wood in his right hand. His voice resounded as he spoke slowly, crying aloud in the city: 'Pearls! Pearls!' (*Acts of Peter and the Twelve*, p. 2).

The mysterious pearl-seller attracts no custom from the rich, who look out from their lofty windows and rightly perceive that he has no pearls to sell; and the poor gather round, asking only to look at a pearl, for they have no money to buy. These latter souls are bidden, however, to make the journey to the pearl-seller's own city where they would freely be given of his treasure. At Peter's request, the man discloses his name—Lithargoel—which means (from the Greek) 'the light bright stone'; and he invites the Twelve themselves to make the hazardous journey to the city of 'Nine Gates'. They are warned of the perils they will encounter on their journey, and that whatever of the world they were to carry with them would attract robbers and dangerous wild beasts. With clear reference to the circumstances of the canonical mission of the Twelve, they must travel unencumbered if they are to arrive safely, without even the necessities of food and water, which, presumably, would be provided for them on the way (cf. Mt. 10.5-10). The Apostles abandon everything, and set out on their journey, conversing of heavenly things as they go; and having escaped the robbers, the wolves, the lions and the bulls, they find themselves outside the gate of Lithargoel's city. He himself, now in the guise of a physician carrying a medicine chest and pouch, meets the travellers at the gate. Peter asks the physician, whom he does not recognize, to conduct them to Lithargoel's house. He agrees—but first addresses Peter by name, and thus reveals himself to be, in truth, the Saviour. The passage is couched in language reminiscent of a Resurrection epiphany:

> He said to Peter: 'Peter!' But Peter was startled that he knew that his name was Peter. Peter answered the Saviour: 'Whence do you know me, that you called my name?' Lithargoel answered: 'I wish to ask you: Who gave you this name "Peter"?' He said to him: 'It was Jesus Christ, the son of the living God—he gave this name to me.' He answered and said: 'It is I! Recognise me, Peter!' He loosed the garment which clothed him, and by which he had made himself unknown to us (*Acts of Peter and the Twelve*, p. 9).

The Apostles—now significantly eleven in number—are given the medicine chest and pouch, and bidden to return to the city of 'Habitation', there to teach and to heal those inhabitants who seek to believe, and who must consequently endure the hardships of the faith. When John, speaking for the Eleven, expresses doubts about their medical competence, the Saviour assures them that his power will enable them to perform such physical wonders as would engender faith; and from this faith would flow the healing of the 'sickness of the heart' also (p. 11). The tractate closes with a practical exhortation to the Eleven to avoid associating with the arrogant rich, or in any way to show partiality to them, 'for many have shown partiality to the rich' (p. 12). Here in these closing words we have an indication that the work was written for a community, some of whose members were in danger of compromising with the world—a facet which calls to mind the warning of the writer of the Apocalypse to the church at Laodicea (Rev. 3.14-22).

The composition of the text is obscure. Various indicators suggest that the author-compiler has used at least two different traditions, merging these together to form a continuous narrative. Some exegetes have distinguished between the story of the voyage to the 'enduring' city (Habitation) and that of the journey to the eternal city (Nine Gates), suggesting that these two narratives represent separate traditions crudely woven together. This theory would certainly solve some apparent anomalies;[16] and the fact that both are concerned with apostolic journeys to cities might well account for the association of the two. On the other hand, despite the inconsistent imagery, to separate the stories in this way tends to obviate the most natural exposition of the narrative—that the two cities represent the antithetical kingdoms respectively of the world and of God; and that those who endure faithfully in this present sphere will secure for themselves the joys and treasures of the next. Such an interpretation would give some credence to the view that the story of Habitation and Nine Gates represents a single tradition—and one which accords well with numerous similar themes in the New Testament.

Interlaced into this story is another tradition, according to which the risen Saviour reveals himself to the Eleven. Disguised now as a physician, he loosens the garment that had hidden his identity, and speaks Peter's name. Clearly there are affinities here with the canonical Resurrection appearance stories. In this epiphany, the Eleven meet the risen Lord at the gate of his city, anxious to enter the kingdom and enjoy their rest, and their merited reward. What they are told is that they must return to the world, and continue his work of compassion and healing. The story seeks to explicate that fundamental problem which the delay of the parousia had created. They had been taught, as Peter here reminds the Lord, to 'renounce the world and all that is in it' (p. 10); and they had done so, abandoning all

---

16. For example, the problem of how the Apostles could leave an island city and find themselves being attacked (in the midst of the sea) by lions and wolves!

for his sake—being concerned only for food for each day as it dawned. Yet here they were being asked to remain in the world, and to continue his work among the sick, the poor and the deprived in the world, and being given the power to perform such a task. Often in the Apocryphal writings, especially those of Gnostic orientation, the disciples cannot understand why they are bidden by the Saviour to endure in the world, while at other times they are invited to follow him into his kingdom.[17] Here, in this post-Easter tradition, which has its rationale in the farewell address of Jesus to the disciples (cf. Jn 13.36-37), they are provided with the reason why they must remain:

> Return to the city from which you came, which is called 'Dwell and continue in endurance!', and teach all those who have come to believe in my name that I (too) have endured in hardships of the faith. I myself will give you your reward. To the poor of that city you are to give what they need that they may live, until I give them that which is better... (*Acts of Peter and the Twelve*, p. 10).

We began this section by recognizing the complex nature of this tractate. Now we must acknowledge further that having identified more than one constituent tradition which focus on quite different themes, it is still difficult to discern the joins. It would appear that the two (or more) stories have been laterally intertwined throughout, rather than one story simply appended to the end of the preceding one. If we were to ask why the author-compiler chose to associate these traditions in his work, the answer must be the complementary nature of the themes. The first concerns the antithetical claims of the two kingdoms, emphasizing that the true follower of Christ must shun the one, and take the difficult and hazardous road to the other. The other theme reminds the disciples that while in the world they have work to do to manifest Christ's power, and enlarge his kingdom, they are indeed to follow him—but not yet!

Because the *Acts of Peter and the Twelve Apostles* has no mention in early literature, and exists in only one fourth-century Coptic manuscript, it is quite impossible to be precise about its date and provenance. The only internal clue, perhaps, is that, while there are no direct quotations from the canonical books, there are many allusions to New Testament themes. The illustration of the 'pearl' (of great price) is the most obvious example;[18] but the whole concept of the renunciation of worldly things in order to

---

17. Cf. the *Apocryphon of James*, Codex I, p. 13: Peter replies: 'Sometimes you invite us to enter the kingdom of heaven. But then again you turn us away, O Lord.'

18. Cf. Mt. 13.45-46; Cf. also, the 'white stone' of the Apocalypse (Rev. 2.17).

attain to the heavenly is a constant motif of the Gospels. Another Gospel theme which we have already noticed concerns the advice to travel without encumbrance if they are to proceed in safety. It may be of some significance that the majority of such allusions relate to the Gospels of Luke and John. These, together with the parallels with the Johannine Apocalypse we noted earlier, might indicate an Asian (or western Syrian) origin for the work. The fact that there are no direct canonical quotations, and no hint of ecclesiastical organization, might suggest a fairly early composition; and a date for the work as it stands of about 200 might be proposed.

Chapter 7

THE CHURCH IN EGYPT

The Gospel of the Egyptians
The Gospel of the Hebrews
The Gospel of Mary
The Epistle of the Apostles
The Dialogue of the Saviour

Despite the impressive array of Christian papyrus fragments and codices which have emerged from the sands of Upper Egypt in the past century, there is surprisingly little reliable evidence about the beginnings of Christianity in this region. We cannot even be sure whether the large contingent of domiciled Jews in Alexandria in the first century would help or hinder the establishment of the new faith, or to what extent Christians might have regarded themselves as a sect within Judaism. We have seen that Philo's mention of the Therapeutae was unlikely to have been a reference to Christian ascetics;[1] and the evidence of the Acts concerning the charismatic Apollos proves at most that among the Alexandrian Jews there were those who knew of Jesus (Acts 18.24-28).

The earliest certain witness to Christianity in Egypt must be Clement of Alexandria who cites a work which he apparently knew well as the *Gospel of the Egyptians*.[2] Some form of Christianity must therefore have been established by the mid-second century. Unfortunately, we are largely limited to Clement's quotations for our knowledge of the contents of this so-called Gospel—though both Hippolytus and Origen make reference to the work in their respective heresiologies. Clement also provides quotations from a *Gospel of the Hebrews*, a book which is generally thought to have been written in Greek for the use of the Greek-speaking Jewish-Christians living in Alexandria. Unhappily, as we have already observed, the inconsistent attribution of quotations by Jerome and Epiphanius, as well as by

1. Cf. Eusebius, *HE* 2.17.3-17. See Chapter 1.
2. Clement, *Strom.* 3. Origen also refers to the work in his *First Homily on Luke*.

Clement himself, has led to some confusion; and we must rely on the passages themselves for their identification—a dangerous procedure which can easily lead to circularity of argument! Both of these early works we shall try to examine in this chapter, with the aim of discovering both the nature of the works, and the purpose of their production, as well as how they relate to the canonical Gospels and other writings.

We shall also consider in this chapter three other works which are generally thought to originate from Egypt—the *Gospel of Mary*, the *Epistle of the Apostles* (*Epistula Apostolorum*), and the *Dialogue of the Saviour*. These, in their respective ways, illustrate the tensions between Gnosticism and orthodoxy which were felt as strongly here as anywhere.

1. *The Gospel of the Egyptians*

It is evident from Clement's quotations that the *Gospel of the Egyptians* was a work which would have been especially attractive to encratite Christians. We must not assume, of course, that the entire work emphasized the ascetic ideal. Obviously Clement would be interested to quote only those passages that were pertinent to his argument, and which he wanted to condemn as being false or heretical. His immediate concern in Book 3 of the *Stromata* was the denunciation of those teachings that denigrated marriage and the procreation of children. Twice he refers to a question put to the Lord by Salome:

> When Salome asked, 'How long will death have power?' the Lord answered, 'So long as ye women bear children'—not as if life was something bad and creation evil, but as teaching the sequence of nature (*Stromata* 3.45).

In another passage, Clement again refers to a saying of Jesus in this Gospel which speaks of the destructive power of sexuality which finds its expression in the female. In answer to a question by Salome, the Saviour replies: 'I am come to undo the works of the female.' Clement comments that this Gospel equates 'female' with 'lust'; and clearly his purpose seems to be to temper the force of the encratite argument by showing that while continence may be considered admirable, neither marriage nor the procreation of children can be in opposition to the divine purpose.

Whether Clement had actually seen and handled a copy of the *Gospel of the Egyptians* is, at least, questionable, for he nowhere intimates that he had. Indeed, he prefaces the words of the Lord quoted above with the comment: 'They [the Lord's words] are handed down, *as I believe*, in the Gospel of the Egyptians.'[3] It would be to go beyond the evidence to suggest, as some have done, that this Gospel was used by the Gentile Christians of Egypt—as opposed to a Gospel used by the Jewish-Christians. The fact that Clement refers to the work as a 'Gospel' might certainly imply that it was well known as such; but we have no evidence to show that it took the shape and form of a traditional Gospel, or that it contained narrative elements describing the ministry of Jesus. From the quotations alone, we could be forgiven for assuming that the so-called *Gospel of the Egyptians* was no more than a dialogue between Jesus and Salome.[4]

Hippolytus, like Clement, seems to be familiar with a *Gospel of the Egyptians*, but his interest is merely to assert that it was used by the heretical Gnostic sect called the Naassenes. According to Hippolytus, the Naassenes believed that true human nature, yet to be achieved, was hermaphrodite. Sexual continence alone could achieve that heavenly state where 'there is neither female or male, but a new creature, a new man, which is hermaphrodite'.[5] Whether Clement associated the *Gospel of the Egyptians* with any particular Gnostic group we do not know; but he, too, refers to this same disparagement of women in this Gospel. Again, when Salome enquires when men should be free of the death of the soul, the Lord is said to have replied: 'When you have trampled on the garment of shame and when the two become one and the male with the female is neither male nor female.' It should be noticed that the *Gospel of Thomas* records a number of similar Logia in which both Mariham (Mary Magdalene) and Salome are prominent; and the androgenic ideal is clearly expressed by the author of that important work:

> Jesus said: When you make the two one, and when you make the inside as the outside, and the outside as the inside, and the upper as the lower, and when you make the male and female into a single one, and a hand in place of a hand, and a foot in place of a foot, an image in place of an image, then shall you enter the kingdom (*Gos. Thom.* 22).

These parallels[6]—of the female becoming male, or of both becoming something other than either—pose the question whether there are textual

---

3.   The emphasis is mine.

4.   Whether this Salome was the mother of the sons of Zebedee, the (step-)sister of Jesus himself, or one who went to the Sepulchre with the other women, is unclear. She appears quite frequently in Apocryphal tradition.

5.   Hippolytus, *Refutations* 5.2.

6.   The *Second Epistle of Clement to the Corinthians* also has this same quotation (*2 Clem.* 12.1).

links between the several works, one borrowing from another, or whether the saying was part of the oral stock of Dominical sayings. What seems quite certain is that among the more ascetic of Christian groups, both in Egypt and in eastern Syria, the belief was prevalent that human beings advance towards their ultimate spiritual goal only as they renounce those fleshly appetites that accrue from the sexual differences separating men and women. It may be that, in addition to this general encratite ideal, some communities refused to countenance women in their midst on the grounds that only the male was capable of true spirituality; and something of that idea may be read into the most hotly debated of all Thomas's Logia, in which Simon Peter is first made to exclaim:

> Let Mariham go out from among us, for women are not worthy of the life. Jesus said: Look, I will lead her that I may make her male, in order that she too may become a living spirit resembling you males. For every woman who makes herself male will enter the kingdom of heaven (*Gos. Thom.* 114).

It may be that the sentiment expressed in all these passages should be seen against the background of that general trend of thought running through much of the Gnostic literature of the period which rejects the natural and the material in favour of a complete reversal of values. What is 'above' must become the 'below',[7] and what is on the 'left' has to be made the 'right'.[8] Thus, within the Gnostic system of 'syzygies' (opposing partners), woman becomes the left-hand (negative) partner to the male 'right'; and until they become one (or all take on 'maleness') sin and death and decay must prevail. We will encounter this attitude towards women in another work we shall consider later in this present chapter, the *Gospel of Mary*.

It would seem unlikely that the so-called *Gospel of the Egyptians* was, in its original form, anything more than some form of dialogue between the Lord and some of his disciples. It may, indeed, have existed simply as a set of Logia, like the Gospels of Thomas or of Philip. The few fragmentary quotations provide little information about who composed the work, and for whom. Its title—'according to the Egyptians'—might indicate that it was written for and by Gentile Egyptians within Egypt; it might, just as easily, have been appended to the work from outside the region by Christians for whom its teaching was abhorrent. That it served an encratite sect within Egypt whose teachings were markedly different from those of the mainstream Alexandrian Church seems to be incontrovertible. It must be assumed that it was written during the first half of the second century.

7.   *Acts of Peter* 38.
8.   *Acts of Philip* 140.

2. *The Gospel of the Hebrews*

Like the *Gospel of the Egyptians*, and the 'lost Gospels' examined in Chapter 3, the *Gospel of the Hebrews* survives only in the quotations predominantly of Clement, Origen and Jerome. The testimony of Eusebius makes it clear that Hegesippus knew this Gospel, and made extracts from it.[9] The indication, then, is that it was a work of some substance, and of early composition. The use of the word 'Hebrews' in the title strongly suggests that the work was composed for the use of Greek-speaking Jewish-Christians domiciled outside Palestine; and because its citations derive chiefly from Alexandrian writers, the assumption is that its earliest area of circulation was Egypt. It is important to recognize, however, that there is no definitive evidence to show that the book was composed by and for Egyptian Christians.

The confusion concerning the attribution of quotations mentioned above adds to the difficulties of determining the content and extent of the Gospel. Furthermore, as with the Egyptian Gospel discussed in the previous section, we must not make the mistake of presuming the character of the whole from that of the part. The passages quoted by the patristic writers might not be representative of the work as a whole, chosen simply because of their divergence from the Matthaean norm. Since we have only these few short citations, however, we must make what we can of these. There is general agreement that some seven quotations are from the *Gospel of the Hebrews*—though at least two of these present some ambiguity. Jerome, in particular, seems not to distinguish between the *Gospel of the Hebrews* and the *Gospel of the Nazaraeans*; and it may well be the case that he himself was confused, referring at times to the 'Gospel according to the Hebrews which the Nazaraeans use', and once to the 'Gospel written in Hebrew and which the Nazaraeans read', when the quotation appears to come from the Greek Gospel. In short, we will be wise to be cautious about Jerome's attestations, relying rather more than is usual on the text itself.

There is hardly less certainty about one of Clement's citations. In the *Stromata* he makes the following assertion:

> As it is also written in the Gospel of the Hebrews, 'He who wonders shall reign, and he who reigns shall rest' (*Strom.* 2.9).

---

9.   Eusebius, *HE* 4.22.8. Eusebius elsewhere lists the work among the spurious writings (*HE* 3.25.5).

This represents what is sometimes referred to as a 'chain' saying, and is more fully quoted by Clement in a later book of the *Stromata*, this time without stating his source:

> He who seeks will not rest until he finds, and when he finds he will wonder, and wondering he shall reign, and reigning he shall rest (*Strom.* 5.14).

This 'chain' saying turns up again, however, as Logion 2 in the Nag Hammadi *Gospel of Thomas*, and even more exactly in the Oxyrhynchus fragment of this Gospel. It may be that the saying which describes the progression that leads to salvation was familiar in Gnostic circles, especially in those regions influenced by the Alexandrian *Hermetica*;[10] for such a progression of seeking and marvelling and finding salvation in oneness with God is a fundamental concept of the *Corpus Hermeticum*:

> Tis from Thy Aeon I have found praise-giving; and in thy Will, the object of my search, have I found rest (*Corpus Hermeticum* 13.20).

The idea of seeking and finding rest in the truth which Christ reveals is, of course, an important New Testament theme, bound up with Jesus' unique relationship with his heavenly Father. Ultimate truth is hidden from the 'wise and understanding'; but those who learn from him who is at one with the Father 'will find rest' (Mt. 11.25-30). It is interesting to note that in the Nag Hammadi document known as the *Treatise on Resurrection*, the anonymous author, writing to his pupil Rheginos, contrasts the wisdom of worldly learning with the *rest* that is available to those who seek heavenly truth in Christ:

> Some there are, my son Rheginos, who want to learn many things. They have this goal when they are occupied with questions whose answer is lacking. If they succeed with these, they usually think very highly of themselves. But I do not think that they have stood within the Word of Truth. They seek rather their own rest, which we have received through our Saviour, our Lord Christ. We received it when we came to know the truth and rested ourselves upon it (*Treatise on Resurrection* 44).

In many of the second-century writings the notion of 'rest' has to be understood not only as the ultimate goal of the seeker after truth, the end of the chain, as it were, which leads to salvation;[11] it also possesses a mystical connotation, descriptive of that unity of wisdom and love which

10. Refer to Chapter 1 for a brief explanation of the *Hermetica*.
11. The concept of 'rest' as the final human spiritual goal is found quite frequently in the Pseudo-Clementine literature.

lies at the heart of the Godhead. It is in this sense that another significant quotation from the *Gospel of the Hebrews* must surely be understood. In his *Commentary on Isaiah*, Jerome makes mention of the 'resting' of the Holy Spirit on Jesus at his Baptism, referring to a passage which he claims to have found in 'the Gospel written in the Hebrew speech, which the Nazaraeans read':[12]

> Further in the Gospel which we have just mentioned we find the following written: And it came to pass when the Lord was come up out of the water, the whole fount of the Holy Spirit descended upon him and said to him: My Son, in all the prophets was I waiting for thee that thou shouldest come and I might rest in thee. For thou art my rest; thou art my first-begotten Son that reignest for ever (Jerome, *Commentary on Isaiah* 4).

The importance of this passage lies in the christological insights it affords. In one sense it might be taken to imply the pre-existence of the Son, rather than his adoption at the moment of his baptism. From the beginning of time ('in all the prophets') the Father had awaited this eschatological moment of union and rest with his pre-existent Son.[13] The Nag Hammadi *Sophia of Jesus Christ*, an early Christian adaptation of the Gnostic *Letter of Eugnostos*, speaks of 'unity and rest' as the first principle of the Godhead; and it is this concept of unity within the Godhead that underlies this pericope from the *Gospel of the Hebrews*. We should recognize, however, that the concept is not wholly incompatible with an Adoptionist interpretation of the passage, and one, moreover, which is in accord both with Luke's account of the baptism and with the prophecy of Isaiah (cf. Lk. 3.22; Isa. 11.2). As the Holy Spirit descends upon the chosen and anointed one, so the Spirit finds that rest which thus far, for all ages, had eluded him; and (if we might finish Isaiah's prophecy), to this root of Jesse, which shall stand for an ensign of the people, shall all the Gentiles seek, and 'his *rest* shall be glorious' (Isa. 11.10). The baptism of Jesus, and the proclamation of his divine Sonship, represents both the culmination of the long human search for rest in God, and, at the same time, the consummation of God's ceaseless yearning from the beginning of time to enfold his beloved creation within himself.

If these foregoing excerpts from the *Gospel of the Hebrews* illustrate the Gnostic influence on the work, others are more orientated towards the

12. The general consensus of opinion is that Jerome means here (and elsewhere) the *Gospel of the Hebrews*, not the *Gospel of the Nazaraeans*, and that he was mistaken about both its language and its readership.
13. Cf. Clementine, *Homilies* 3.20.

Palestinian and Jewish tradition. One in particular seems to want to raise the profile of James of Jerusalem above that of his fellow Apostles. Once again, it is Jerome who relates the episode:

> When the Lord had given the linen cloth to the servant of the priest, he went to James and appeared to him. For James had sworn that he would not eat bread from that hour in which he had drunk the cup of the Lord until he should see him risen from among them that sleep. And shortly thereafter the Lord said: Bring a table and bread! And immediately it is added: he took the bread, blessed it and brake it and gave it to James the Just and said to him: My brother, eat thy bread, for the Son of man is risen from among them that sleep (*Gospel of the Hebrews*, in Jerome, *de viris inlustribus* 2).

The giving of 'the linen cloth to the servant of the priest' is redolent of the Resurrection itself; and it will be observed that this account of the events seems to imply that it was James, rather than Peter or Mary, who first witnessed the Lord's risen form. This manifestly contradicts the New Testament evidence, though the story may be seen as an extension to the tradition recorded by Paul that Jesus appeared to James, and 'then to all the apostles' (1 Cor. 15.7).[14] While it is true that the linen cloth represents clear proof of the suffering and death of Jesus, and his physical presence in the grave, to suggest that this is a deliberately and polemically anti-Docetic is to overstate the case. We may say, however, that if this Gospel-like narrative does in fact originate from the *Gospel of the Hebrews*, despite the Gnostic overtones of other quotations from this Gospel, it serves to demonstrate the non-Docetic character of the work, as well as its Jewish-Christian orientation.

The other interesting issue raised by this passage is its use of the Last Supper tradition. Again, it would be to go too far to suggest that the purpose of the account is to show James's participation in that unique and sacred meal; but the account does emphasize the central position of James *from the beginning* within the Lord's inner circle of disciples. The pretext for this claim is, of course, James's vow of abstinence. The implication is that, at some point prior to the death of Jesus, James had shared, as others had done, in 'the cup of the Lord'.

We may speculate that the *Gospel of the Hebrews* began with an account of the baptism of Jesus—though some have identified a mythical story of the Incarnation in a work by Cyril of Jerusalem as deriving from this Gospel. A strange version of the temptation follows, in which Jesus himself

---

14. This appearance, of course, was by no means the first; already 'five hundred brethren at one time' had seen the risen Lord.

speaks of how the Holy Spirit (whom he calls his mother[15]) had lifted him by one of his hairs onto Mount Tabor—there, no doubt, to survey 'all the kingdoms of the world and the glory of them' (Mt. 4.8; cf. Ezek. 8.3). There is just a hint of the teaching ministry of Jesus in two brief quotations from Jerome in which the Lord exhorts the disciples to brotherly love; and the evidence of the quotation concerning the Resurrection appearance to James indicates that the Gospel ended in the traditional manner. From the small amount of extant material available to us, however, it is impossible to estimate precisely in what ways this Gospel differed from the Matthaean Gospel; but the influence of Alexandrian Gnosis, the Hermetic writings, and the Jewish Wisdom literature are much in evidence. The work was probably composed during the early decades of the second century.

3. *The Gospel of Mary*

The *Gospel of Mary* is the first of a group of three Dialogue-type texts which first came to light at the end of the nineteenth century with the purchase in Cairo of a fifth-century Coptic codex.[16] Copies of two of these books—the *Apocryphon of John* and the *Sophia of Jesus Christ*—were also subsequently found at Nag Hammadi.[17] Fragments of a Greek version (the original language) of the *Gospel of Mary* have more recently been discovered at Oxyrhynchus, and these Greek papyri have assisted in the task of uncovering the original text. Unfortunately, much of the Coptic manuscript is missing. Only eight of the original eighteen pages are extant, the first six pages and four pages in the middle being lost entirely.

The work as we have it begins with a Gnostic discourse between the Saviour and Peter on the nature of matter, and the origin of passion and sin. Mary Magdalene has no part in this discourse, a fact which might conceivably suggest that the section comes from a separate source from the rest of the work. It is quite possible, of course, that Mary figured in the missing earlier section, but there is no hint that this might have been the case. The discourse ends with a series of aphorisms addressed to all

15. The Lord is designated 'the son of the Holy Spirit' in the *Apocryphon of James* (p. 6).

16. Codex Papyrus Berolinensis 8502. These texts were not actually published until after the discovery of the Nag Hammadi documents.

17. Because the *Apocryphon of John* and the *Sophia of Jesus Christ* are basically Gnostic works, 'Christianized' by the addition of a few Gospel allusions and the inclusion of the names of Apostles, they fall outside the scope of this book.

the disciples which are manifestly from the canonical Gospels, culminating in the command to preach the Gospel, without initiating further legalistic restrictions:

> When the Blessed One had said this, he saluted them all saying: 'Peace be unto you. Receive you my peace. Beware that no one lead you astray with the words: "See here!" or "See there!" For the Son of man is within you. Follow after Him! Those who seek him shall find him. Go then and preach the Gospel of the kingdom. I have issued no command save that which I appointed you. Nor have I given any law like the lawgiver, that ye may not be constrained thereby.' When he had said this, he went his way (*Gospel of Mary*, p. 8).[18]

In the second section, Mary plays the dominant role. The disciples are anxious and aggrieved that they have been bidden to undertake so dangerous a mission—to go to the Gentiles and preach the kingdom. Interestingly, it is the *Gentiles* who are blamed for the persecution of Christ; and the disciples fear the same fate as befell him. It falls to Mary, now, to reassure them of the Lord's protection, and to encourage them in the task. They turn to her as the one whom the Saviour loved 'more than the rest of women', asking her to pass on to them the teachings which he had secretly vouchsafed to her. Mary begins by recounting the circumstances of her vision in which the secret revelations were made. Tantalizingly, at this point in the manuscript, four pages are missing. What follows—presumably the closing words of Mary's testimony—is a wholly Gnostic exposition of the soul's upward journey through the inquisitorial powers of darkness and ignorance that seek to control its rise to the kingdom.

The final section relates Mary's confrontation with the Apostles, some at least of whom resent her privileged position in the Lord's favour, and doubt her testimony:

> When Mary had said this, she was silent, since the Saviour had spoken with her up to this point. Andrew answered and said to the brethren: 'Tell me, what think ye with regard to what she says? I at least do not believe that the saviour said this. For certainly these doctrines have other meanings.' Peter in answer spoke with reference to things of this kind, and asked them about the Saviour: 'Did he then speak privily with a woman rather than with us, and not openly? Shall we turn about and all hearken to her? Has he preferred her over against us?' (*Gospel of Mary*, p. 17).

'Hot-tempered' Peter is rebuked by Levi, who comes to Mary's aid. 'You are treating her as if she were one of our enemies', he remonstrates. 'If the

---

18. Page refs. are from the Codex Papyrus Berolineusis 8502.

Saviour made her worthy, who are you to reject her?' (p. 18). The book ends with a united resolve to 'separate as he commanded' and to preach the Gospel, once again affirming the Saviour's warning that they were not to lay down any other rule or law beyond what he had given.

It has been generally recognized that we have here a complex text owing its origin to both Gnostic and Christian sources. The question that has so far found no definitive solution, however, concerns the nature of the composition. Does the book, like so many others among the Christian-Gnostic works, represent a 'Christianizing' of an older Gnostic writing, or is it rather a Gnostic revision of early Christian traditional material? It will be observed that the same fundamental questions apply to other works considered in this chapter. Such questions are by no means as easy to resolve as they might appear. For one thing, it is rarely obvious whether the Gnostic content in any given work postdates or predates the Christian framework; for another, it is not always apparent whether the Gnostic material has been accommodated to Christianity, or whether it represents a movement away from and beyond Christianity. What would seem to be of primary importance is first to consider how the specifically Christian material fits into the whole, and then to ask whether the narrative framework might once have stood as an independent tradition. If we apply these fundamental questions to the first discourse section of the *Gospel of Mary*, we find that the Gnostic author has employed familiar Gospel aphorisms to punctuate his material so as to provide a Christian setting to his work. Gnostic pronouncements are several times concluded with a familiar Dominical comment:

> The Saviour said: All nature, all formations, all creatures exist in one and with one another, and they will be resolved again into their own roots. For the nature of matter is resolved into the roots of its own nature alone. He who has ears to hear, let him hear (*Gospel of Mary*, p. 7).

It does not appear to be the case, however, that the author is adding Christian sayings to an already existing Gnostic text. Rather, the whole discourse seems to be an integral composition, the author obviously wanting to provide Christian authentication for his Gnostic thoughts by including the words of Jesus; and to be on the safe side he concludes with a string of well-known, though quite unrelated, sayings.

The second (and wholly Gnostic) discourse, which purports to represent the Saviour's secret instructions to Mary, is entirely different in character. Here there are no punctuating aphorisms. The whole passage has clearly been inserted into a Christian narrative tradition in order to make its teaching appear to come directly from the risen Christ. In Gnostic-Christian literature, Mary Magdalene is frequently portrayed as the revealer of truth;[19] and here, in contrast to her male companions, slow in understanding as they had been in Gospel tradition, she makes known to the Apostles the truth concerning the Saviour, and about the destiny that awaits the true believer. It is important to notice that the narrative could stand on its own —and, doubtless, once did; and we should recognize, too, that it is more firmly embedded in canonical tradition than at first might be imagined. The Apostles, daunted and dismayed at the task they have been given, are especially worried about the inclusive nature of the mission. They are to go to the *Gentiles*, a task which they obviously feel to be not only dangerous, but wholly inappropriate. Twice they are told that legalistic restrictions must not hinder their universal mission. Once before, in a pivotal and salutary waking dream at Joppa, Peter had made the mistake of rejecting what God had pronounced clean (Acts 10.14). Now, in this story of Peter's angry disapproval of Mary, he is reproached by Levi for his presumption in the face of the Lord's patent approval of her: 'If the Saviour hath made her worthy, who then art thou, that thou reject her?' (p. 18). The first readers of this Gospel would clearly understand that just as Peter's earlier conservatism at Joppa had threatened to jeopardize Christ's plan of universal salvation, so his present angry refusal to countenance Mary's (Gnostic) insight into the true teaching of the Saviour might, unchecked, cost the Church and her mission dearly.

Was it sheer jealousy that was responsible for Peter's truculence? Did it issue, rather, from a deep-seated conviction about the natural inferiority of women? We could well imagine that both of these sentiments played some part in the altercation. Modern feminism might justly want to emphasize the age-old prejudice of the male against his female counterpart. In a passage of the *Pistis Sophia*, Peter objects to the Lord that Mary is dominating the conversation to the exclusion of those who are naturally fitted to speak; and, despite Paul's dictum that in Christ there is neither male nor female, his derogation and disapproval of women, whom he considered to have been created for the sake of men, and who should not be permitted to speak in the Assembly, is well known (1 Cor. 11.9; 1 Tim. 2.12). Yet we need to reckon with the historical fact that such prejudice was engendered at least as much from theological considerations as from sociological ones.

19.   In the *Dialogue of the Saviour*, for instance, Mary is said to be the one who 'knows the all' (Codex III, p. 139). See also the *Gospel of Philip*, where it is stated that 'the Saviour loved Mary Magdalene more than all the disciples' (*Gos. Phil.* 55).

Apart from any personal elements in the quarrel, Peter is here merely reflecting the contemporary orthodox recognition, which many (though not all) Gnostics challenged, of the divinely ordained hierarchy which made women secondary and inferior to men. Encratite Christianity, of course, would go further, pointing to the corruptive and destructive influence of women as the paramount obstacle to be overcome in man's quest for his spiritual return to God. We must notice, however, that notwithstanding the modern distaste for such outdated doctrines, Mary herself, in some sense, recognized that only in 'maleness' could she discern the truths revealed to her: 'Let us praise his greatness', she says to the Apostles, 'for He has made us ready, and made us to be Men'! (p. 9).

It is sometimes asserted that Peter and Andrew are, in this Gospel, representatives of western (Roman) orthodoxy, implacably opposed to the Gnostic claims to be in possession of esoteric truth denied to Christ's appointed Apostles. The pointed references to Peter's difficulties with the *Gentile* mission, however, and the implication that the Apostles might wish to erect even more barriers against Gentile inclusion, would rather more suggest an alignment with Jerusalem than with Rome. The message of the Gospel would then seem to be that if Peter's narrow Judaic conservatism could hinder Christ's universal mission, how could he be expected to appreciate that eternal truth might be entrusted to others than the circumcized—even to Gnostics and women! While it is impossible from the text to assign the work to a particular region, it seems more than likely that the *Gospel of Mary* orientates to Alexandria, where a Jewish-Christian 'orthodoxy' would inevitably join battle with Gnostic ideology. A relatively early date might be envisaged, and certainly no later than the middle of the second century.

4. *The Epistle of the Apostles*

If the *Gospel of Mary* displays hints of the tension between Jewish, Hellenized and Gnosticized forms of early Christianity in Egypt, the *Epistle of the Apostles*—usually known as the *Epistula Apostolorum*—is representative of that syncretic movement within the Alexandrian Church which permitted an accommodation of all three. The work is fundamentally anti-Gnostic, if not polemically so; yet it contains concepts which clearly derive from Gnosticism, a fact which should not surprise us in view of the early influence of Valentinus on Hellenized Egyptian Christianity. The title of the book, derived from its opening lines, establishes the purported nature of the work: it claims to be a letter from the Apostles to the worldwide Church containing the true teaching of Christ, relayed specifically to counter the false and impious teachings of Simon (Magus) and Cerinthus. In an earlier chapter we observed the antithetical relationship between this document and the *Apocryphon of James*. No doubt both books originate from the same period—though not necessarily from the same place. We shall see that there is much in the form, style and content of this present work to suggest an Egyptian provenance; but the influence of both Simon and Cerinthus seems to have been ubiquitous, with links to Palestinian Christianity as well as with the churches of Asia. The *Epistula Apostolorum* has come down to us largely in two versions, the Coptic and the Ethiopic. This latter version begins with a résumé of Jesus' holy birth and ministry (chs. 1–6), not included in the Coptic, and is often the more expansive of the two versions. Which text might be nearer to a probable Greek original is uncertain.

The Ethiopic version's introductory section lays great emphasis on the fleshly appearing of the Son of God 'through the holy virgin Mary' (3). It will be recalled that in an earlier chapter we considered the distinctive teaching of Cerinthus. It is this teaching that the author of this present work wants above all to repudiate, repeatedly drawing attention to the essential commixture of the divine and human nature of Christ, and the reality of his suffering, death and resurrection. The first indication of the unique character of Jesus finds expression in the story of the holy child's schooling, a tradition which, as we have seen, occurs elsewhere:

> This is what our Lord Jesus Christ did, who was delivered by Joseph and Mary his mother to where he might learn letters. And he who taught him said to him as he taught him, 'Say Alpha.' He answered and said to him, 'First you tell me what Beta is.' And truly it was a real thing which was done (*Epistula Apostolorum* 4; cf. the *Infancy Gospel of Thomas* 6.3).

Several of the Gospel miracles are selected by the author of the Ethiopic résumé to illustrate the heavenly qualities of the God-man Jesus: the wedding at Cana of Galilee, the woman with the haemorrhage, the man possessed by demons, the coin and fish, the feeding of the multitude. In this last miracle we may discern the Alexandrian propensity for scriptural analogy, for the author draws out his own interpretation of this wonder as 'a picture of our faith concerning the great Christianity' (5). Whether this first section of the Ethiopic text appeared in the original Greek work is problematical, for the Coptic version (probably the earlier) begins simply with the statement that Simon and Cerinthus are enemies of Christ, and then proceeds with a testimony of Christ's crucifixion at the hands of

Pilate and Archelaus, how that Jesus the Saviour was crucified between the two thieves, and buried in a place called the place of the skull.

The Resurrection account is particularly noteworthy, because it conflates a number of Gospel traditions. It begins (with minor variations in the two versions) with the women mourning and weeping at the tomb.[20] There follows the strange story of how Martha and Mary, in turn, tried vainly to convince the Apostles that the Lord had risen, and how, in the end, the risen Lord needed to show himself alive to them. The story is an embellishment of the command to Mary to acquaint the Eleven with the news of the Resurrection, drawn out in this account to emphasize the initial disbelief of the Apostles, and how their subsequent conviction was based on solid and tangible evidence. 'What have we to do with you, O woman?' they said to Mary. 'He who has died is buried, and could it be possible for him to live?' Even the risen Lord's presence among them could not entirely convince them that he was not a ghost, until they had seen and touched the visible evidence of his suffering:

> Put your finger, Peter, in the nailprints of my hands; and you, Thomas, put your finger in the spear-wounds of my side; but you, Andrew, look at my feet and see if they do not touch the ground. For it is written in the prophet, 'The foot of a ghost or a demon does not join to the ground' (*Epistula Apostolorum* 11).

We may contrast this anxiety to demonstrate the corporeality of Jesus, even in his risen state, with the recollection of John in the *Acts of John*, as he describes for his audience his own experience of being with the Lord. He explains that sometimes when he reached out to touch Jesus he experienced a solid, material body, but at other times it felt as though he did not exist at all; and John goes on to confess that he would often look to see whether Jesus was leaving footprints on the ground, or whether his feet were raised, in fact, above it.[21] Clearly, the author of the *Epistula Apostolorum* wants to emphasize both that Christ's earthly state was fleshly and real, that in truth he died and was buried, but also that in his resurrected appearance he was no phantom or figment of the imagination. In all of this, the author displays his solidly orthodox Christology.

Now Jesus begins to reveal to the Apostles the manner of his coming in the flesh, how that during his earthly life he was both here with them on earth and also with the Father in heaven; and how they were to remember

20. The phrase 'mourning and weeping' occurs only in the spurious ending of Mark's Gospel (Mk 16.10).
21. Cf. *Acts of John* 93.

his death, until his return in power. He speaks to them of their redemption, and of the resurrection of their flesh at the last day. Much of the central section of the work is concerned with answering the problem of how, and in what manner, those who are saved will enjoy their 'rest' in the kingdom. Here there is no equivocation:

> He said to us, 'What is it then that passes away? Is it the flesh or the spirit?' We said to him, 'The flesh is perishable.' Then he said to us, 'What has fallen will arise, and what is lost will be found and what is weak will recover, that in what is thus done may be revealed the glory of my Father. As he has done to me, so will I do to all of you who believe. Truly I say to you, the flesh will rise alive with the soul, that they may confess and be judged with the work which they have done, whether it is good or bad' (*Epistula Apostolorum* 25).

It should be noted that the author of the *Epistula Apostolorum* entertains not even the slightest doubt concerning the vexed question of the resurrection of the flesh for those who truly believe. Pauline thought on this important matter is capable of a variety of interpretations; and some have suggested that the Apostle actually had a change of mind on the subject, his Jewish ideas gradually tempered by Greek concepts of the immortality of the soul.[22] Others have supposed an adaptation by Paul of the Gnostic notion of casting off the garment of the flesh in order to enable the divine self to rise to its destined and eternal rest. Even the Gnostic *Gospel of Philip* in one passage recognizes the complexities of the issues, asserting that neither the flesh alone, nor the spirit alone, can rise.[23] The teaching of the *Epistula Apostolorum*, strangely enough, is not too far removed, emphasizing, as it does, the inseparability of soul and body. All will rise together: 'He [the Lord] answered us, saying, "Truly I say to you, the resurrection of the flesh will happen while the soul and the spirit are in it"' (*Epistula Apostolorum* 24).

The passage which follows concerns the coming judgment, with a reiteration of the traditional Judaeo-Christian belief in the end-moment of history, when each will reap his due reward. Such a belief has no place, of course, in the realized eschatology of the Gnostics. The *Gospel of Thomas* records that when Jesus was asked when the new world would come, he replied, 'What you await has come, but you do not know it'.[24] Here, in the *Epistula Apostolorum*, the souls of the underworld are not forgotten, as

22. Cf. 1 Cor. 15.12; 2 Cor. 5.1; Rom. 6.4.
23. Cf. *Gos. Phil.* 23.
24. *Gos. Thom.* 51.

Jesus relates how he has preached in the 'place of Lazarus' to enable the righteous below to share in that day which will surely come. In language which would be well understood by his Gnostic opponents, Christ assures his elect and righteous ones, and those after them who through their preaching will believe in him, that as the judgment comes they will be protected from all that would harm them:

> You, the children of life [the Ethiopic has 'light'], I have redeemed from all evil and from the power of the archons, and all who through you will believe in me. For what I have promised you I will also give to them, that they may come out of the prison and the chains of the archons and the powerful fire (*Epistula Apostolorum* 28).

The discourse now takes up the theme of the mission of the Apostles. They are to 'preach to the twelve tribes, and also to the Gentiles and to the whole land of Israel from sunrise to sunset and from South to North' (30). The story of Saul's conversion is now introduced as an endorsement of the universality of their task; and the urgency of their common mission is set against the background of the signs of the coming judgment. The book ends with a warning that, before the judgment comes, false teachers will arise (an implicit reference to Simon and Cerinthus) who will produce worthless teaching, turning away many of the faithful who formerly had kept the commandment and believed in him:

> Woe to those who use my word and my commandment for a pretext, and also to those who listen to them and to those who turn away from the life of the teaching, they will be eternally punished with them (*Epistula Apostolorum* 50).

The book has numerous allusions to, and direct excerpts from, the Gospels and Acts, as well as from several of the canonical Epistles. Clearly the composition could not have been earlier than the second century. On the other hand, the date of the parousia is explicit and precise (17); and this would tend to indicate that the work was in circulation earlier, rather than later, in the second century. It is interesting that the two versions do not quite agree. The Coptic text states that the parousia will happen after 120 years, while the (probably later) Ethiopic version has 150 years—an understandable revision as the delay becomes more apparent with the passage of time. We might also note that both versions speak of the *Father*'s return (not the *Son*'s), explaining that the Father and the Son are one: 'I am wholly in the Father and the Father in me' (Jn 10.38). Undoubtedly the book was intended to strengthen the traditional faith of its readership, and to warn those who sought to pervert or undermine it of the dire consequences of their action. Its Christology is essentially Johannine, with a strong emphasis on the Word becoming flesh, and the corporeality of the risen Lord: 'We have heard and felt him after he had risen from the dead' (*Epistula Apostolorum* 2; cf. Jn 1.14; 1 Jn 1.1). It is more than likely, in view of its avowed purpose, that the book was composed in Egypt, primarily for Egyptian Christians. It may well have enjoyed a much wider circulation in Ephesus and in Rome, however, where Simonian and Cerinthian doctrines were in vogue until at least the end of the second century.

5. *The Dialogue of the Saviour*

The short Nag Hammadi tractate entitled the *Dialogue of the Saviour* might be said to be equally at home in a Mesopotamian setting, as in an Egyptian, for it has much in common with the Thomasine writings, and in particular, as we shall see, with the *Book of Thomas the Contender*. There are, however, sufficiently cogent reasons for considering the work in this final section of our survey. The book, as its title declares, is of the Dialogue genre, in which the disciples ask questions of the risen Lord, and receive his revelatory answers. This 'question and answer' type of dialogue —sometimes labelled *erotarokrisis*—with its literary roots, perhaps, in the dialogues of ancient Greece—has greater affinities with Alexandria than with Edessa, or even Antioch. In company with other works considered in this present section—the *Gospel of the Egyptians*, the *Gospel of Mary* and the *Epistula Apostolorum*—this tractate may confidently be assigned to Egyptian origin. The *Sophia of Jesus Christ*, not included here because it is essentially a Christianized Gnostic tractate, is of the same genre. We might also note that yet another text from Nag Hammadi, this time the wholly Gnostic work entitled *Zostrianus*, reveals the same preoccupation with the concepts of *light* and *darkness* as does our present text, a feature shared by both the Johannine and Hermetic literature of this region. So far as the apparent kinship between the *Dialogue of the Saviour* and the Thomasine tradition is concerned, it will be recalled that in Chapter 5 it was suggested that part of the *Book of Thomas the Contender*, or even its final compilation, may well derive from Egypt.

   The book begins with a discourse by the risen Christ to the Twelve, and Mary Magdalene, who features prominently in the text, along with Matthew and Judas.[25] The Saviour is about to depart; and for them, too, the time is

---

25. Note that the double name of Thomasine tradition (Judas-Thomas) is not used in this book.

fast approaching: 'The Saviour said to his disciples, "The time has already come, brothers, for us to leave behind our labour and to abide at rest. For whoever abides at rest will rest for ever"' (*Dialogue*, Codex III, p. 120). It is clear, then, that the book is set in the end time; but the disciples are not yet ready to follow him into rest. With phrases redolent of the farewell address of John's Gospel (ch. 14), the Saviour assures the disciples that because they have known the Father and believed in the truth, their place in the realm of tranquillity is assured. Later in the subsequent dialogue, when Matthew asks when they would follow him, the Lord replies, 'When you lay down these burdens…when you abandon the works which will not be able to follow you, then you will rest' (p. 141).

The Saviour then proceeds to instruct the disciples about how they are to avoid the powers of darkness which will seek to impede their crossing from this present world to the heavenly sphere, at the time of the dissolution. This section of the manuscript has not survived without considerable damage, and there are many lacunae in the text. The general theme, however, is clear, and typical of many of the Christian-Gnostic writings. The disciples are not to fear their upward journey, for they have *within themselves* the teachings which the Lord has given them. The power of the archons is considerable, but not insurmountable. As long as they 'know the things within them', they will make the crossing in safety. The disciples begin, now, to question the Lord about the nature of mind and spirit; and his reply, replete with concepts of light and darkness reminiscent of passages in Matthew's Gospel (cf., e.g., Mt. 6.22), prompts Judas to enquire about cosmological matters:

> 'Tell us, Lord, what existed before heaven and earth came into being.' The Lord said, 'There was darkness and water and spirit upon water. And I say to you…that which you seek and inquire after, behold it is within you…' (*Dialogue*, p. 127).

There follows an exposition of the creation myth, based on the story of Genesis, the Word of the Father being sent forth to establish and order all things on the earth, yet standing outside as a great light ruling over all; and 'when Judas heard these things, he bowed down and he worshipped and he offered praise to the Lord'. When Matthew asks to see this place where exists only pure light, and no wickedness at all, he is told that as long as he is 'wearing flesh' he will not be able to see it—a motif which we have encountered in more than one other of the Gnostic documents. Judas now returns to the cosmic theme to ask about the movement of the earth, and of its foundations, to which the Lord responds by affirming the sustaining power of the Word, illustrating his explanation by picking up a stone, and holding it in his hand. He goes on to warn, however, that ultimate reality can be understood only from its roots. The soul must search within, to know and understand. 'To him who will not know the root of all things, they remain hidden. He who will not know the root of evil is no stranger to it.' In the same way, no one can know the Father who has not known the Son.

After Judas, Matthew and Mary have been taken to the 'boundary of heaven and earth', and given a partial vision of things that are yet to come, they pose a series of eschatological questions which are given stock Gnostic answers. Several of the questions closely mirror those of the *Epistle of Peter to Philip*: What is the fulness and what is the deficiency?; How have I come to this place?; In what way can we fight the archons? The Lord's replies, in turn, reflect those of other 'catechetical' documents of early Gnostic Christianity. We might instance the question of Judas and Matthew concerning the garment of the soul in the life which is to come:

> 'We wish to understand the sort of garments in which we shall be clothed when we leave the corruption of the flesh.' The Lord said, 'The archons and the governors possess garments which have been given them for a time and which do not last. But you, as children of truth, are not to clothe yourselves with these transient garments. Rather, I tell you that you will become blessed when you strip yourselves!' (*Dialogue*, p. 143).

Although the *Dialogue of the Saviour* could not be described as a thoroughly encratite work, there are occasional pericopes which indicate that its author (or redactor) was at least sympathetic to encratite teaching. Judas asks an innocent question about prayer: 'When we pray, how shall we pray?' Instead of the reply that might have been expected, the Lord pronounces an invective against the female:

> The Lord said, 'Pray in the place where there is no woman.' Matthew said, 'When he says to us, "Pray in the place where there is no woman", he means, "Destroy the works of womanhood", not because there is another way to give birth, but because they will cease to give birth'. Mary said, 'Will they never be obliterated?' The Lord said, 'They know that they also will dissolve, and the works of womanhood here be destroyed as well' (*Dialogue*, p. 143).

We could hardly fail to notice the striking similarity between this passage and an equivalent extract attributed by Clement of Alexandria to the heretical *Gospel of the Egyptians*, in which the Saviour is reported to have said, 'I am come to undo the works of the female'.[26] Clement suggests that

26. This passage was quoted earlier in this chapter.

the Egyptian Gnostics here equate 'female' with lust, and 'works' with birth and decay. So close are these conceptual parallels that we might reasonably conjecture that the author-redactor of the *Dialogue* was not merely familiar with the Egyptian Gospel, but made use of it in his work. Certainly the passage quoted above, characteristic of encratite thought, is not fairly representative of the *Dialogue* as a whole. This, of course, is not to imply that the main body of the work is not ascetic in tone. The author is anxious throughout to emphasize that the body needs to be controlled by the inward self; yet he does so generally in terms which are no more extreme than we might expect to find in the canonical writings. Indeed, his terminology and phraseology is unmistakably Matthaean:

> The Saviour said, 'The lamp of the body is the mind. As long as the things within you are kept in order, that is […], your bodies are luminous. As long as your hearts are dark, the luminescence you are waiting for… (*Dialogue*, p. 125; cf. Mt. 6.22).

It was proposed at the start of this section that the *Dialogue of the Saviour* exhibits theological affinities with the Thomasine literature. We might disregard a possible link through the name 'Judas', for its coupling with 'Thomas', which is clearly important in the Thomasine books, is not in evidence in the *Dialogue*. Similarly, the invective against the 'female' in the *Gospel of Thomas* (114), which is of the same order as that found in the *Dialogue*, may well prove to be an addition to that work. In both the *Gospel of Thomas* and the *Dialogue of the Saviour* these passages seem quite out of keeping with the remainder of the text, and may well prove to represent a late second-century, or even third-century, encratite redaction. However, that there are thematic links between all these works is undeniable. The extreme asceticism of the *Book of Thomas the Contender* may not be present, and there is no indication in the *Dialogue* that the community it serves has yet become an isolated sect; but both communities clearly share the same eschatological viewpoint. Close parallels with many of the sayings in the *Gospel of Thomas* also suggest that this Egyptian Gnostic community was familiar with the Thomasine tradition, and may have been rapidly moving towards withdrawal and separation from the mainstream Church. The solitary ideal, common to all these books, was clearly important to the author; and the concept of enlightenment as the first step towards rest and salvation is a dominant motif. Above all, the notion that salvation comes from *within* the self, not from outside, is the fundamental truth which, in company with the Thomasine books (and many other Gnostic writings), the *Dialogue* wants to affirm: 'They said to him, "What is the place to which we are going?" The Lord said, "Stand in the place you can reach!"' (*Dialogue*, p. 142; cf. *Gos. Thom.* 24).

Recent attempts to identify a number of different sources behind the composition of the *Dialogue of the Saviour*, on the basis of the various Gnostic traditions which it contains, have much to commend them. We should not underestimate the difficulties involved in such a task. Certain indicators do present themselves, however. At times in the text the word 'Saviour' is used; at other times, the word 'Lord' appears instead; and these deviations do seem to correspond to theological emphases, the former passages having a more Gnostic orientation than the others, which more closely resemble the content and style of the traditional dialogue of the New Testament. The book ends with a fine example of the latter style, in which the call to asceticism is shown not to be an end in itself, but to lead to a very practical ethic: 'The Lord said, "It is proper for whoever has understood the works to do the will of the Father. And as for you, strive to rid yourselves of anger and envy, and to strip yourselves of..."' (*Dialogue*, p. 146). It might be proposed, then, that the original *Dialogue* comprised a conversation between the Lord and some favoured disciples —Matthew, Judas and Mary Magdalene—into which was later inserted one or more blocks of Gnostic teaching. Whether the earlier material was of Syrian or Mesopotamian origin, or whether, like the final composition, it came from Egypt, we cannot know, though its Thomasine links must certainly be acknowledged. We may hazard that the work as it stands will not be earlier than the middle years of the second century.

EPILOGUE

'When Judgment is pronounced and we are all brought up to heaven, we shall see clearly in God secrets that are now hidden from us.' With such wise words does Mother Julian of Norwich bring to a conclusion her celebrated *Revelations of Divine Love*—the book that enshrines the substance of her 16 visions (or 'showings') of the nature of God.[1] Julian is utterly convinced of the validity of the truths revealed to her of the love and providence of God; yet, with a humility inspired by a lifetime of prayer and meditation, she is able to acknowledge that the God who thus reveals himself remains unknowable this side of heaven.

In this brief survey of many of the so-called Apocryphal writings of the early Church—the 'hidden Scriptures' of Christianity—we cannot fail to have been inspired by new insights that even the most seemingly bizarre of the books have afforded. Like the documents that constitute the New Testament, most of these 'secret' books purport to be, or to contain, revelations of ultimate truth mediated through Christ. Yet the very fact that God's revealed truth is presented in so great a variety of ways, and in a manner which at times is wholly at variance with any traditional New Testament understanding of the Lord's teaching, should suggest that we need to approach all revelatory experience—and particularly that which translates into the written word—with that same intellectual modesty and reasoned restraint that characterizes Julian's every thought.

The pious recluse *might* have expressed the same concept in another way: 'When we arrive in heaven, we should expect to laugh to see how wrong we were'! Cautioned thus, we must first acknowledge that, because so few Apocryphal writings have yet come to light, and so little definitively known about them, categorical assertions about their provenance and origin are usually inappropriate, and speculative attributions must always be tentative. In this survey of pseudepigraphical writings—books which might at one time have vied with the canonical works at least for popularity, and perhaps even for intellectual respectability—we have been bold enough to

1. Chapter 85. Julian of Norwich was a fourteenth-century anchoress.

assign, if not always a place of origin, at least an area of association. In doing so, while due regard has been paid to whatever internal and external evidence might present itself, the primary aim has been not so much to arrive at definitive conclusions on questions of provenance, as to try to provide an ordered critique of the various works in their associated geographical groups. It is certainly the case that regional considerations can and do have an important part to play in determining the probable origin of some documents. Extremes of asceticism in a text, for example, may tend to point to a location east, rather than west, of Antioch; again, the prominence of Logos theology, and parallels with Hermetic literature, will strongly suggest an Alexandrian source. So it is that books are brought together in association, just in the same way that textual similarities will often persuade us of a genuine connection between two or more works. While such groupings can be helpful, however, it is important to remember that associations of this kind may in reality exist only in the mind of the reader. There are few certainties in Apocryphal research; and the prudent student will want to admit his or her fallibility.

Interesting and consequential as questions are about the origin of the Apocryphal books—who wrote them, where, when and why?—it is the fact that they exist at all, and must therefore inevitably challenge our traditional understanding of the faith, that presents the really crucial issue for the Church at large. It has to be acknowledged that, thus far, the Church has managed to disregard the challenge, apparently content to rest on a nineteenth-century appraisal of these 'heretical' documents. To be fair, it would hardly be an exaggeration to say that Nag Hammadi has taken the Church by surprise. A few avant-garde scholars have sought to show how Gnostic beliefs in the early centuries threatened to become a powerful alternative to orthodox Christianity; but by and large the subject hardly figures in academia. It may actually be the case that few Church leaders have studied a single Christian Apocryphal document; and fewer still of their faithful congregations have yet even heard of Nag Hammadi. It is fascinating to speculate on what Mother Julian would have made of the 'hidden' Scriptures of the second century. Had she been acquainted with the patristic citations, we could well imagine that she might have sympathized with the early condemnation of works which were patently spurious, for Julian would not have allowed herself to take issue with the judgment and decree of Holy Church. Yet we might also imagine that, had she been able to peruse these strange works which emerged from the Egyptian sands more than half a millennium after her time, she would at least have deemed them worthy of study. Indeed, while she would certainly have been puzzled and dismayed at the Gnostic repudiation of Redemption through the blood of Christ, the mystical and spiritual qualities of many of these works might well have given her particular joy.

The aim of these concluding pages is to try to assess how the faith might have developed in its formative years if anti-heretical orthodoxy had not stifled free debate, thus provoking entrenchment on both sides. At the same time, we shall want to explore whether recent manuscript discoveries, which established Christianity cannot for ever ignore, might offer the Church a timely opportunity to meet the aspirations of a world in desperate need of spiritual direction. Before we can attempt such a task, however, it will be necessary to say something about the criteria adopted for the foregoing survey, and explain why some important early works have not been included. To fail to do so would be to invite the same charge which has been levelled, whether fairly or not, at the early heresiologists—of selecting only those books which tend to uphold a particular point of view.

It hardly needs to be said that *some* selection has had to be made, for an exhaustive survey was never the object of this present volume; and since, as the Evangelist Luke pointed out, there were many in the ancient world who were anxious to compile an account of the things which had been accomplished in the time of Jesus, and to interpret those sacred events, such an enterprise would in any case prove impracticable (Lk. 1.1). What has guided this present selection has been the intention to include all those second- and early third-century Christian documents, of whatever theological inclination, that are directly illustrative of the course of the faith during this crucial period. It may be argued that the five major Apocryphal Acts only just meet the criteria, depending on the date to which, as finished works, they are assigned. Their undisputed popularity for the Manichaeans, however, and the probability that quite early apostolic traditions are enshrined within them, furnishes enough of a pretext for their inclusion. From the standpoint of sheer interest it would have been tempting to include the considerably later *Acts of Philip*, which adds colour to the Philip tradition in Asia Minor; but the line had somewhere to be drawn. By the same token, the *Gospel of Matthias* and the *Acts of Pilate* are not considered here, along with other works of either a fragmentary nature or of dubious provenance. The primary aim has been to avoid the confusion of a multiplicity of documents which, however important they may be for the later development of Christianity, contribute little to our understanding of the progress of the faith in the earliest period. It will be noticed that several third-century Gnostic works of considerable influence have not found a place in the book—among them, the *Pistis Sophia*, the *Sophia of*

Jesus Christ and the *Gospel of Truth*—largely because it has been considered that these works represent Christianized versions of basically Gnostic material, rather than essentially Christian works with Gnostic inclusions. Such decisions are admittedly arbitrary; but they have been made solely to further the aim of providing a concise introduction to the Church's earliest popular literature which eventually failed, for a variety of reasons, to achieve canonical status.

It is important to remember that, by the close of the second century, Christianity was fast assimilating ideas and teachings from an array of existing philosophical systems and religious movements—from precursorial Mandeism and Zoroastrianism in the east, Philonic Judaism and the *Hermetica* in the south, and magic and mystery in the west. Whatever were the antecedents of Gnostic thought, its various forms had by this time begun to influence Christian literature and thought in many regions of the empire; and all this, of course, against the background of the Neoplatonic and Stoic ideals of the Hellenistic Roman world. Christ's original teaching, whatever this may be understood to have been, would inevitably take on new interpretations with the expansion of the faith; and the fact that Christianity was a syncretistic movement, able to accommodate to its surroundings, and to transform them, was doubtless one of the chief reasons for its unparalleled and continuing success, despite the attendant tensions and conflicts within the Church which were symptomatic of that achievement.

What we can never be quite certain about is whether Christianity borrowed ideas directly from these various systems, or whether all dipped into a common pool of thought. Did the Logos Christology of John's Prologue, with its very close affinities with an equivalent concept in Philo's writings, derive from the writings of Hermes Trismegistus (or vice versa!), or did it stem from the common philosophical currency of this region? What of the Johannine concept of God as 'life' and 'light', again much in evidence in Philo's work, as well as in the *Hermetica*? Could this, perhaps, be a consequence of a singular Alexandrian fusion of Greek and Hebrew thought? Nor is it difficult to find instances of conceptual parallels between the Neoplatonism of Philo and the Jewish Wisdom literature, giving substance to the hypothesis that Gnosticism owes as much in origin to Hellenistic Judaism as it does to Christian mysticism or to Persian dualistic thought. We have seen that the eschatology and the encratism of many of the second-century writings examined in this survey have their roots not only in the New Testament, but also in the ancient eastern religion of Zoroaster—though we must allow the very real possibility that later forms of ancient religions may just as conceivably have incorporated Jewish and Christian ideas at a comparatively late date. What we may confidently assert is that just as Gnosticism owes its origin, in all its various forms, to a multiplicity of sources, so few Christian texts, whether those within the canon or those outside it, can claim to be entirely free of its influence.

Yet, at an early stage in the history of the Church, the bishops and theologians of the established centres of the faith settled the standard of scriptural orthodoxy, and pronounced their verdict for all time on books which failed to meet that standard; and, as we have seen, many of those books which, according to the criteria, were adjudged to be spurious and dangerous have survived only because they were hidden away in the sand. Other books which managed to secure a place within the canon largely on the grounds of their assumed authenticity would probably not have done so today—at least, under the same criteria. It is no part of this present work to make a hindsight judgment on the wisdom or justice of the work of the heresiologists—except, perhaps to submit in their defence, that the rationale of their criteria would have seemed so much more relevant and defensible in their time than in ours. Furthermore, few would doubt that, without this measure of disciplined conformity, the Church would not have survived as a cohesive worldwide power for good. It is now generally allowed that there were social and political reasons for the wholesale condemnation, by an increasingly institutionalized Church, of books that failed to bolster mainstream orthodoxy. Clearly, the Gnostic emphasis on individual self-determination would hardly commend itself to a hierarchically governed Church. Similarly, the belief in the reality of the suffering, death and bodily resurrection of Christ, rejected by the Docetics, was essential to Christian orthodoxy at a time when so many of the faithful were suffering persecution and death in the name of Christ. To suggest, as the Gnostics did, that Christ himself was not subject to actual bodily suffering would hardly represent an encouragement to anxious and frightened souls on the verge of apostasy. It was important for those about to shed martyr's blood that there should be no doubt that the Lord had suffered in the same way too. Politics aside, however, there were important *theological* reasons why Christian orthodoxy was anxious to suppress the 'heretical' writings —though not all these reasons appear as absolute now as they once did.

The modern reader does not find it easy to comprehend how the fanciful cosmological principles of the Gnostics—from Simon Magus and Menander to Basilides and Carpocrates—could have gained such a measure of intellectual approval among so many adherents of so very diverse cultural milieux. Yet such was the philosophical thirst of the age for new ideas that it required adversaries of the standing of Irenaeus to combat the very real threat posed by charlatans who claimed to have been sent as Saviours of humankind. The more bizarre and mythological the system, of course, the easier it was for the Gnostics' teachings to be discredited. We cannot but wonder, however, whether their increasingly extravagant and defiant claims were as much a *consequence* of their persecution as its cause. If, as Irenaeus claimed, the Gnostics were accustomed to branding themselves behind the right ear lobe to mark their eccentric singularity, we could hardly expect conformability in their teaching. What is certain, however, is that, underlying the mythology and angelology that characterized their systems, there lay a comprehensible principle of cosmological duality which had its roots in the religions of the ancient east. How was it conceivable that the ultimate deity could create a world in which evil abounds? This is the very question that exercised Marcion in his rejection of the Old Testament, and his repudiation of the creator God of the Jews. Despite the protestations of mainstream theologians that the world was not under the sway of a malevolent Demiurge, the Christian Scriptures, along with those of the Jews, provided clear affirmation of the ongoing cosmic struggle between good and evil (cf. Col. 2.20); and it is this phenomenon (and how these elemental powers were to be overcome) that dominates the Gnostic writings, as our survey has shown.

If the Gnostics found it helpful to devise mythological explanations for the human fall from grace—variants and embellishments of the Genesis myth—they also needed to recognize and solve the very real dilemma concerning ultimate human deliverance. Clearly, Christ (the Saviour) had a crucial revelatory role in the process of redemption. Yet it was inconceivable to the Gnostics that salvation could be achieved through some once-for-all vicarious act. Human individual salvation lay, in large measure, within oneself. It was also unimaginable to the Gnostics that *all* human beings were capable of salvation, since not all had within them that remnant 'spark' or 'seed' of divinity which guaranteed their return and reunion with the Godhead. Many of the writings we have examined focus on this fundamental tenet of Gnosticism—that within each individual 'pneumatic' soul there lay, often dormant and unrecognized, the very means of the individual's deliverance. We may find wholly unacceptable the deterministic notion that only *some* human beings are by nature capable of salvation, while the remainder are predestined to oblivion. It is a very modern concept, however, that the process of achieving wholeness of being, and of shaping one's individual destiny, begins within the self. Moreover, that those exclude themselves from eternal rest who deliberately reject the good, and turn to the evil is an essential concept of Christianity, and very much a part of the Gospel message. Early apocalyptic literature (both Jewish and Christian) contrived to remind disobedient souls of the inevitable consequences of their recalcitrance. The Epistle of Jude witnesses to the spread of antinomian liberalism within the Church, as the parousia and day of judgment become ever more a distant and, perhaps, illusory prospect; and it is hardly surprising that, in an age of profligacy and apostasy, spiritual souls might reckon a qualified determinism (giving some responsibility to the pneumatic soul to ensure his or her own salvation) to be a more agreeable notion than the popular universalism based on faith in the salvatory cross of Christ.

Tertullian once described Paul as 'the apostle of the heretics', because of Marcion's partiality for Paul's teaching.[2] However, it might be nearer the truth, in view of Peter's midway position between the legalism of James and the liberalism of Paul, to give to Peter this somewhat dubious title. It is manifestly the case that Peter's authority is claimed by the pseudepigraphical authors more frequently than that of any other Apostle, partly, no doubt, because, as Prince of Apostles, he was undisputedly the key figure among the Twelve, but partly, too, because his particular 'third way' form of Christianity would seem to offer a suitable basis for the Gnostic's spiritualized conception of the faith.[3] It is tempting to wonder whether the course of Christianity might have taken a different turn altogether if Peter had not so early 'departed to another place', never again to reappear.[4] It may be that fewer Apocryphal works would then have been consigned to the fire, or to a lengthy obscurity. Such a work as the *Acts of Peter and the Twelve Apostles*, for instance, with its marked insistence on the incompatibility of material and spiritual things, and the shedding of earthly ties as the only guarantee of the kingdom, might well have become the popular Christian classic it deserved to be. Yet despite the fact that this is a prominent theme of the Gospel, it was not exactly the message that a Church would want to promulgate which was more anxious to establish itself as a

2. Tertullian, *Adversus Marcionem* 3.5.4.

3. 1 Peter, clearly a late 'establishment Epistle' written for the Jewish-Christians of Asia Minor, as Colossians and Ephesians were to the Gentile Christians, is an exception.

4. Acts 12.17. The record of his appearance at the Conference in Acts 15 is thought by many to be out of sequence. Whether Peter's disappearance signalled his removal to Rome (or elsewhere), or his demise, as some believe, the fact remains that he takes no further recorded part in the fortunes of the Church.

respectable and influential entity *within* society than remain peripheral to it.

Gnostic eschatology is by no means easy to determine. One obvious reason for this is that each Gnostic community (insofar as we are able to speak of 'communities' of Gnostics) would have developed its understanding of the 'last time' (*eschatos*) in its own way; and, by the very nature of Gnosticism, there would be many whose eyes and hearts were fixed not on some point of future time, when the sheep would be separated from the goats, and a new world order inaugurated, but on the 'here and now' time of their own individual escape from imprisonment in the world. A few of the earlier writings envisage something of both an immediate release and a coming cataclysmic judgment; and we can in some measure trace the development of thought in the writings themselves. It may be that both 'realized' and 'future' eschatological ideas find expression in the Fourth Gospel. The notion that the kingdom has already come, and 'is within you' certainly differentiates this Gospel from the Synoptics; but a future judgment is also implied when the Evangelist speaks of the hour which is coming when those who have done good will come forth from the tombs to the resurrection of life, and those who have done evil, to the resurrection of judgment (Jn 5.29).

The one absolutely basic belief of Christian orthodoxy which ran entirely contrary to Gnostic thought was, of course, the notion of the promised return of Christ to the world, whether this might be conceived as being concomitant with the judgment or not. The early Christian Apocalypses, as we saw in Chapter 4, moved gradually towards a merging of the two happenings—the parousia and the judgment; and the further idea of a new cosmic beginning (the rule of Christ) is introduced. The delay in the parousia unquestionably had its effect on these expectations; though it has to be admitted that well into the second century, despite the scornful reservations of some doubters, most Christians remained hopeful that Christ would one day usher in his kingdom, with power and judgment (cf. 2 Peter; Jude). During the course of the second century the Church devised a variety of explanations for the delay: the final consummation would follow an interim period during which the Gospel was to be offered fully to the world; God's time-scale is different from ours; the judgment was *already* taking place in the space–time continuum as the gospel is received or rejected. The gradual diminution of parousial expectation, however—or rather the spiritualizing of these hopes within some form of a realized eschatology—enabled the Church to develop and deepen its theological base to meet the spiritual and intellectual needs of the Hellenistic world of the third century. By the same token, it sounded the death knell for Gnosticism, because its distinctive notion of 'the kingdom within' was being appropriated by Christian orthodoxy, which at the same time was ordering the kind of outward institutional framework that would ensure cohesion, growth and stability for the faith.

If the development of the canon of authoritative Scripture, the establishment of a firm hierarchical Ministry, and the gradual formulation of doctrinal consensus all contributed to the demise of Gnosticism, we should not assume that the Gnostics were simply incapable of making the progression from their amorphous and unorganized position to a rational appreciation of the evolutionary advances of mainstream Christianity. It should not be forgotten that Gnostic precepts significantly influenced the writings that finally came to form the New Testament; and there can be little doubt that both the common parlance and reasoned convictions of Christians in their everyday lives would continue to reflect that same influence, long after Gnostic systems had lost their credibility.

It is in the matter of the nature and being of Christ, however, that 'heretical' Christianity—Gnostic and Docetic—provided the impetus for an orthodox consensus. The concept of the essential divinity of a pre-existent Saviour is affirmed throughout the later writings of the New Testament, in clear contradistinction to the many prevalent and popular Adoptionist theories of Judaic forms of the faith. It is worth remembering, however, that there was no definitive orthodox doctrine of the nature of Christ before the fourth century, and that second-century 'deviant' Christologies might have, as one of their sources, the canonical Scriptures themselves. Two of the Synoptic Gospels explain the dual nature of Christ in terms of his miraculous conception and virgin birth. Such a theory might seem to make Jesus the 'Son of God' only from the moment of his birth, and does not, in any case, answer the dualistic problem of the incompatibility of flesh and spirit. It was only a short step from here to what many Gnostics would consider a far more reasonable hypothesis—and one no more fanciful, yet preserving the notion of Mary's virginity—that the eternal Christ passed through Mary as water through a tube, his fleshly form on earth being a mere semblance of reality.[5] If these respective theories seem to overemphasize either the humanity of Jesus, or his divine status, the writer of the Fourth Gospel offers what appears to be a more satisfactory answer to the problem. For him, Jesus the Christ existed on two planes. His earthly, fleshly existence was real; and it could properly be said that he was 'sent

5. Cf. Irenaeus's description of Valentinian Christology, *AH* 1.7.

by God' (as John the Baptist had been sent, and the Prophets before him) as a human delegate of God. His humanity, however, was an expression of his essential nature, which was divine. He 'came from the Father' and would return to the Father (Jn 13.3; 16.28). In no sense did he *become* the Son of God, whether at his birth, or at his baptism; he was, in the fullest sense of the expression, 'of God', and remained a stranger on the earth.

It was precisely this idea of 'Christ the stranger' that lay at the heart of Gnostic Christology; and once more it was a small step from the Johannine concept to the Gnostic representation of the temporary fusion of the eternal Christ with the human form of Jesus, settling upon the chosen and anointed one for the period of his earthly visitation, and leaving him before the Crucifixion. We have seen how a form of this theory—that of Cerinthus—met with intense opposition in Alexandria and Asia.[6] We might imagine that sincere attempts to explain so great a mystery as the life and being of Jesus, however far such hypotheses might have deviated from an emerging orthodox consensus, at least deserved dispassionate and reasoned examination. Instead, they were perfunctorily anathematized. By the same token, since the passion narrative of the Gospels was capable of wider interpretation than that which eventually prevailed—the vicarious sacrifice of Christ, his blood being shed for the sins of humankind—Gnostic objections to what seemed to them to be a crude and repugnant theory of atonement might have been given a fairer hearing. It is true, of course, that the Gnostics themselves would scarcely have advanced their cause either by their disposition of superiority, or by their lack of cohesion and solidarity. There were (it has been said) as many Gnostic systems as there were Gnostics; and the different groupings, as the Coptic *Apocalypse of Peter* clearly attests, seem to have been no more accommodating to each other than the mainstream Church was to them. The modern student of the Christian Apocrypha will recognize, however, that the Gnostic writings do indeed have something to contribute, especially to an age that is searching for new ways to interpret the ancient *kerygma*, and yet which seems at times quite as doctrinaire as the age in which the documents themselves were composed.

If the 'hidden Scriptures' provide us with a freshness of insight into the nature of the Godhead, they also reveal much about ourselves as human beings, and our assessment of our place within the eternal scheme. The Jewish-Christian Apocryphal writings, it is true, tended to adopt a traditional theism, wanting largely to emphasize the ethical demands of the faith,

6.   Cf. the *Apocryphon of James* and the *Epistula Apostolorum*.

and the supernatural potency of Christ's apostolic representatives. Many works of eastern origin, like the *Book of Thomas the Contender* and the traditional *Apocalypse of Peter*, were primarily concerned to promulgate the ascetic ideal. Doubtless the tenets and exhortations of these important books had their influence on the later Christian writings, and on the whole course of the faith in the west. Indeed, the Petrine Apocalypse has a mention in the Muratorian Canon, though it was even then beginning to be deemed unsuitable for use in the churches. Ascetic forms of the faith persisted in the east long after western Christianity had adopted a more worldly and liberal attitude to sexual matters. Orthodox theologians of the third century roundly condemned the ascetic ideals of celibacy and chastity; but if these ideals had not become so inextricably interwoven with Gnostic precepts, with the result that offending books were proscribed, normative Christianity might have developed rather more rigidly and austerely than in fact proved to be the case. We should not forget, however, that saintly Christians in every age have warned of the incompatibility of flesh and spirit. The Church accommodates to the world at its peril; and there are few Apocryphal writings that fail to emphasize this fundamental teaching of Christ himself.

If the movement away from asceticism inevitably brought with it a certain loss of 'holiness', a diminution of that Godly fear and piety which intrinsically defines spiritual beings, the repudiation and systematic elimination of Gnosticism in all its forms was yet more consequential. The Gnostics recognized the divinity within themselves—and that, like the eternal Christ before them, they came from God and would return to God. Christian orthodoxy required a mediator, a 'go-between' whose compensatory sacrifice would countervail and expiate the sins that separate humankind from God. So powerful and fine a concept as this, especially in its exemplary aspects, requires from us neither approbation nor justification. However inadequately it has been construed at times, the idea of the vicarious sacrifice of Christ has undergirded the most successful religious system the world has known. Yet the notion of total dependency on a power outside the self for one's salvation has not always received unqualified approbation. Satisfying and comforting a notion though this may be, there is an alternative view which contends that at least part of the responsibility for the individual's destiny lies within his or her own conscious self. Few today would entirely concur with the Gnostic belief that what separates humanity from God is not sin, but ignorance; but the Gnostic emphasis on self-knowledge, and the individual's need to understand and realize his or her own destiny, reflects an essential element of human spirituality, and one, moreover, which resonates well with the modern mind.

It has not at all been the aim of this book to suggest that the non-canonical literature of early Christianity might in some way represent a superior alternative to the books and thought of the New Testament. We cannot doubt, of course, that, had these hidden books not suffered suppression and interdiction, the faith would have developed more esoterically, and with a far greater emphasis on the spiritual authority of the individual. Whether such a religion would have survived through the centuries is quite another matter. If the foregoing study has encouraged a greater awareness and understanding of the important contribution of the Apocryphal writers, however, it will have served its purpose. It may be that as these treasured documents gradually attain the same critical respectability that the books of the New Testament enjoy, they may even contribute to a deepening of the Church's liturgy, and find a place in its lections. God is to be found, so the *Gospel of Thomas* reminds us, in all kinds of places—within the wood, and under the stone.[7] May it not be that these sacred Scriptures, hidden under the sand for so many centuries, will yet help to bring a new spirit of openness and truth to the ancient faith?

7.   *Gos. Thom.* 77.

Index of References*

* References in books marked with an asterisk indicate the page number of the manuscript or manuscript.

OTHER ANCIENT REFERENCES